Canadian Samurai
One Man's Battle for Acceptance

By Russ Crawford

Canadian Samurai
© Russ Crawford 2020
Published by Agrinomics Publishing.
For more information visit www.CanadianSamurai.ca.
Cover and book design by Castelane.com.
Bushido icons designed and produced by Keiko Onodera., Ideogram.us
All rights reserved.

No part of this book may be reproduced, scanned, or distributed in any printed or electronic form without permission. Please do not participate in or encourage piracy of copyrighted materials in violation of the author's rights. Purchase only authorized editions.

Paperback ISBN: 978-1-9992805-0-5
eBook ISBN: 978-1-9992805-1-2

BIOGRAPHY & AUTOBIOGRAPHY / Cultural, Ethnic & Regional / General

Contents

Prologue	7
Chapter One	
Remembrance Day 1967	14
Chapter Two	
Samurai and Bushido	25
Chapter Three	
Coming to Canada	40
Chapter Four	
The Fight to Fight	68
Chapter Five	
World War 1	78
Chapter Six	
Between the Wars	128
Chapter Seven	
Pearl Harbor and Internment	182
Chapter Eight	
Life After World War 2	225
Chapter Nine	
The Sixties and Seventies	235
Chapter Ten	
Some Final Bows	243
Chapter Eleven	
Redress	252
Epilogue	255
Acknowledgments	262
Bibliography	263

This book is dedicated to the 22,000 Japanese Canadians who were wrongfully and inhumanely interned or otherwise detained in Canada during World War II. These detainments were the worst kind of racism and intolerance in our country and around the world.

Perhaps we want nothing better than to forget the raw wounds of yesterday, to cover the scars with delusions of security, but what was once taken away can be taken again. Who knows but that the next time will be made easier by the plunderers because we shrugged and said: shikata-ga-nai (it can't be helped).
—Muriel Kitagawa

PROLOGUE

Port Coquitlam, British Columbia, Canada April 1, 1951

He knew exactly where to dig. Nine years had passed since George last set foot on the rich delta soils of this small family farm in British Columbia's Fraser River Valley. The sun had set an hour ago leaving the countryside in darkness. Even with limited visibility he knew it would be easy to find the hidden package. This had been his home for nearly twenty years.

His heart raced. His pulse throbbed, almost pounding in his ears as he anticipated the discovery of the package, a treasure he had buried during that fateful week in 1942. It felt much longer than nine years since their world had been shattered. Slowly they were recovering—financially, mentally and emotionally. George knew the lives of his family members could not be restored to what they once had been but he knew this one article could bring some comfort. Beyond his family, the lives of all Canadians of Japanese descent would never be the same. His mission this night was simple: to reclaim one small vestige of his family's honor and to recover an important symbolic memento for his family.

Like many spring evenings on the coast, this one was cool and humid. It had been pouring for four straight days. This was nothing new. The dampness in the air created a wall of low hanging mist that left a film of moisture on George's clothes as he walked through it. Everything was soaking wet—the ground, buildings, fences and the lush foliage. Water dripped from the lowest points on branches and buildings as it accumulated on surfaces, collected into droplets and sought the fastest route to ground. The air was succulent with the aroma of cherry blossom trees in full bloom.

The sights, sounds and smells triggered many memories for George as he waited patiently before the final leg in his quest—memories of the farm, his childhood and then of racism and hatred.

George Mitsui waited until he was certain no one was at home at the farmhouse which just nine years ago was his family's home. It wasn't like he was stealing anything, or was it? No, he was retrieving his family's property, hidden to protect it from the thieves who stole everything else belonging to them.

"I am just recovering what is rightfully ours," he justified to himself. So why did he feel like he needed to do this in secrecy, under a cloak of darkness? Why was his pulse racing and why was he behaving like a thief? He had become suspicious, untrusting, even cynical since he, his family and all Japanese Canadians had become personae non gratae in Canada.

Just shy of thirty years old, George was strong and agile. He was shorter than the average Canadian, more typical of men who shared his Japanese heritage. He moved adroitly along his route in the familiar terrain. The sights and sounds and smells—oh the farm smells—were all too familiar to him, taking him back as if he had been here just yesterday. He crept toward the rear of the yard, passing the well they'd dug for water, the brooder house they'd built to raise chickens and then behind the barn. He paced out ten steps along the post and wire fence line and located the spot. He plunged his small shovel into the soil and hastily but carefully began excavating the small dig like an archeologist at work. Thanks to the rain, the earth was soft and yielded to the blade with little resistance. George worked cautiously, careful not to damage the precious package he had buried here in haste before he and his family were forced to leave.

He moved a half-dozen shovels of soil, tossed the spade aside and proceeded to remove the dirt by hand. He had wrapped it well to protect it from moisture and decay, never dreaming that it would be nearly a decade before he would return to reclaim it. Nor did he ever imagine it would be one of the few family possessions remaining after their devastating personal experience. Yet, in all those years, the cache never left his mind because it represented more than just a family heirloom; it represented his father's courage and dignity as well as the historic pride of his Mitsui ancestors.

After a few minutes of pushing the soil and rotted leaves aside, he reached the package. The heavy burlap with a waterproof liner should have protected it, he hoped. After ten minutes of effort, he pulled a two-foot-long parcel from the hole and brushed off the loose dirt. Quickly, he filled in the hole and scurried back to his car, hoping no one would think he was a thief running from the property in the cover of darkness with a bulky package under his arm.

George's original plan had been to let his father unwrap the package once he returned to Ontario, but his plan changed when he finally held it in his hands. He couldn't stand to wait. In fact, he couldn't even wait until he got back to his hotel room. He lifted the trunk of the car to gain some protection from the mist, shook off the remaining dirt and unwrapped the object. Layer by layer he tore back the wrapping and cheesecloth, finally revealing its mysterious contents under the light of a near full moon breaking through gaps in the cloud cover. The familiar orange and black silken *furoshiki* wrap was still in place and the gently curved shape was unmistakable.

Beautiful, he thought, *simple but so symbolic.* George removed the silk, revealing the familiar arched case. Reverently grasping the case with his left hand and the handle with his right, he drew a sleek sword from its scabbard. The blade glistened in the evening moonlight as small droplets of mist collected on the surface. This was not just any sword; it was his great grandfather's sword and his father's before him. It was a samurai's sword.

Five days later in Hamilton, Ontario

Back in the small family home in Hamilton, Ontario, George Mitsui sat on one of the yellow vinyl-covered chairs at the chrome and

Arborite kitchen table across from his father, Masumi. His mother, Sugi, stood behind George facing her husband so she could watch Masumi's reaction as he opened the parcel. Their family had endured so many horrible experiences in the past decade and they were long overdue for a happy moment.

The modest house and furnishings were substandard in comparison to their beautiful farmhouse in Port Coquitlam, but this was all the family could afford now. Their furniture was well used and a bit tattered, but the home was clean and well kept.

At sixty-three years of age, after a lifetime of personal trials and tragedies, Masumi Mitsui should have been thinking about relaxing and reaping the rewards of his life in his well-earned retirement years. But he didn't feel like he could relax, and he couldn't afford to retire. Instead, he had been forced to rebuild a life for his family after being uprooted, losing everything he'd owned and worked a lifetime to build.

Masumi looked younger than those sixty-three years. He was fit and strong and stood straight and proud—all five foot four inches of him. Only when he walked, with an obvious limp, did he reveal any weakness. His life had been a series of challenges and new beginnings but, until December 1941, those challenges had been of his own making—not thrust upon him against his will.

"I found it Dad!" declared George, laying his hands over the familiar orange and black silken-wrapped bundle.

As George slowly and almost reverently passed the bundle towards him, Masumi's thoughts returned to the reason George had hidden the package in the first place. He was drawn back to the life changing day for his family and, in fact, the entire Japanese community in Canada. The day was December 7th, 1941. It was the day Japan declared war on the Allied forces of the Second World War—a day triggering events which would uproot all Japanese Canadians, or JCs as they were often called, and thrust them into the dehumanizing experience of segregation.

For most Canadians, the actions taken by the Canadian government toward Japanese Canadians after the bombing of Pearl Harbor, were just a brief report they heard on the radio or read in the paper. They were more concerned by the larger story of an escalating world war. But for the Mitsui family and all other Japanese families in North America, the bombing was the beginning of a nightmare, a dreadful period in their lives that left them permanently damaged and outcasts in their own country. For all people of Japanese ancestry living in Canada, that day triggered far more than the frequent and incessant racial slurs or cultural hatred they experienced day after day. The heinous attacks escalated bigotry to new levels of hatred toward undeserving targets.

"Good job, son," said Masumi. "You know I really didn't want you going back to British Columbia because we were treated so badly there, and I definitely didn't want you to take any risks. I told you it would be dangerous to go to B.C. and to our old home, but you never listen to me, George. You should take an old man's advice sometimes. But now that you are back here and safe with us, I am relieved. I have to admit, I am excited to see it," he went on, as he admired the cloth and the treasure within.

"May I?" He looked up to make eye contact with George and held out his hands in anticipation.

George's two sisters and younger brother were also gathered around the table in the kitchen to participate in this important moment. Unable to contain their excitement, they were smiling before Masumi even began to unravel the layers of silk. All eyes were riveted on him as he reverently gathered back the smooth cloth just as he remembered his grandfather doing for him over fifty years earlier.

This package was the only important physical article left of the Mitsui family's legacy of forty years in Canada. They'd lost their farm and their family home. They'd lost their furnishings, their car and every other personal possession they had accumulated. In losing their seventeen-acre farm, they'd also lost their livelihood as chicken farmers Despite these humiliations, they'd retained their spirit and pride.

With his parents and siblings gathered, George provided a detailed account of his adventure in recovering the sword.

"It was right where I buried it, untouched, undiscovered. It was a good hiding place," he said proudly. "The farm still smells like chicken poop Dad." Then he added more quietly, "I hate chicken poop." The grinning faces revealed he had said it loud enough for even his siblings standing behind him to hear.

"It was a chicken farm, George." Masumi grinned. "What would you expect it to smell like—cherry blossoms? We made a good living on our farm, son. I miss it every day." It was nice to see everyone smiling, Masumi realized. Some good was already coming from the presence of the sword in their home once again.

They all watched with great anticipation as Masumi unwrapped the parcel, revealing the contents. He gently and ceremoniously pulled the sword from the bundle—first the scabbard, then the collar and finally the hilt. This was the Mitsui family *wakizashi,* a samurai short sword. It represented their deep ancestral roots tracing back over four-hundred years in Japanese history. As he held the sword in his hands, a broad smile spread across his face. He became very silent, clearly lost in the thoughts and fond memories triggered by this iconic family treasure.

The sword symbolized honor, a virtue which was most important to Masumi. This treasure had survived the samurai weapons purge at the end of the failed Shogun feudal uprising in 1867, as well as the collection and demolition of Japanese swords after World War 2. It, and the larger *katana* sword, had been a family treasure hidden by the Mitsui family in Japan. As he held the sword reverently, palms up, in his two hands, Masumi felt the sense of pride and connection with his ancestors flowing through him like an electric current. The energy was real and palpable to him. Samurai swords are said to hold the spirit of the warrior. Masumi believed this to be true. He felt the spirits of his ancestors, and particularly the spirit of his grandfather, as his eyes took in this simple and yet beautiful artifact in his hands.

The recovery of this lone object, this singular connection to his family lineage, stirred pride and passion in Masumi. The sword aroused many memories of his father and grandfather, of his connection with his own past—a symbolic heirloom binding the generations of warriors in his family together over history. It was the sword of the Mitsui samurai, not a modern-day replica, this was the real thing, the weapon of an ancient warrior.

This was the second time George had presented the sword to Masumi. The first occasion was in 1941 when George returned to Canada after a three-year trip to Japan. Masumi had sent him there as a young teenager to learn some personal discipline after a series of mischievous events. The sword was a gift to Masumi from their living relatives in Japan. It was not ornate or decorative in any way, just a simple sword used by his revered ancestors in a very different place and time. His distant Japanese relatives learned of Masumi's heroism during the First World War. The sword was a symbol of their pride and honor towards Masumi as a true warrior of the Mitsui clan. They granted the responsibility of the sword to Masumi recognizing him as the best person to hold one of the family's symbols of warrior tradition.

The Mitsuis once again enjoyed the reconnecting of this symbol of their heritage with their small Canadian family. The moment in the kitchen brought them closer together with a physical reminder of who they were and where they came from. Their gathering was also a reminder of the events in their lives over the past decade and the effects on all of them, particularly Masumi.

"This sword will always remind us of our family legacy and the noble values it represents," said Masumi. "It is a symbol of honor and the warrior spirit flowing in our blood. It will always be a part of our family, a part of who we are."

"It is also a reminder of the injustice and abuse inflicted on our family by the Canadian government," he continued. "I can never forgive the government for their actions against us and against all Japanese Canadians during the Second World War. They owe all of us an apology!"

CHAPTER ONE

Remembrance Day 1967

Hamilton, Ontario   November 11, 1967

The brilliant hues of red and orange common with an Ontario autumn had faded and most of the fallen leaves had been collected from the grounds of Dundurn Park on the shore of Burlington Bay. Once a critical military outpost built by the British in 1813, the park was home to Dundurn Castle, a stronghold in its day and now a small museum archiving some of the earliest recorded Canadian historical events in the Hamilton area. The dreariness of winter was just a few short weeks away. The overcast sky with its grayish white clouds blended with the smoke emanating from industrial smokestacks scattered across the harbor. Hamilton was a steel town—the Pittsburgh of Canada. Numerous foundries and fabrication plants dotted the shoreline, all contributing to the omnipresent smoke and ash in the air. Even on sunny days, a gloominess hung over this southernmost reach of Canada.

The Mitsui family home on York Street was a short walk from the castle and surrounding park. Once a small connector route out of the community, this street had evolved into a well-traveled artery connecting Hamilton and nearby Burlington. Many commuters used York as an alternate to the busy King's Highway 403, just a few blocks to the west. Historically, York Street had military significance as the main roadway connection between the Niagara River on the west, all the way east to Kingston on the northeast shore of Lake Ontario at the entrance to the St Lawrence River.

Today was Remembrance Day in the year of Canada's Centennial. It marked one-hundred years of confederation, with a coincidental military significance as the 50th anniversary of the famous World War 1 Battle at Vimy Ridge—the battle that gave birth to Canada as a nation in the eyes of the world. It was also the fiftieth-year anniversary of another important conflict of the same war—the battle for Hill 70, the battle that distinguished Masumi as a war hero. Today should have been a special day for Masumi Mitsui. Not only was it an important day in his military history, it was also his 80th year on this planet Earth. During those World War 1 conflicts, Masumi had shown himself worthy as a warrior in the many brutal battles during the "war to end all wars." In his heart and in his mind, he had proven to all that he honored the legacy of his family and his culture as a brave warrior—a Canadian Samurai. But the reality of the circumstances framed in these anniversaries was something quite different. Heroism had not been remembered; honor had not been bestowed—at least not to this soldier.

On this particular Saturday, Masumi and Sugi's family members were gathered at their modest home for breakfast. Family gatherings were common for the Mitsuis, even though they were often tumultuous and quarrelsome as a result of a highly competitive spirit amongst the children. But in the end, his family has been through more than their share of difficult times together. But this day had some surprises in store for Masumi. His daughters, Amy and Lucy, had been busy arranging visitors for their father to bring to light his role in Canadian history.

Masumi Mitsui was not large in stature, but carried an air of authority and confidence in his manner. He could be assertive when he needed to be, using short, sharp commands and stern, serious looks. A glimpse into his past revealed a history filled with examples of heroic leadership and inner strength. Normally a man of few words, when he spoke his voice was crisp and forceful, and his words carried great weight. His hair was dark, and he sported a thin, well-manicured mustache. Friends and family knew him to be serious most of the time, but he always had a smile for the love of his life, Sugiko or "Sugi" as he affectionately called her.

Sugi was small of stature but deceptively strong with exceptional endurance. As an early immigrant to Canada from Japan in the 1900s, she survived and thrived during difficult times. After the untimely death of her first husband a few years after arriving in Canada, she and her young son were forced to adapt. Marrying Masumi brought together two great survivors, two hard working people with a desire to build a better life for their family.

As they raised their family in British Columbia, Masumi and Sugi made sure all five of them felt safe, knowing they belonged in this world. The children maintained their self-esteem thanks to the character and inner strength of Masumi and Sugi Mitsui.

Two years after moving to Ontario, near the end of World War 2, the Mitsuis were able to make a down payment on their modest home in Hamilton. Dick was living on his own in Toronto but Masumi, Sugi and their four youngest children lived here. They all had jobs, and together they worked to recover from the loss and devastation they had suffered. As small as the house was, they made do. They shared bedrooms and respected each other's space. Over time the three older children married and moved on with their lives. But 490 York Street would always be the family anchor they called home since moving to Ontario—at least that's what they thought.

Family gatherings became larger events with the addition of spouses and children. The space, however, remained the same size. As a result, with the whole family gathered, it was hectic. Often people collided in the small kitchen and narrow hallways, and other times emotions got bumped. But today was an important occasion, a day to put aside small differences and come together in honor of their father.

For Masumi, today was a somber reminder of the vicious war he and his comrades had fought and the ultimate sacrifice many of them made. On November 11th each year, civilians remembered the war by paying tribute to honor the sacrifices made by others. But remembering the war from a soldier's perspective was something very different, something painful and unpleasant. Soldiers most often preferred not to tell war stories because the heart-wrenching, vivid and disturbing recollections were really the last thing any of them wanted to relive. For Masumi, Remembrance Day brought back harrowing memories of the harsh realities of the First World War, and the deaths of many Canadian soldiers, some of them his close friends. Remembrance Day also reminded him of the horrendous experiences endured by his family at the hands of the Canadian government during the Second World War. It was a day he preferred to spend alone with his thoughts and memories. His recollections vacillated between the positive, fond memories of acceptance by his fellow soldiers, and the negative discrimination white Canadians held towards Japanese Canadians when they returned home from the war in Europe. He was also reminded of the anger he carried in his heart and mind towards the government for its betrayal of his loyalty.

Masumi kept his comments to himself on most matters, but inside he was passionate about many things—his family, his ancestry, his culture and his honor. Every year, on the 11th of November, Masumi became even more quiet as he relived his history and struggled with the highs and lows of his life experiences. One day a hero, the next an enemy alien. One day a respected citizen of Canada helping build a community, and the next day a virtual prisoner stripped of all his property and accomplishments, of all that he and his family had built. It was impossible for him to understand how immigrants to Canada from other countries such as England and Scotland had blended into the fabric of this new nation, but those who looked different, like the Japanese and Chinese were treated as intruders or unwanted outcasts. Racism was an ugly thing, but it persisted in this "young" hundred-year-old country.

In his own mind, Masumi wrestled with his loyalty to his country and the injustices he and his family had endured. For all of Masumi's life in Canada he had faced an enemy most other Canadians would never even know—the subjugation of his heritage and hatred from white countrymen. The pledge so familiar on this day—*Lest We Forget*—rang hollow with Masumi. He would never forget and that was just fine with him.

Masumi's children had a different agenda. They felt the day deserved special attention. Special for Canada yes, but special for this man who was their father and a World War 1 hero. In honor of the day, his four children arrived—Amy, George, Lucy and Harry along with their families. Masumi's good friend Hirotaka, or "Hiro" as Masumi called him, was also here. In addition, the local CBC TV station newsman and his crew were scheduled to arrive mid-morning to interview Masumi, and after lunch they expected a Japanese World War 1 historian and author, Ken Adachi. The interviewers were the work of Amy and Lucy, determined to honor their father as the Canadian hero they knew him to be.

Compared to a normal day when Masumi and Sugi would be alone with their youngest son, Harry, the house was crowded, ready to burst at the seams. Masumi had just turned 80 one month ago. He filled his time by watching soap operas on television, taking unplanned naps and playing the occasional game of "*Go*" with his old friend Hiro. The aim of Go was to surround your opponent's stones of one color with connected lines of your own color on a 19x19 inch grid game board. It helped to keep his mind sharp and his time occupied. Plus, he reveled in beating Hiro on a regular basis.

"Like my grandson says, Hiro, you suck at this!" Masumi would offer with a sly grin and a chuckle.

But today's schedule would be very different than his usual routine. The house was full of relatives. Masumi enjoyed having his family come to see him even if the chaos would be close to overwhelming.

"How can a few small children make so much noise?" he asked Hiro with a bewildered look on his face as two grandsons scurried through the living room squealing with laughter.

Masumi had slowed quite a bit over the last ten years, but for most of his life he had worked very hard. He had championed many causes before, during and after the First World War. It was the only way he knew. These principles had been instilled in him from an early age by his father, his uncle and his grandfather. But now, time was catching up with him, and he had become much less active.

While it was satisfying to have many of his children and grandchildren visit, his wife's absence saddened him. Sugi had been through so much with Masumi over those years. She'd been strong when he was not. Sadly, her poor health and confusion had forced the family to move her into permanent care after she suffered a stroke. She went as far as she could go, Masumi supposed. She would have loved to have the whole family around, but sadly, she was too sick to ever leave the hospital. He hoped to visit her there later and share stories of the day that would please her, rowdy grandchildren and all.

In the kitchen of the Mitsui home, little sandwiches and colorful snacks were filling the table along with drinks and desserts. Preparing food for family and guests was always the job of Masumi's daughters, Amy and Lucy, and George's wife Nancy. George had the full-time task of keeping his two sons, Victor and David, and Amy and Lucy's sons, Stan and Mark, out of trouble, while the youngest of Masumi's children, Harry, would just poke his head into various rooms in a rather socially inept manner. Masumi's daughters, Amy and Lucy, were close in age as well as in their relationship. They had bonded through a lifetime of hardship and developed their own inner strength from their mother's example. They tended to run the show at family events and no one challenged them, including Masumi—except on this day, on Remembrance Day.

While they worked on lunch prep, Amy and Lucy whisper-yelled back and forth to each other. They focused on the meal preparation as they spoke to each other without making eye contact.

"You talk to him Lucy," encouraged Amy. "He listens to you."

"Not about Remembrance Day he doesn't." Amy shook her head.

"Well he really should attend the service this year. Every Canadian is proud of our military, the stories of heroism and our victory at Vimy. Father was a hero in that war and people want to honor him."

"I know, I know. You don't have to convince me. We have to convince father. Mom would make him go if she were here."

"Well, talk to him like she would."

"Yeah, sometimes I think she kind of scared him, didn't she." Lucy grinned.

"Oh yeah. Tough old soldier and decorated war hero catching it from a little Japanese woman," Amy said. "That was always fun to watch."

"Okay, okay." Lucy wiped her hands on her apron. "I'll try. I'll give it my best shot and see what happens."

Lucy glided into the living room with a plate of sandwiches and placed them on the dining room table.

"Sandwiches are ready," she announced. She fixed two small plates with sandwiches and a couple of Masumi's favorite pickles for her father and Hiro and delivered them. She noticed her father was sneaking in a nap. He did that often now. She gently nudged him and told him to eat a little food. It was going to be a long day. Her eyes caught a glimpse of the Mitsui family samurai sword proudly displayed blade side up on the top shelf of the credenza beside Masumi's chair. He took great comfort in having this link to his ancestors nearby. It meant something to everyone in the family, almost like a talisman bringing good luck and protection to its owner.

Disturbed from his nap and reaching for the plate, Masumi broke her train of thought.

"Thank you," he said. "You are a good daughter Lucy. You and Amy take good care of an old man."

With his expression of gratitude Lucy thought this might be the best time to broach the subject.

"Father, will you please go with us to the Remembrance Day ceremony today?" She retreated into the circle of family members, hoping for safety in numbers and trying to create the impression she was speaking for everyone in the room. "It's the fifty-year anniversary of Vimy Ridge. It's an important anniversary. It has great meaning for you. We know that. And many people will be gathering to pay tribute to those who have fallen as well as those who survived." She took a deep breath. "George and his family have driven here from Smithville to be with you, and the rest of your family are here too, to be with you and support you today. You are one of the oldest survivors of the war father." She was on a roll now, buoyed with strength at his silence, assuming he must be considering her proposal. "You would do more to honor your friends and fellow soldiers by representing them than by holing up in the house with your private ceremony like you usually do on this day. We think it's time," she concluded with a smile of satisfaction on her face, proud of herself for the speech.

"Oh, *you* think it's time, do you?" Masumi said.

Lucy's smile quickly disappeared. She had woken the bear.

Since the end of the Second World War, Masumi had refused to participate in public ceremonies on November 11th. He and his fellow Japanese Canadian World War I veterans had been dishonored by his government at the start of the war and throughout its duration. But an even deeper cut was the treatment of all Japanese Canadians after the bombing of Pearl Harbor. Hurt deeply by this treatment, he could never forget and probably never forgive. This act had disrespected all Japanese Canadians. He was on a one-man mission to boycott the Canadian government's military ceremonies.

"I'll tell *you* when it's time. Not this day. Not any day! You know how I feel about this Lucy." Masumi angrily rose from his chair and watched her as she turned to leave. This is what Sugi used to do he recalled. She would get him riled about something and then walk away, usually into her turf, the kitchen.

These women, he thought. *Like mother like daughter, they know how to get to me.* But Lucy looked a little uneasy as she reached the kitchen only to find Amy had made a quick exit to the bathroom, deserting her to defend herself alone.

Few things stimulated an emotional response from Masumi, at least not one as charged as this. He was generally calm and solemn, showing little reaction or emotion—except when he laid a whipping on Hiro while playing Go. He was just wired that way. But in this case, his emotions were clear, and his family knew well enough not to push him on the subject—at least that's what he thought.

Masumi limped after Lucy as she made her quick exit to the kitchen.

"It was our Canadian government who broke up our family, stole our possessions and imprisoned us!" he barked at anyone and everyone. "I will always honor my comrades. You all know this! But I do not honor the ceremonies of our government because they dishonored me!"

Masumi understood today was a different kind of ceremony and an important milestone for him and other World War I veterans. It had been fifty years since the Canadian Expeditionary Force fought and won control over a critical piece of high ground known as Vimy Ridge, a German stronghold and strategic position for the first three years of the war. His heroism and the loss of the lives of many of his unit's soldiers—and the additional losses four months later on Hill 70—changed the course of the war. These confrontations were well known and made for good news coverage on this historic day.

But all these considerations were not enough. Not enough to forgive and forget. Not enough to undo the indignities of his family's imprisonment and the racism he and his countrymen experienced both then and to this day. Not enough to compensate him for all they had lost since the bombing of Pearl Harbor.

"No Lucy, I will not go to the ceremony today! Like every other year, I will honor my fellow soldiers who died in the war in the privacy of my own home," Masumi asserted. "Go if you want, but I am staying here!"

Masumi pivoted on his heel and in formal military fashion marched right out of the kitchen. He headed for his chair, the one nobody else would dare sit in it, partly out of respect for an old man, but mostly because it was a ratty old chair that looked like it also survived World War 1. Tired from the emotional charge, he settled into this relic by his TV to finish his nap. His grandson David had other ideas. Before Masumi could settle in David plopped down on a small stool beside his grandfather's old chair. Masumi knew this visit was all about his medals. At the age of twelve, George's youngest son David was curious and engaging. He moved too fast for Masumi to keep up with him, but one thing always slowed him down long enough for them to share a bonding moment: It was when Masumi brought out his shiny war medals.

David and his older brother Victor had traveled to the Mitsui home in Hamilton with their parents to participate in what David understood to be some kind of ceremony for his grandfather's service in the war. Masumi didn't like to speak about the war much but unbeknownst to David, his grandfather's story was one of the biggest war stories in Canadian history, and Grandfather had played an important role in the victory. After the battles, Masumi had been awarded several medals for his part in the conflict.

Masumi walked over to the credenza where the samurai sword sat on display and opened a small wooden case stowed safely inside one of the sliding front panels. Removing a velvet sack, he returned to his chair and pulled opened the drawstrings. He watched David's eyes sparkle and shift from one medal to another as he peered into the bag.

"You like these, don't you, David?" said Masumi, as David admired the three shiny medallions, two silver and one gold medal, each with brightly colored ribbons attached.

"Yes, I do Papa. Please tell me again what they are for?" he asked for the umpteenth time. Masumi didn't mind. He was proud of the honors and it pleased him whenever his grandson wanted to know more.

One by one, Masumi removed the medals from the pouch and pinned them to his blue blazer over his heart as was his custom on this day, every year. With the third one in place, the medals hanging by their colorful ribbons, Masumi turned back to David. "This is the British War Medal." He touched the first one. "It was awarded to Canadians who served overseas during the Great War. This one is the Military Medal and represents bravery." Then he pointed to the last. "This gold one is called the Victory Medal and it was presented to all Canadians who served in the war. It represents our victory."

"Can I have them?" David asked innocently.

"One day they will be yours David," he pledged. "But today I need to wear them in honor of all the men who died while fighting bravely for our country, for our freedom. It's important you know this. Many of them were my friends and I miss them very much."

As Masumi sat with David in the comfort of his home surrounded by his close family, his thoughts recalled a similar scene in his past, a time when another small boy listened to his grandfather tell stories about being a brave warrior. Seventy years ago in fact, in Fukuoka-ken, Japan. He remembered himself as a ten-year-old boy spending time with his grandfather and asking many questions about his shiny swords and armor—one of which now held a place of honor just feet from his chair.

Masumi's grandfather had been a samurai warrior and, as a young boy, Masumi wanted to know all about that too.

CHAPTER TWO

Samurai and Bushido

Fukuoka-ken, Japan October 1897

The only light in the central room of their small home emanated from the flickering flame of an oil lamp on a simple table against the wall. The sparsely furnished sitting room with bare floors and walls typified the Japanese working-class homes of this time. Masumi's father, Hachiro, preferred traditional Japanese customs, but the spartan decor also reflected the difficult economic times and their limited financial ability to afford luxuries.

The Mitsui family all lived together in this small house in the village of Fukuoka-ken. Masumi's mother, Yoshiko, had died two years before and left a large void in their family. When Hachiro was away at sea, Masumi and his younger brother Tomoyoshi, or "Tomo" would live with their uncle but now, with their grandfather moving in with them, they were able to stay in their own home.

Masumi didn't mind having Grandfather close at hand; it was exciting for him. After all, not everyone's grandfather was a samurai warrior. Despite his humble and unassuming presence, stooped posture and balding head with long gray hair on the sides, this man was a legend among the people of his village. He went for short walks daily and had risen in popularity with the neighbors. He was revered by many and shown great honor by the people he met during his daily stroll. There was something peaceful and yet powerful about Grandfather. He spoke softly but purposefully and everything he said held meaning to Masumi. Both Masumi and Tomo felt close to Grandfather and were proud to have him living with them. They imagined themselves as great warriors one day, just like their grandfather.

Returning home from school one afternoon, Masumi was anxious to share his lessons from school with Grandfather. They had been speaking about the history of Japan and, in particular, about samurai warriors. He knew more about this than most of his fellow students because of his grandfather, but he realized there was a lot he didn't know, so he asked Grandfather for tales of samurai adventures. Grandfather promised he would tell Masumi the tales of the samurai and Japanese warlords but he would have to start at the beginning. Masumi didn't really understand what that meant. He just liked to imagine stories of adventure and great battles, of swords and weapons. All these things were magical and mystical to a young boy.

After dinner, he couldn't contain his excitement as Grandfather finished his evening routines of meditation, writing or painting and drinking tea or saki—more mysteries Masumi wanted to learn about. He hoped his grandfather would let him hold a sword tonight. He would wave it in the air and banish the enemy just like a samurai.

Masumi's father was also a warrior, a modern-day warrior though. As an officer in the Japanese navy, he spent much of his time at sea defending his country. Masumi's ancestors were all samurai, from his grandfather and back many generations. But the feudal culture of shoguns and warrior armies had been banned by the government over thirty years earlier or most surely his father would have been a samurai too. He wondered if his future would continue the family tradition of honor and respect, serving as a proud and respected defender of his country. Maybe they would allow samurai again in the future, and one day, maybe he and Tomo could be brave warriors, wearing armor and fighting great battles side by side with their grandfather's swords?

When Masumi's father was home, he and his grandfather would play a game in the evenings called *"Igo"*. It was a board game with colored stones, far too complicated for Masumi. He just wanted to play with Grandfather's armor and weapons anyway, even though he wasn't allowed to touch the swords.

"Masumi, come," called his grandfather. "Sit here beside me and I will tell you about our family and about bushido."

"Bushido? What is that?"

"Without bushido there is no samurai. Bushido is the *way of the warrior*," explained Grandfather. The lessons had begun.

"First I will speak of your ancestors. The Mitsuis were known in both the ruling Tokugawa clan and the Satsuma clan. The House of Mitsui helped build the great nation of Japan since the year 1100. Our family comes from right here in Fukuoka-ken, the southern region where the Satsuma reigned. For several hundred years, Mitsui men in both clans were samurai. They served many shoguns and were respected and feared as fierce fighters and brave warriors. But not every man is destined to be a warrior Masumi. Each man must find his own destiny.

"In the years from 1600, there was a great deal of fighting in Japan. Shoguns battled for lands and riches and many samurai died during this period. Japan then went through what was called a unification period of strategic alliances bringing peace across the land. This peace meant less fighting, so many samurai were forced to do something different to survive. In 1650, one of our ancestors, Sokubei Mitsui, put away his samurai swords and armor and went into business. He began making soy sauce and sake for a living. Other Mitsuis went into the banking business while some remained samurai. That's how the family split into two different lines—business and soldier.

"I'm sure you have learned about the Meiji Restoration in 1868 at school," Grandfather continued. "The Emperor seized all shogun lands and made samurai illegal by 1876, so those of us who were warriors had to find a new path. This was an opportunity for the Mitsuis who had chosen jobs over fighting many years earlier, especially those in banking. The Mitsui Bank aligned with the new government, moved from our homeland in Kyoto to the new business center named Tokyo and built the great Mitsui business empire.

"For those of us who remained loyal to the principals of samurai, the treatment was not as favorable. Some samurai found their way into high level jobs in the government, but there were too many of us for too few jobs. Some, who refused to renounce their warrior ways, found the future was not kind to them. They became outlaws in their own land and many were eventually hunted and killed. This was a very sad time in the history of our land," Grandfather solemnly recalled.

"But the culture and belief of samurai continues today, even though the fighting is no longer our way. The virtues of being a samurai warrior are still part of who we are as Japanese people. This is what I was talking about when I spoke of bushido. It is part of our culture," he said with reverence.

"So, before I tell you about wars and weapons, you must understand what it means to be samurai, Masumi. It was a great honor and privilege to be a shogun warrior. The meaning of samurai is 'those who serve.' In days gone by, long before the Meiji Revolution, samurai were respected across the land. During the revolution we were disgraced and disbanded, forced to fit into a new world. We were warriors without a battle. But we were still full of pride, and now, even though we no longer engage in battle, we honor the warrior way—bushido."

At that point Grandfather paused to let some of the lesson sink in.

"I want you to stop and really embrace that word Masumi—bushido. It is the most important thing in my life. It makes me who I am. Bushido is not a religion in the traditional way. In the beginning it was a set of moral principles or a code of conduct observed by Japanese warriors but it has become much more over the centuries and is now more commonly practiced by many Japanese men and women.

When the ancient Japanese warlords fought for territory, their armies battled and only the strongest of the warriors survived. Originating from a rough breed of men, the samurai who served the warlords became a privileged class. This evolved warrior felt the need for standards of behavior like other professional classes, a code of conduct befitting honorable men.

The roots of bushido come from many sources, Masumi. The art of Zen mastery, the Shinto religion and the writings of Confucius and Mencius are all part of bushido. They have all become part of what I am about to teach you."

"I have prepared a writing for you with all of the elements of bushido. This is what you will learn about if you ever want to become a samurai." Grandfather handed Masumi a single sheet of fine paper with eight words in Japanese symbols. It was written in Grandfather's fanciest script. For Masumi this was already a treasure to him, a step to becoming a warrior.

"Let us resume," said Grandfather.

"The origin of these beliefs and practices for samurai goes back to the 1600s and the religions of Shinto and Zen Buddhism. They are a code of conduct and chivalry for warriors to follow. In some cases, warriors took their dedication to bushido very seriously and those samurai who failed to uphold these beliefs would choose to commit *seppuku* which is a ritual suicide. But in today's world they embody the very best characteristics of a good person. However, in those early years, in order to become a samurai, a warrior was required to demonstrate mastery of this code of conduct. These are the virtues of bushido which I will teach you…if you want to learn."

"Yes, Grandfather, please teach me the way of the warrior. I want to be a great warrior too," pleaded Masumi.

"Very well. I will share them with you now. Look at the paper I gave you and follow along. The virtues of bushido are:

~ Politeness and Respect
~ Honesty and Integrity
~ Benevolence and Mercy
~ Loyalty and Duty
~ Courage
~ Self-control
~ Justice
~ Honor."

Grandfather paused briefly, and Masumi could see he was lost in his memories of greater days. "I will say to you again Masumi, the days of the samurai are over," he continued. "Bushido is the code of moral principles samurai were required to observe. But the virtues and practice of bushido continue as the national moral code of Japan. What was founded in samurai culture has now become a part of Japanese culture."

Masumi listened very closely to every word his grandfather revealed. He knew not to be rude and interrupt or ask too many questions. He would learn everything from his grandfather in time. But he was still very anxious to get his hands on those shiny swords.

"As I told you, before a man can become samurai, he must learn bushido," stated Grandfather. "He must learn how to conduct himself and how to treat other people. There is a right way and a wrong way of doing everything. Samurai must know which way is the right way and how to behave. For hundreds of years samurai warriors were chosen for their strength and bravery, and over time the samurai became armies of the most powerful and fearsome fighters anywhere in the world. But our teachings also included virtues of fairness, mercy and chivalry. We learned the difference between right and wrong. We learned this moral code.

"You must learn and remember the virtues of bushido," explained Grandfather. "You can memorize these eight virtues in a single day but mastering them will take a lifetime. Everything we do is an opportunity to act with honor and respect. If you want to learn, then each night for the next eight I will tell you the meaning of one virtue which is a part of bushido. But it will take you a very long time to comprehend them and to understand how different your life's experiences will be if you follow bushido. Your journey with bushido will be different than everyone else's," Grandfather concluded.

Masumi sat silently, through this solemn lesson, engrossed in every word. Most children would be bored and fidgeting if they had to take even more lessons after school! But Masumi remained motionless, focused, intent on every word. His grandfather was sharing something important and very personal with him and, even at ten years old, he could comprehend the august nature of these words.

If I am to be a samurai, thought Masumi, *I must learn everything there is to know.* This wasn't at all like school. This was like sharing an adventure with a brave man who had lived these stories, one who dedicated his life to bushido.

"So, let us start with RESPECT," suggested Grandfather. "This means to be sympathetic to the feelings of others. It also means to respect yourself, so others will respect you too. It means you must be kind and polite and respect all people in your life. This is how the Japanese culture is known to the world," he stated with pride.

"Do you mean I should be kind to Yoshi at school, Grandfather?" asked Masumi. "He's bigger than everyone and mean to me and the other kids. No one likes him."

"Him most of all," replied Grandfather. "There is a reason he behaves the way he does. For you to be a master of bushido you must look deeper into the soul of things in order to understand them more fully. This starts with respect. With it comes tolerance and understanding Masumi. All these behaviors make you a better person."

"Well I don't think I like your idea very much," said Masumi. "He's horrible and mean to everyone."

This was starting to sound like it was going to be more work than Masumi had thought. Yoshi was an ass. It would be hard to try and respect him. Maybe this bushido stuff wasn't going to be so great after all.

But later, lying in his bed, Masumi's thoughts were on his grandfather's words, well one word at least—respect. He thought about respecting his parents and his teacher, about respecting other elders and being sympathetic, kind and polite to others. This was how his parents and his grandfather behaved he realized. This was how he should behave, if he wanted to be like a samurai.

The lessons carried on for the next seven nights. Grandfather spoke with reverence and detail about the other virtues of bushido. He spoke to Masumi like he was a grown man adding even more importance and sanctity to his words. He spoke of bushido in the words handed down over time, from generation to generation of samurai warriors, just as Grandfather was doing now with Masumi.

He spoke of:

~ COURAGE: perceiving what is the right choice and acting on your decision

~ BENEVOLENCE: mercy, love, magnanimity, affection for others, sympathy, and pity are all traits of benevolence

~ HONESTY: to be truthful and trustworthy beyond any doubt

~ LOYALTY: to display unfailing homage and fealty to a superior or a country

~ RIGHTEOUSNESS or justice: the power to decide on a certain course of conduct in accordance with reason without wavering; to strike when it is right to strike or even to die when it is right to die

~ SELF CONTROL: the discipline of fortitude and mental strength to remain stoic and unemotional under all circumstances faced by a samurai

~ HONOR: a vivid consciousness of personal dignity and worth

It was a lot to take in. But Masumi listened and learned. By the third night he knew he needed to start making notes of these "lessons" from his grandfather. He couldn't remember it all. One day in the future, he would remember all the virtues like his grandfather could. When he had to start making notes the sessions began to feel a little bit like school, but so much more fun. They were something special just between him and his grandfather. Masumi could visualize the kind of man he could become, a man like his father or grandfather. A man of dignity and honor respected by his community and loved by his family. These were goals worth striving to achieve.

On the fifth night (loyalty) Masumi thought he would try to hurry things along a little bit. "Can we look at your swords and armor tonight, Grandfather?" he ventured. He thought it was pretty hopeless, but the wait was killing him.

Not surprisingly, Grandfather said, "Not yet, young one. Don't be so eager. The young bird must display great patience and stay in the nest until he grows muscle and feathers and is strong enough to fly. You are like that young bird. You must wait for your feathers."

As the week progressed, Grandfather went into great detail on the virtues of bushido and their meaning and application in life. He repeated many times the importance of acting out these behaviors as a foundation of being a good person. Some were obvious to Masumi. Things like loyalty and honesty. He understood what those things meant, but words like benevolence and justice were unclear to him.

Grandfather told Masumi a story about each virtue. He liked those parts best as the tales often included past adventures Grandfather had experienced as a samurai. Courage in battle. Loyalty to a fellow samurai or a shogun lord. These stories filled Masumi's head with colorful, powerful images of the history and culture of his country and its people. They taught him what it meant to be Japanese and the descendant of a Mitsui samurai.

On the last night Grandfather knelt beside Masumi, put his hand on his shoulder and complimented him on his dedication to learning the bushido way.

"You have been a good student Masumi," said Grandfather. "But your journey for this knowledge is only just beginning. You have a long way to go. Tonight, we will talk about honor—for me, the most important of all bushido virtues. I think, if you follow all the virtues I have taught you for all of your life, you will achieve honor. This is not one thing or one act. It is the sum total of everything you say and do. It is how others see you, how you see yourself. It is knowing you lived your life the best way you could and knowing in your heart you did things the right way."

Masumi's gaze was locked on his grandfather intently as he listened to him speak of honor. He idolized the man and wanted to be just like him. He didn't need to write the words about honor. It was almost like he already knew what his grandfather was going to say. All the other virtues seemed to flow together into this last and most important one. Knowing he would have many conversations with Grandfather in the years to come and this was just a beginning made him feel empowered and special to have begun his journey in the warrior way. He would not disappoint his family, not ever.

After dinner on the ninth night, Grandfather entered the sitting room with a bundle wrapped in the most beautiful black and orange silken material. Masumi knew this cloth covered the swords. Grandfather asked if he was tired of learning about bushido and wanted to take a break. But Masumi had been paying attention. He knew the math—eight nights and eight virtues. That meant he was finished and it was time to see the samurai armor and swords. Did Grandfather have another diversion in store for him? Was there more schooling in bushido before he could actually get to the prize of seeing and touching his grandfather's prized possessions?

"No, Grandfather, please. It's time to see your shiny swords."

"Very well then, young bird. You have earned it," he said with a knowing smile.

Ceremoniously unwrapping the silken furoshiki-covered bundle fold by fold, grandfather revealed the treasure. Masumi finally got his chance to see the real samurai swords, not the wooden toys he and his brother played with in their backyard battles.

"These swords are a sacred symbol of our family and of the samurai culture," said Grandfather. "They were given to me by my father and to him by his father before him. Your ancestors were all part of the Mitsui clan. At one point the Mitsui family was the richest and most eminent family in Japan. We were powerful businessmen and possessed one of the most feared samurai armies in all the lands of Japan. Not all families named Mitsui are related to each other Masumi, but we are all connected to the roots of Japanese culture.

"Each samurai warrior had these two swords." He stood, a sword in each hand. "Together they are known as *daisho* which means big and small. The katana (or *tachi*) is the larger sword and the *wakizashi* (or *tanto*) is the smaller one. In battle, a samurai would fight with one in each hand as both could be used as defense from an opponent's blow or as a weapon to kill." As he spoke, he gestured both attack and defense positions with the swords, deftly waving them in smooth, circular patterns seemingly in every direction at the same time. It was mesmerizing to Masumi to watch this great warrior maneuver these beautiful weapons with both grace and strength.

This brief description and demonstration sent a chill through Masumi as he looked at his Grandfather holding one sword in each hand in battle stance and pictured him actually killing an opponent.

"Japanese legend says the spirit of the warrior is contained in the swords. This is very powerful Japanese magic," said Grandfather.

"Did you ever kill anyone, Grandfather?" Masumi suddenly asked.

Grandfather paused and looked toward the ground in a humble and thoughtful manner. Masumi waited patiently as his grandfather weighed the question before answering.

Hamilton, Ontario November 11, 1967

"What did you say, David?" Masumi turned his mind back to the present.

"Did you ever kill anyone, Papa?" David repeated.

Shocked out of this memory which had taken mere seconds, but felt like an hour passing, Masumi thought, *What a remarkable coincidence.* This was a déjà vu moment, but different. Different because he now faced answering the same question he posed to his grandfather so many years ago. This was a serious moment to be handled carefully. Of course he had killed men. That's what war was about. Thousands of men on both sides had perished in a wasteful loss of life. But to be held accountable now and by his son's son was a moment he had never prepared for. Digging deep into his early childhood memories he recalled the words his grandfather had shared with him seventy years ago.

"A warrior is faced with life and death decisions many times during the battles in his own life, David," Masumi began. "It is important for you to understand, when you enter into a battle, you fight for what is right and you defend the lives of your friends and family. In many cases you defend your whole country. The warriors in our family—me, my father, my grandfather and our ancestors before them have all taken lives in order to defend our families and our beliefs—the bushido code. My hope is you never have to face a similar decision in your life. Sadly, American soldiers fighting in Vietnam right now must make this choice and my heart is with them every day." His speech slowed reflecting the emotion these thoughts evoked.

His grandfather's counsel continued to flood his memory. "It is also important for you to understand a warrior must be benevolent," he continued. "To be benevolent means to have sympathy and mercy towards your adversary. To know when it is time to kill and when it is time to show mercy. This is also part of the bushido code—*the warrior way*.

"But there is no glory in killing another man, David. In battle you must defend yourself and fight for what you believe to be right. Today, more battles are fought with words than with swords. This is how you and your brother should act. Even with words you can still fight for what is right and be merciful to your adversary."

Masumi could tell David's initial curiosity regarding his medals had shifted to rapt attention to the story he was sharing. Masumi had never talked about warriors and fighting with his grandchildren before. David had heard the stories of his samurai ancestors and even the story of his grandfather's bravery on Hill 70 during World War 1, but this was different. This was the sharing of a grandfather's deepest feelings and wisdom. Like Masumi when he was a young boy, David knew nothing of bushido and he certainly didn't know he was in the midst of a life lesson.

Eventually the spell was broken, and David's thoughts shifted away from Masumi's war memories and ancient Japanese wisdom. As quickly as he'd appeared to see the medals, he leapt from his chair in search of new adventure.

Masumi rose, stretched out his stiffened knee and poured a couple of small drinks.

"Hiro san, here's your schnapps." Masumi handed him the small pinwheel crystal glass filled with an orangey liquid.

"Peach?" asked Hiro.

"Of course." Masumi grinned. "It's the best kind!"

Masumi settled back into his chair opposite Hiro with the go board between them, covered in a seemingly haphazard arrangement of black and white stones. Each of the men had bowls of their corresponding stones ready to be placed on the board and they continued the game with intense concentration.

"It's my turn." Masumi had Hiro on the ropes yet again. This brought a small grin to his face, but he quickly erased it. Cockiness or overconfidence were not acceptable in the bushido code.

As Masumi placed a white stone on the board, capturing another of Hiro's clusters of stones, Hiro asked, "What do you think about this fellow Muhammad Ali being sentenced to jail for five years for not reporting for military duty?"

"I think it is his duty to fight for his country when he is called," replied Masumi. "Mr. Ali said he had no quarrel with the Vietcong, but I didn't have one with the Germans in 1916 either. I went to war because my country needed me. If my country is at war with another country, then so am I. That's loyalty!

"This war in Vietnam is very different than the Great War though," Masumi conceded. "It is not a war of honor and moral difference. It is a war based on suppression and power. Many citizens in the United States aren't supporting their soldiers in this war. They don't feel like it is the United States' war. It would be very hard to fight and risk dying for your country while so many people are opposed to Americans even being involved."

"That's what I say too," said Hiro. "But how can someone who fights for a living not be willing to fight for his country?"

The room grew quiet as Hiro refocused on the game and pondered his next move, realizing it didn't look good again. He mumbled a swear word in his native tongue as he looked over the board. Masumi managed to suppress a smile. He liked winning.

As he placed what would turn out to be his last black stone on the board, Hiro said, "I agree with your decision today Masumi, you don't have to go to the ceremony if you don't want to go. I'm getting a bit tired of all these centennial celebrations myself. This one is just like all the others."

"No, it isn't." Oddly, Masumi found himself defending the Remembrance Day event. "Today is about the war, not Canada's 100th birthday. Lucy and Amy are right. We should make sure all Canadians know about the Japanese role in the Great War. Many people today weren't even born when we fought in France. And many other Canadians, those who should be old enough to remember, have forgotten the sacrifices made by the Canadian Expeditionary Forces."

Getting a little heated and passionate about the war, Masumi leaned forward in his chair causing Hiro to retreat in his. Masumi's voice became louder as he continued, "At Vimy Ridge, Hill 70, Passchendaele and all through Europe, our battalion, the Fighting Tenth from Calgary, fought bravely. Many men gave their lives over there, men who came from different countries originally, all fighting for their new country, Canada." He waved his hand to the east, in the general direction of Europe. "Back then, men and women came to Canada from a lot of different places looking for a new start and a better life than the one we had in our homelands. As we both know, it hasn't been easy, being *issei*, the first Japanese generation in Canada, but the war brought us together. At least, that's what I thought back then. Men from many countries fought as a unit for Canada. It made me very proud. But you know what it was like when we returned after the war?"

"I sure do," said Hiro. "It was like we never left. The racism and hatred resumed almost immediately. It flared like someone blowing on a glowing coal."

Deliberating his next move, Hiro realized he was beaten. Buying a little more time, he asked, "Why did you come to Canada in the first place, Masumi? You have never told me your story."

"I thought I was going to work on a fishing boat and they let me off in Victoria!" Then, a wry smile spread across his face, and Hiro realized he was joking.

"Honestly, it was sixty years ago, Hiro. I'm not sure I can remember everything, but I am very clear on the days leading up to my departure from Japan. It was a difficult time for me and for my father and brother too."

Masumi's thoughts drifted back to his last days in Japan. Was it really almost sixty years ago? How did he get to be an old man old so fast? He could still picture the dirt road ascending to the top of the hill and their small home with his mother's garden in the front.

CHAPTER THREE

Coming to Canada

Politeness and Respect
...a sympathetic regard for the feeling of others. In its highest form politeness approaches love. Respect yourself, and others will respect you.

Fukuoka-ken, Japan December 1907

Late autumn leaves clung desperately to their branches in Masumi's village in the southern part of Japan. The first snowfall would come soon. Shorter days and the overcast skies added to the somber mood Masumi felt in his heart.

He sat with Tomo outside their home in the small garden first planted by their now departed mother and then by their grandfather until he passed. It was a serene and peaceful place—a quiet sanctuary, fitting for their conversation. Small clouds of mist escaped from their mouths in the cold, damp evening.

Tomo had a bewildered and concerned look on his face as Masumi spoke. They had shared many adventures together as young boys. They were best friends—*shinyuu*—and together constantly. Although Tomo did not know it yet, this was about to change.

With his heart heavy, Masumi ended the silence. "I have decided it is time for me to leave our home Tomo. I am leaving Fukuoka. I am leaving Japan," he said.

"Why do you say this Masumi? Where are you going? What will you do?"

"I have brought disgrace to our family honor," lamented Masumi. "I have failed, and I am full of shame. There is nowhere for me to go, nothing I can do. If I am to help our family, I must find work, so I am going to go to Canada and start a new life. Many others have already left here for a better life and I know I must go now and seek out this new adventure."

"But why? What has happened? What about your plans to join the Navy?"

"I will tell you later. I must first speak to father."

Masumi rose from the small wooden bench leaving Tomo staring after him with a concerned and saddened look.

It was going to be even more difficult for Masumi to tell his father he had decided to leave his family and his homeland. His small family was very important to him, and the bond he shared with his father, although sometimes challenging, was a powerful force that was the foundation of his values and beliefs. This relationship played a large role in who he was as a young man. He admired his father as a brave and honorable man and an officer in the Japanese navy, a career direction he had hoped to emulate. Hachiro was much like his own father, Masumi's grandfather. The same pride, honor and fearless dedication to their military careers had been instilled in Masumi. He wanted to be just like them. His decision to leave was not going to be well received by his father, but it seemed like his only alternative.

All his dreams and hopes had come crashing down in a single moment. He felt ashamed and believed he had dishonored his family. Masumi had planned to join the Navy to earn a living and do his part to look after the family. Now, with this road closed to him, his only option was to go to North America and make money to send home.

Like his father and his ancestors before him, Masumi had the warrior spirit in his heart and in his mind. He had a vision of following in the honored footsteps of his grandfather as a samurai warrior. However, the lifestyle of the samurai had ended a decade before Masumi was born. When he was a young boy, these legendary warriors, their shoguns and feudal lords were already Japanese lore, history to be taught in school. "One day, in your own way, you will be a respected warrior, Masumi, like all the men in our family who came before you," his grandfather had told him. The importance and special nature of these stories had become deeply etched in his psyche.

Masumi had continued to study and embrace bushido—the samurai code—from his first lessons with his grandfather to his twentieth year. He knew the code of moral principles which the samurai upheld better than ever. To him this knowledge was also a requirement of the Mitsui clan. Before he was twelve years old Masumi knew the eight virtues of the bushido code. Maybe he still didn't comprehend the full meanings of these words and the depth of commitment needed to embrace each of them, but he knew this was important to his father and grandfather, and therefore it was important to him. He drew great pride in his samurai ancestry. It gave him a feeling of belonging to something greater than himself. In their youth, he and his brother used to draw glorious and elaborate pictures of samurai warriors in their full armor and head gear and pretend to be them. They played with carved wooden swords and waged imaginary battles between great warriors. The clash, or more accurately, the clunk of the wooden swords and the warrior screams echoed across their mother's garden and throughout the neighborhood. These encounters were at the core of his childhood, some of his best memories. But the samurai had disappeared. They were a thing of the past, a journey he would never be able to take as a man. Still, it didn't mean he couldn't be a defender of his people and his country just like his father.

The early 1900s in Japan was a challenging time for the nation and its people. Wars and unrest existed between Japan and Russia, South Korea and China. Citizens were either involved in the war effort or in the commercial development brought about by the Meiji Restoration and Modernization. Like many other families, the Mitsui samurai found their warrior roles diminishing and ultimately disappearing. Some found work in the new Meiji government but, for many, this was not the life they wanted to lead. Ultimately, they became outcasts because of this new, young ruler and his vision of national restoration based on peace and economic success.

The Emperor's Meiji Restoration plan, which ended the samurai warrior reign in Japan, had so far failed to improve the Japanese economy. The cost of transforming the entire country proved to be prohibitive. Citizens struggled to find jobs that could pay higher taxes and support their families at the same time. In many cases families lost their land because they could not pay their bills.

By mid 1907, Japan had declared war with China and South Korea, immediately following the end of the Russo-Japanese conflict of 1904–1905. Masumi's father managed to keep his family home by blazing a new trail for Mitsui warriors. He followed a career as a soldier in service to his country in the Japanese navy. The military needed good men who would serve and risk their lives for their country. This, Masumi believed, was how he could follow family tradition and fulfill those childhood dreams.

Leaving a bewildered and confused Tomo in the garden, Masumi entered the house, left his shoes in the *doma* (an area of hard compacted dirt near the entrance of a Japanese home) and found his father having tea in the *washitsu* or sitting area. His eyes scanned the room, pausing on the samurai sword. The lump in his throat grew even larger as he thought about the meaning of the sword to his family and what he now had to share with his father.

"Ah, Masumi, how are you and your brother today? Tell me how you did at the Navy exam." His fatherly pride was evident as he anticipated the answer.

Masumi summoned the courage to break the news to his father.

"Father, the test is what I have come to speak with you about. I failed the entry exam today. They told me I was not a good candidate to be in the Navy. I don't know what to do now. I always thought I would join the Navy like you. I think I must find work elsewhere since there are no opportunities for me here. I think I should leave Japan and seek work in the United States or Canada."

"This is a very serious decision, Masumi. Tell me exactly what happened."

Masumi recounted the events to his father as he flashed back to the registry office of the Japanese Navy, to a small induction room where he was informed he had failed the exam and did not meet the requirements necessary to become a sailor in the Navy.

"How can this be?" Masumi asked the officer. "The Navy needs recruits. I am volunteering to join. I am loyal to my country and only wish to serve."

"I am sorry to tell you this, young man," replied the officer with little sympathy or emotion. "The report simply says 'Rejected' because you failed the exam. There is nothing more I can do for you here. You can apply again next year."

Masumi's spirit was crushed. His dream of a career in the Navy alongside his father was not going to come true. How could this be happening to him? He was nineteen years old, strong and willing, so naturally this confused him and was also a great embarrassment. How could he stay? How could he face his family and friends with this disgrace hanging over him? And, without a military career, what would he do? If Masumi could not help in supporting his family in his chosen path in the military, he really had no idea what work he could find. Jobs were not easy to come by right now. Alternate options popped into his head as he scrambled to make a new plan, but he immediately vetoed most of these for one reason or another. It became clear that he would have to leave Japan and start over somewhere else—anywhere else.

These thoughts raced through his mind as he spoke with his father. All he could think about was his failure, remembering the painful words of the officer at the registration office. He didn't understand what had happened and why he had failed the exam. In his heart he knew they were wrong and he would be a great warrior, just like his father and grandfather. But in that moment in the registration office, his dreams were shattered and now he needed to leave.

After recounting the meeting at the naval office to his father, Masumi was unable to make eye contact with him. He looked to the wooden floor in shame.

"I understand how you must feel," his father said sympathetically. "You are a man now and it is time to find your path. There is little future here in Japan for you and your brother. These are sad times for our great nation. I too had hoped you could join the Navy and fulfill your dreams. You do not disgrace our family though. I am proud of the young man you have become. You are brave and honorable."

"I do not feel like I have honored our family, Father." Masumi was unconvinced by his father's encouraging words. "One day I will bring honor to myself and my family. I will prove the samurai blood in my veins is strong and I honor bushido."

"I have no doubt you will, my son. What do you know about North America? Why do you think your future would be better there?"

"Many of the people leaving our country are going to Canada. I spoke with the Japanese emigration officer this afternoon and he told me over eight thousand people left Japan for Canada this year. It is a very big country with many cities and great opportunities, welcoming people from all lands to start a new life. I hope to earn money there and send it back here to help our family in some way. There are also many Japanese people living there already, so I will not be alone," he added. "Who knows what adventures might lie ahead for me?"

"Very well then, this will not be an easy thing for you to do," said his father. "I think you are brave to make this decision and begin this bold quest. Go with my blessing and send letters of this new land and your adventures."

Over the next few weeks, Masumi arranged to travel from his home province in Japan across a vast ocean to a new country in North America. His emotions left him conflicted. On one hand, the prospect of new adventures and self-determination were exciting. But, on the other hand, leaving the relative safety of his family and traveling so far without knowing what lay ahead of him was frightening. He stood by his decision to make the journey, determined to show everyone he was an honorable man with the courage and strength to succeed. He remained in Fukuoka-ken for the New Year celebrations of 1908, then packed a bag of clothes and some personal items and said his goodbyes to his uncle, father and brother.

"Good luck, Masumi," said his father. "Write many letters to me and Tomo and come back to Japan as soon as you can."

"I will father. I will make my family proud of me."

Tomoyoshi and Masumi were brothers, best friends and samurai kindred, making Masumi's departure particularly painful for the younger teenager.

"Take care of father, Tomo," said Masumi. "You will have to care for him as he gets older. This is a very big responsibility I am passing on to you. I know you will honor him."

Leaving his brother was the most painful part of Masumi's decision to leave and he knew his brother was extremely upset as well. The young men wanted to remain strong and stoic and hold their emotions in check but, as they embraced, they sobbed and grasped each other tightly.

"Good-bye, my brother, I love you." Tomo managed to say. "Maybe one day I will join you or you will return to Japan. We will be together again!"

"My heart is sad, Tomo." Masumi choked back the tears and emotion. "I will miss you very much. But in an odd way this feels like the right choice for me. I think it is part of my life path and will take me to my destiny."

Honesty and Sincerity
...means truth, faith, fidelity, sincerity, trust and/or confidence. Be honest in everything you do.

On January 2nd, 1908, Masumi boarded the train to begin his journey. His voyage to Canada was going to be a long, arduous journey from his small village. The recent nationalization and consolidation of all the smaller private rail networks meant he could at least travel all the way to the vessel port of Yokohama on a single ticket. He found seating beside a window, giving him something to look at besides the inside of the car. But by the second day, the accommodations on the train became quite unpleasant. The seats were not at all comfortable or suited for sleep while the train rattled along towards its destination. The cars had an icy chill to them this time of year and the train was noisy with the incessant clackity-clack of the heavy metal wheels on the iron rails and the constant noise of the steam locomotive. Masumi bundled up, tried to sleep or, alternatively, watch the Japanese countryside roll by his window.

He traveled on the train north and east across half of the country for the next two days, over a thousand kilometers, past two extremes of Japanese civilization, an exciting contrast of the old and the new. The first section included Hiroshima, dating back to the late 1500s and then on to the ancient city of Kyoto, resplendent with meticulous gardens and magnificent historic structures dating as far back as the seventh century. Further north, the train passed through the modernized seaport of Kobe with new docks and ship loading, electric lights and motorized equipment.

Traveling through Kyoto held a particular interest for Masumi. The Mitsui family had a long and storied relationship with this part of Japan. His grandfather spoke with great reverence of the ancient city in their many conversations over the years. Many temples and pagodas in the city, as well as in the hills surrounding, were visible from the passing train. Masumi had seen pictures of the ornate, majestic Japanese buildings and he had learned about the historic Emperor's Imperial Palace and the Shinto temples in this earliest of communities. Sadly, he was not be able to stop and experience them for himself. He might never see this most beautiful of ancient cities again as he followed his path to Canada. One day he vowed, he would return to Japan and see all the things important to his culture and his own family's history.

The snow-covered trees and mountains offered beautiful scenery for the train travelers, but Masumi had a difficult time enjoying the view. The sadness of leaving his family and birthplace weighed heavily on him as he journeyed toward his port destination.

The city of Yokohama contrasted sharply to the picturesque serenity of Kyoto and even more so to his country hamlet. It was an industrial port with wide streets, motorized vehicles everywhere and constant noise from the frenetic activity. Modern buildings filled a downtown core and people wore western clothing he had never seen before. The designs were odd but clean and tidy at least, which were important measures for him.

He felt out of place and unsure of himself in this new, robust environment. After three hours of wandering the busy streets of Yokohama on foot, adroitly dodging the automobiles and trucks, he navigated his way to the harbor, located the ticket agency and booked fare on an ocean vessel to North America on the NYK Line (Nippon Yusen Kaisha), one of the most modern ocean fleets in the world.

He used all of his savings and some money his father had given him to pay for his trip and to get him started in Canada. He had the large bills bound together and secreted inside his vest. He also had some bills tucked inside his shoe as further security. He kept a close watch on his money. Not everyone was as honest as he was. His youth and small stature made him a good target for thieves who worked in gangs. In this massive city he felt insignificant and suspicious of everyone. Maybe he was overly cautious but, alone in a strange place, he decided to be extra careful. Ironically, once he got to Canada his Japanese Yen would be of little value, and he would have to find work and earn Canadian money in order to live.

He found an adequate boarding house close to the port which would be his home until his departure day. It was a decrepit three-story building stinking of fish and other port smells he couldn't identify, but it was the right price and the right location. It would only be for a few nights prior to departure, all part of the adventure.

He kept to himself in Yokohama, mostly because the busy city was intimidating, making him acutely aware that he was on his own for the first time in his life. Was this part of becoming a man? Had he made a good decision to leave? Did he have any other choice? Doubt started to set in, but he suppressed it and resisted yielding to failure. This was a skill Masumi would learn to rely on in the most difficult times in his life.

As the days ticked slowly by until his departure, Masumi's solitude escalated the feelings of loneliness. He could no longer rely on the support and comfort of his family and the familiar surroundings of his small village and welcoming home. The people of Yokohama were not friendly and, in some cases, very hostile. He wasn't the only person struggling to find happiness and a place in this world as unemployment remained high and, like him, many Japanese people were leaving their homeland in search of a better life.

The old boarding house had a way of communicating in the quiet of the night, as the building's boards creaked and pipes banged. This was probably an ancient Japanese structure, of no historical significance other than it somehow, remarkably, remained standing. At least it sounded several hundred years old. In the quiet of his bed at night, amidst the creaking and groaning, Masumi would reflect on the words of his grandfather. This was what he was talking about when he spoke of the virtue of self-control and character. This journey would be a source of character building. He would embrace the challenge, build his fortitude and carry on this journey, not only to Canada but towards becoming a better person, someone who could find his own way and look after himself and, one day, his family. His grandfather's words gave him strength and a moral compass which he knew would help him in his life ahead.

~

January 10th, 1908 was another cold, rainy winter day in Yokohama. The streets were covered with ice and snow making it difficult to get around. Despite the frigid conditions, the stink of rotting fish still hung in the air. Fresh breezes coming in off the ocean freshened the air with a pleasing salty sea fragrance, but when the wind diminished, the ever present and over-powering fish industry stench persisted.

He arrived at the port two hours before departure and stood on the passenger loading dock looking up at the Iyo Maru, his ocean liner bound for North America. On the dock, many other Japanese emigrants waited anxiously to board. They were mostly young men around his age, along with one dignified older man in his seventies. He wondered what their stories were and hoped he would get to know some of his fellow travelers on the twelve-day trans-Pacific journey to North America.

Outwardly, Masumi appeared shy and quiet to most people. This was his nature. But he wasn't really shy, just measured in his words and actions. He thought about many things deeply but was cautious in sharing his views or saying too much. In this sense he was a private man but not shy, confident but not brash, and humble, definitely not a braggart. He wanted people to see him as a man of integrity and honesty, not prone to self-aggrandizement and truthful in his words and deeds.

The Iyo Maru was a mighty steel ship with twin smokestacks capable of carrying over 250 passengers and crew on the voyage, an impressive ship and one of the largest Masumi had ever seen. It was resplendent with multiple levels, brass fittings and many windows for viewing the ocean during the journey. Masumi's lodging was a small inside cabin with no window, but it was fine with him. It had a bed and would be a significant improvement over sleeping on the train and probably the boarding house too. He was anxious to continue his travels and start his new life. His final destination was Victoria, British Columbia. The name had an exotic, foreign appeal to him.

Masumi was also thankful he had saved enough money to take a steamship rather than making the journey by sailboat. He would be at sea about one quarter of the time and living in much more comfortable conditions than in the hold of a sailing ship. The steamship was a lot more money, but he justified the expense in calculating he could send money back to Japan sooner and his Japanese currency wouldn't be any good to him in Canada anyway.

Weeks earlier he had applied for his passport and permission to emigrate to Canada. He finally received his authorization after a two-month waiting period. Upon his arrival in Yokohama he heard people at the ticket office speaking about some kind of agreement being put into place between Canada and Japan to restrict the number of people entering the country. He knew very little about this situation and felt it had little to do with him. But hearing these rumors, he felt even luckier to have his application accepted, and he was excited to board the ship and begin the next stage of his journey. So, with his immigration paperwork in hand, he was undeterred in his goal to reach Canada and start a new life.

Just before 11:00 a.m. the crew on the dock untied the huge ropes securing the Iyo Maru and the vessel gently coasted away from the pier, steaming eastward out of Yokohama Harbor on the first leg of its journey to the west coast of North America.

As they left port, Masumi watched the wake of the ship from the stern, taking a long last look at his homeland. The reality of leaving his country, his village and especially his family had never been more vivid than at this very moment. Leaving land—leaving Japan—was symbolic to him, much more so than leaving his village. The lump in his throat seemed large enough to choke him and his eyes welled with tears. He was truly alone. Would he have the strength to finish what he had begun? Could he start a new life and find his path in the world? Masumi's mind turned to the teachings of bushido to find his inner strength. He looked for self-control, morality and integrity. These would be the attributes necessary for him to succeed. Not that he wouldn't need the other teachings of bushido. He was certain they would all be a part of who he was to become. As the ship picked up speed, the city grew smaller and the distant wake of the boat wider as they headed out to sea.

During Masumi's journey across the Pacific Ocean, he met many of his fellow passengers. Most of them were Japanese, but some Russians had boarded earlier in Hong Kong along with a few Chinese. The language barrier prevented any hope of conversation with them, but they communicated cordially with a shared enthusiasm for adventure and a new beginning. The other Japanese travelers came from many different areas. They were fisherman, carpenters, laborers and merchants—each one hoping to find new opportunity and a new life in North America.

No women traveled on the Iyo Maru. About half of the male passengers were married, but they left their wives and families behind to start their new lives and would send for them once they were established with a job and a home. Masumi was glad he was free from the extra concern of a wife and children. He felt enough pressure to succeed on his own without having to think about the responsibilities of family.

The voyage across the Pacific Ocean was difficult. The seas were seasonally rough, and to Masumi's surprise, the ship rocked with an erratic and sometimes violent motion through the choppy waves. He imagined traveling over these same rough seas in a small sailboat and felt even more pleased with his chosen mode of transportation. Trying to stay in bed in his cabin turned out to be a very bad idea. The motion of the boat was not at all to the liking of his stomach. To better deal with the sea-sickness, Masumi spent much of his time outside on the deck of the ship.

Most of the crew were Japanese so he was able to communicate with them in his own language. Once, while trying to suppress the urge to vomit, he met his first new friend, Kiyoji Iasaki, one of the crew members. Kiyoji had sailed back and forth to North America several times and Masumi enjoyed speaking with him each day.

"Tell me about Canada," Masumi begged. "What is it like?"

"It is a wonderful and beautiful country," Kiyoji began. "There is so much land, not crowded like Japan at all. But Japanese and other Asians have many problems in Canada. Last year there was a terrible fight in Vancouver when thousands of white people rioted in the streets of the Chinatown area, breaking windows and threatening the lives of Chinese families. After they rioted in Chinatown the gang moved on to Japantown, but the Japanese were ready for them and fought back, throwing bottles from roof tops and defending themselves with bricks, stones and knives."

"That sounds dangerous." Masumi was genuinely concerned. Where was this conflict rooted? He had heard nothing about these threatening conditions, only that Canada was welcoming and offered immigrants a new opportunity, a new life, with "welcoming arms," the emigration agent had told him.

"You should stay in Victoria rather than go to Vancouver. It is not good there either, but safer I think than living in Japantown in Vancouver, at least from the rumors I have heard in port. And you must learn to speak English," Kiyoji advised. "This is very important if you want to find a good job and become a Canadian. It is the best way."

Masumi also became friendly with the older man he had noticed while boarding the ship. He was a dignified, well-dressed man, clearly a person with responsibility and status. His name was Kokichi Omoto and he was an ambassador to Canada for the Japanese government as part of the Japanese-British Alliance. Masumi often joined Omoto in the comfortable leather chairs in the ship's lounge to learn more about Canada. Omoto was always formal, wearing a three-piece suit and a gold pocket watch with a gold chain, as he strolled on deck or dined for lunch or dinner. Through their conversations, Masumi learned more about Japanese people living in Canada and what the future might be like for him there.

Omoto told Masumi it was true that over eight-thousand Japanese immigrants came to Canada in 1907, but in 1908 only about five-hundred Japanese citizens would be allowed into Canada. In the years to come an annual limit would be set at four-hundred people per year.

"You are very fortunate to have been approved to immigrate to Canada," said Omoto. Clearly Masumi had been privileged to be one of the lucky applicants but, it was beginning to feel like the hardest part was still ahead of him and being described as "one of the lucky ones" might be a premature statement.

Omoto shared with Masumi his version of the riots and violence and the racial difficulties happening in British Columbia.

"Last year there were a few race riots targeted at Japanese and Chinese immigrants. In addition to Asian workers accepting low wages and dangerous conditions, they were also being used by company owners to break labor strikes," said Omoto. "It can be a dangerous place at times for Asians. It puts them between the business owners and the white workers. Very unfair in my view. The Japanese don't want to fight with anyone, they just want to earn a decent living, but locals see them as a threat to their jobs.

"The Canadian government decided to limit immigrants by using permits or a *head tax* for the Chinese to try and calm the racial hostility. The actions helped a little, but skin color was, and remains, a dividing force in human relations in Canada. Also, Japanese immigrants tend to work harder and longer than white Canadians. They're better carpenters and fishermen than Canadians and this has fueled the fires of resentment.

"Over time, as the Japanese Canadians settle in Canada, they are becoming more integrated into the fabric of society, but the hostility and anger runs deep Masumi san. You will encounter challenges as you try to fit in."

Mr. Omoto was staying at the Union Club in Victoria during his visit to Canada. He had stayed there on previous diplomatic visits and was acquainted with the finest hotels and business clubs.

"Masumi," he called to him one morning near the end of their voyage, "you seem like a good man to me, honest and dependable. I know some people at the Union Club in Victoria. I could try to get you a job there if you would like me to arrange it for you."

"Thank you, Mr. Omoto," replied Masumi. "That would be very kind of you. I would be very grateful. I am pleased you see me as an honorable man. It is important to me to possess the integrity of my ancestors and behave in a manner which honors them."

"You understand, the jobs available for Japanese are menial and low paying, but at least it is work and, with some effort, a hard-working man can get a new start there. I will get a contact for you at the club. Come and see me when you get settled in Victoria and I will help you get a job."

"I am just looking for an opportunity, a new start. Thank you for your kindness Mr. Omoto san."

The view from the bow of the Iyo Maru early in the morning was magical. Looking to the eastern skyline, Masumi watched as the sun rose out of the ocean, a perspective he had never seen from his home in Japan. He also noticed two gradual changes during the voyage. Temperatures were dropping and the sun was setting earlier as they traveled north. He wasn't sure he liked either of these changes. He wasn't sure about a lot of things. He had learned more about what awaited him in Canada during his voyage, but the stories he heard weren't anything like the future he had imagined, quite the opposite in fact. Was he heading into an exciting and prosperous future or was he heading to a place where he was not wanted? Would he be able to honor his family by achieving great things? Would he be able to fulfill his dreams of one day becoming a great warrior? Masumi had these questions and more, but no answers. Only time would reveal what was in store for Masumi Mitsui in Canada.

Victoria, British Columbia, 1908

On January 22nd, 1908 the Iyo Maru docked in Victoria, British Columbia, Canada. The buildings of the inner city wrapped around the harbor and there, centrally located, was one of the grandest hotels Masumi had ever seen. The Empress Hotel was a beautiful brown and gray brick building with many windows and turrets. It reminded him of pictures of castles in Europe, but with a lot more windows. There were many banners and colored decorations which, according to the Iyo Maru crew, celebrated the grand opening of the hotel just two days prior to their arrival. In that moment, Masumi felt reassured that this was a magical place and offered a wonderful future. The feeling did not last very long.

As he and the other passengers disembarked, the familiar smell of a fishing industry wafted toward them. But somehow, the cool air and the lush vegetation of the harbor counteracted the familiar stink, at least a little. The combination of smells was oddly pleasant and added to the beauty before them.

On the dock, their luggage was transported to a nearby red brick building where the sign "Immigrants Report Here" was clear for all to see. Of course, this meant nothing to the Japanese, Chinese and Russian passengers who did not speak or read English. Ahead, on an elevated platform, they saw and heard a surly, scruffy man barking out orders. Was this a typical Canadian? Surely not. He was not the least bit friendly or welcoming. In fact, he was decidedly the opposite—untidy and rude, bellowing and waving his arms in a threatening manner. As the passengers drew closer to him, close enough in fact to experience his exceptionally foul odor, it became clear he was some form of authority acting in an official capacity.

"All you Japs over here!" he yelled. They moved as a herd in the direction of a warehouse building. He continued to gesture and yell, knowing full well most of the passengers did not speak English.

"Keep moving your asses! You need to show your papers and then go to medical!" he roared as they passed. None of the verbal instructions meant anything to Masumi or the other travelers. It wasn't until years later, when he could speak English and he witnessed other immigrants entering Canada that he understood how callous that first welcome was.

"*Japs.*" Masumi repeated the word to himself in his mind as he followed the crowd in the direction they were instructed to go. Even with his limited knowledge of the English language, he understood the nature of the word. And he didn't care for the tone and disrespect it imparted, especially out of the mouth of this unsavory character. The man's voice was full of anger and hate, not at all a good first impression.

Masumi had no idea where he would eat or sleep upon arriving in Canada, but there seemed to be procedures in place for all immigrants to follow. He could not read the signs saying "Immigration" and "Medical Inspection" but he could follow along with the human surge of traffic as it merged and flowed into the first building. He noticed Mr. Omoto walking past the lines for the general passengers into a side door. It would seem his status gave him special privilege and advance clearance.

The immigration building was a large open space with tiled floors and walls. It echoed the many simultaneous conversations and the stamping noise of approval or denial emanating from the desks at the far end of the hall. A clatter at a side door caught their attention as several men pulled large carts loaded with the travelers' luggage. Passengers gathered their bags from the carts and formed lines in front of two desks. At each desk sat a white man and a Japanese man acting as interpreter. One by one they showed their paperwork and were then directed to two different areas. He learned later one area was called "detainees," for people who would likely be refused entry. While the second group, the one he was in, went to see a doctor for a medical inspection. Apparently, previous passengers had arrived with smallpox several years ago and the government had established a screening process to prevent further incidents of a breakout.

The Medical area was equally impersonal and stark as the main space, though smaller, with a dank odor of human sweat suggesting he might be here for a while. Rows of wooden chairs, occupied by his fellow travelers, filled the room. At the far end, two doors opened to small examining rooms where a man and woman in each called people forward based on a piece of paper they had received during processing.

A younger man helping guide people through the medical process grasped Masumi's shoulder and motioned for him to proceed to the room on the right side of the hall. Without a translator, the language barrier persisted through the exam. The doctor and nurse proceeded using gestures and tugging him in one direction or another as they examined him from head to foot. The doctor animated actions directing him to remove his shirt, shoes and socks. At one point the doctor opened his mouth widely and nodded towards Masumi indicating to him to copy the action. As he did, a large spoon-shaped wooden object flattened his tongue and the doctor looked down his throat. Masumi was given a complete body exam right down to the condition of his feet. It was invasive and rough, but he had little choice as the alternative surely meant rejection from Canada.

Masumi really had no idea what they were examining him for, but he knew he was healthy and did not expect any problems. Communication continued with hand gestures even though the doctor spoke continually. Masumi had no idea what he was saying. This man was not as rude as the one who yelled at them on the dock, but he certainly wasn't friendly and didn't seem happy about performing his job.

It was clear Canadian immigration was prepared to handle large groups of people entering the country from all over the world. And it wasn't that they generally refused entry or were opposed to the arrival of new Canadians, but they were concerned about the health of passengers and their legal entry into the country.

Masumi's initial reaction to their reception in Canada was not as he had imagined. Where were the people welcoming them with open arms? Where was the Canadian courtesy, offered by those who were happy to see these new countrymen? Instead, they were treated like animals in a pen. There were not enough translators for them upon arrival, adding to the intimidating and humiliating experience. This was not how his parents had taught him to treat guests who come to your home. Through his learnings of bushido, he knew it was proper to be compassionate and respectful and treat all people with honor. His treatment at the hands of these immigration officers was a profound message and its underlying hostility gave Masumi pause to consider again. Did he make the right choice? Was Canada going to be his new home or had he made a horrible mistake? Should he return to Japan? Alone in a new country, thousands of miles from the safety of his family he felt afraid, uncertain and sad.

"No" he said to himself. "This is how I will prove to myself and my family I have character. I am worthy."

Following the medical examination, he and his fellow travelers (excluding Mr. Omoto) sat on benches in an otherwise empty warehouse waiting until everyone was processed. A general air of confusion and anxiety hung over the room. Some voiced their concerns.

"Where will we sleep tonight?" asked one of the Japanese travelers in his native tongue while they sat in a collection room.

"I need to find a job right away," said another traveler. "Is there someone here who can translate for us and help us find work and a place to stay?"

No one answered.

"Can I exchange my Yen for Canadian dollars somewhere?" asked another.

No one answered.

"I have heard there are rooms where immigrants can stay for a few nights until they find a room or move to another city," said another.

Ultimately, that was exactly where Masumi settled for the evening—an old, poorly maintained hotel two blocks from the harbor which had been converted to immigrant accommodations. It was obvious many people had passed through this worn out building on their way to a better life in Canada. Had they found that life?

In the hotel he was forced to share a small sleeping room with two other travelers and a bathroom with six people in total. The rooms were cold and drafty, and the roof leaked during the constant rain. Meals were provided, but the food was not to Masumi's liking. He decided to pursue Mr. Omoto's offer and get out of this place as quickly as possible and hoped he would never have to endure these horrible accommodations in his life again. This disrespect of human beings and the depersonalization of the experience was a shock to Masumi. How was it possible for one race of humans to treat others so badly? Feeling sad and defeated, this was by far the lowest point in his life and an experience he wanted to be over with as soon as possible. He had no way of knowing his future would see this experience repeated many times along with this theme of racial discrimination and in much more devastating and acrimonious ways than he could possibly imagine.

Hamilton, Ontario, November 11, 1967

"Your experience sounds a lot like mine, Masumi," said Hiro. "I came to Seattle but moved to British Columbia to work on a fishing boat belonging to my cousin. The white men hated us and threatened us often. We had some physical encounters with many of the whites while we were out on the water fishing too. I got beaten more than once."

"I made sure to meet with Mr. Omoto the following day at his hotel. Thanks to his recommendation I did get a job at the Union Club," Masumi continued. "I worked there for four years in the kitchen and finally in the dining room. I changed jobs in 1912 and started as a porter and waiter at the Empress Hotel, the magnificent building I spoke of with grand rooms and banquet halls. It is the one I saw when we first landed, right on the inner harbor in Victoria. The roofs are made of copper! Can you believe it? Copper! It was a brand-new hotel, the most prestigious in Canada when I was there. I was very lucky to have the job and they treated me well.

"One other thing, I took the Iyo Maru's sailor's advice and learned English as quickly as possible," Masumi said. "It might have been the best advice I ever received, as it helped me the rest of my life. White Canadians complained Japanese couldn't be assimilated into the country because we were too different. Learning the language opened many doors for me in my later years, during and after the war.

"In the Japanese community in Victoria, I learned many of my countrymen had taken jobs which were often dangerous and paid low wages. These men were desperate to find work and earn enough money to survive or to bring other members of their family to join them in Canada. This threat of cheap labor angered white Canadians and was at the core of the increasing racial hostility.

"Another problem you will remember was Japanese immigrants in the province of British Columbia had not been given the right to vote in any elections (municipal, provincial or federal) even though, except for race, they were exactly the same as other new citizens arriving in Canada from Europe and the United Kingdom. Those immigrants were allowed to vote! I joined the Canadian Japanese Association to fight for our civil rights as new Canadians. I didn't like to see or be the victim of unfair conditions or treatment like this."

Masumi paused to take in the hustle and bustle of his home. This was not a usual day on York Street for the Mitsuis. It was a family gathering day bringing with it many traditions and emotions. He could hear women arguing in the kitchen. What would a family gathering be without the banter? Boring. He missed hearing Sugi's voice in the furor though. She could squabble with the best of them and keep things under control at the same time. An infrequent smile passed across his face from this small memory. His woman had more fight in her than a whole German platoon.

"So tell me, what were those first few years like for you? I know it was the hardest time of my life," said Hiro, breaking Masumi's daydream. "And how did you volunteer for the war?"

"Ah, my friend, very good questions," replied Masumi. "The weather in Victoria was quite similar to Japan and there was a small community of Japanese living in the city. Those were the good things, the familiar things about coming to Canada. But there was much hardship in the city for all Asians. I wouldn't say they were my hardest years, but they certainly tested me in ways I couldn't have imagined. It was hard to maintain personal dignity and a strong character."

Victoria, B.C., April 1908

"Hey, you! Go clean up the mess in the members' lounge. Get to it, now!" barked the kitchen manager.

After three months working in the kitchen at the Union Club no one there even knew Masumi's name. The unbalanced treatment of the staff at the club, and the Asian population at large, was a source of deep emotional despair. White people starting at the club were given better jobs and higher pay than he or the other Japanese-Canadian workers. This was an injustice. It didn't take long to feel the harsh burn of racism, the insult of white superiority, the dagger of hate.

"Yes sir," replied Masumi obediently, abandoning the trash disposal area and heading for the lounge.

"Take a broom you idiot!" shouted his boss.

Omoto had been right, Masumi reflected. The job was menial and the pay barely adequate to sustain one person, never mind trying to support a small family or save for vessel passage for their loved ones, as some Japanese in Canada were trying to do. They were accused of working too hard or taking less in payment and these things were true, but certainly not by choice. It was their only means of survival.

Masumi now understood the aggressive response by the Japanese in Vancouver's Japantown back in the 1907 riot when the white people threatened the Asian population. He would have fought back hard as well and thrown a brick or two. Now, just seven months later, the hostile attitudes on both sides were still on an active boil.

But the general attitude of the Japanese was to keep their heads down, work hard and try to stay out of trouble. And that's what Masumi set about to do. He studied the English language keenly. He made friends, including a young man named Kumakichi Oura, who was four years older than Masumi but shared many of the same views and frustrations. Oura came from a small fishing village in central Japan. They spent hours together discussing their views on many topics as well as helping each other become more proficient in speaking, reading and writing English.

Their initial meeting had come about one night after Masumi had been working extra hours to clean a disgusting food storage area and battling more than one rat laying claim to rotting bags of unrecognizable food. Like every night after work, Masumi walked the eight-block route to his apartment, which included a section along the waterfront. As he passed by a small group of men sharing drinks from a bottle in a brown paper bag, he tried to give them a wide berth and avoid trouble, but one of them noticed him and called out.

"Hey, you, Jap!" yelled one of the rowdies. "What are you doing out this time of night?"

"It is not past curfew," Masumi replied in his broken but understandable English, already regretting even speaking out, let alone in a contradictory manner.

"What are you saying to me, you little shit?"

"Nothing, sir. I am just going home from work."

"Sure you are. Taking more of our jobs like all you other Japs!"

"I don't mean any harm, sir." Masumi tried to diffuse the situation, but now the others moved towards him, threatening.

"Well I mean to harm you right here and now," growled the most vocal of the four as he advanced.

"Stop right there!" came a voice from the darkness just ahead.

A Japanese man of larger stature than Masumi moved toward the confrontation. His air of authority caught the agitators off guard. Not only did he change the odds of whites versus Japanese, he was also sober with a commanding voice. It was enough to cause the whites to stand down.

"Ah, you can all go to hell," grumbled the drunk as they carried on, leaving a clearly shaken Masumi standing beside his savior.

"Thank you for coming to my rescue, sir," said Masumi sincerely. "I am certain if you hadn't come along, I would have been beaten by those beasts. My name is Masumi Mitsui. To whom do I owe a great debt of gratitude?"

"You owe me nothing, good sir," said Oura. "Mostly these goons are more talk than action unless they have a strong advantage like four to one." He waved four fingers in the air. "My name is Kumakichi Oura but you can call me Joe. It is my pleasure to meet you."

"I assure you sir, the pleasure is all mine," grinned Masumi with gratitude.

After their encounter, Masumi and Oura became close friends. As a means to bring some normalcy into their lives, they joined the Canadian Japanese Association where they could socialize with other immigrants and discuss the problems Japanese Canadians were facing. Intolerance, bigotry and hate were predominant, but it wasn't just from citizens. The federal and provincial governments had great disdain for Asian immigrants and some representatives were very open about their racist views.

The deck was stacked against them. No Asian was allowed to vote. The word used to describe this was "disenfranchised." By disenfranchising the Asian immigrants, elected officials didn't have to cater to or even listen to their grievances. European immigrants could vote. The generation of Canadians preceding Masumi's arrival had mostly been immigrants themselves from many countries, just like him, looking for a better life. And yet, they had the right to vote while Asians did not. If you came from a country on the other side of the Pacific Ocean rather than the Atlantic Ocean, you were ostracized, labeled untrustworthy, devious and even lazy. Someone coined the phrase "yellow peril" and it became an accepted reference. This situation infuriated Masumi. It wasn't fair!

Victoria, B.C., April 1914

For the next six years Masumi Mitsui disappeared into the invisible world of domestic servants.

He was present sure enough but, like all Japanese Canadians, he was unseen. It couldn't be called slavery because they were paid for their work, albeit below fair wage. And they were certainly free to come and go as they wished, although no one had enough money to go very far. So, in addition to being overlooked by society, they were virtual prisoners. All they heard from white Canadians was "If you don't like it, then go back to where you came from!"

Masumi's burning inner desire for justice and his expectation of fairness governed his actions during this lonely, isolating period in his life. His grandfather had taught him what is right is right, and what is wrong is wrong. He felt driven to balance these scales of injustice as it related to the treatment of himself and all Japanese Canadians. But he had no platform. He had no way to make a stand, no way to expose the immoral actions of white Canadians.

Masumi was pleased to secure the job as a porter at the prestigious Empress Hotel. Working conditions were an improvement from the Union Club, and he was treated much better by the passing clientele than by the regular members of the Club who held the staff in such low regard. He worked hard and respectfully and tried not to offend anyone. He presented himself as a good person worthy of equal treatment in his new country. None of it seemed to matter. He was tolerated by white Canadians but never accepted as an equal.

Then, on June 28th, 1914, a series of events began in Europe which would, curiously, offer a glimmer of hope for Japanese Canadians to demonstrate their loyalty and equality. The Austrian Archduke Franz Ferdinand was assassinated by a Serbian extremist group. This incident was the catalyst which forced countries in Europe to take sides in what became a global conflict, eventually escalating into World War 1.

On August 4th, 1914, the British Empire declared war in Europe against the German and Austro-Hungarian empires. As a member of the Commonwealth, it meant Canada was at war too. The country would need warriors to help in the defense of its allies.

Like all Canadians across the country, Masumi and other members of the Canadian Japanese Association in Victoria discussed the war and what it might mean to them at great length.

"It's not our fight," said Aoki. "Let them sort it out over there."

"We are part of the Commonwealth," countered Oura. "Canada is going to send troops to fight for sure!"

"So, you are telling me you want to take sides with these people who treat us like dogs?" challenged Aoki. "Go ahead and try. You won't even be allowed to enlist."

"Don't you understand Aoki san?" said Masumi. "This is an opportunity to show everyone we are loyal to Canada. We have courage and an opportunity for equal status as fellow Canadians. They cannot deny us the right to vote if they allow us to fight and even die for our country. Not that I want to die, but I am willing to fight!"

This plan for JCs to enlist came to Masumi quickly as he learned more about the conflict in Europe and the probability that Canadian soldiers would be sent into battle. This was more than a fight for equality, it was a chance to redeem himself for the rejection by the Japanese Navy nearly a decade ago. Like his ancestors, Masumi felt his destiny was to serve as a warrior, but he never believed he would get the chance. He couldn't be a samurai but he could be heroic and loyal and fight for a cause he believed in, the rights and freedom of all men.

"Go ahead," said Aoki. "But don't get your hopes high that they will let you fight as an equal or give you the right to vote in Canada."

Masumi, Oura and several other younger Japanese Canadians living in Victoria began making calls to the local armed forces recruitment offices to join the Canadian military. They learned quickly that Aoki had been right. They weren't eligible to join any branch of the armed services because they were of Japanese descent. Their requests were denied. No reasons were given, but a clear racist argument unfolded as Japanese citizens started pushing this idea forward. Government representatives realized that allowing Asians to join the military would indeed put them on an equal status with white Canadians. For many citizens and influential politicians in British Columbia this was an unacceptable possibility which had to be prevented before it could gain any momentum.

The war waged on into 1915 and then into 1916, and despite numerous attempts to enlist, the Japanese Canadians in British Columbia were still denied permission to become part of Canada's Expeditionary Force in Europe even though Canada was aligned with Japan in this conflict and other Canadian provinces were accepting Japanese Canadians in military forces.

The casualties in the war were beyond anyone's imagination and many Canadians were returning home with horrible injuries or worse, in coffins. Recruitment became more challenging as the stories and the realities of this deadly and gruesome conflict reached back to Canada. Those at home who were eligible to fight learned from returning soldiers that fighting in a war was not at all as glamorous as it was once heralded by the government. And yet, two years into the conflict, Asian Canadians were still deemed ineligible.

Early in 1916, Masumi and Oura learned of a group of Japanese Canadians in Vancouver who were forming a Japanese Canadian battalion. The Victoria Daily Colonist newspaper ran a series of stories on the efforts of two men, Yasushi Yamazaki and Lieutenant Robert Colquhoun of #9 Company of the Canadian Army Services Corp in Vancouver, who had formed an all Japanese troop and were actively recruiting.

"Why are the Canadian forces still refusing to take us?" Masumi wondered aloud to Oura. "We are willing to fight and even die for our country, but they still say 'No.' I'm going to Vancouver, Oura. I'm going to find these men and join this Japanese battalion!"

"I don't want to quit my job here in Victoria, Masumi. But send me word if you think we can join the fight and I will go to war with you," Oura promised.

"I will hold you to your promise, my friend."

CHAPTER FOUR

The Fight to Fight

Hamilton, Ontario, November 11, 1967

The doorbell at the Mitsui home rang around 10:00 o'clock bringing Masumi back to the present.

"Great!" Masumi said softly to Hiro. "Just what we need, more people!"

George answered the door and greeted two men, one carrying a huge bag and a bundled assortment of telescopic poles. George escorted them into the dining room where they opened the bag and assembled some equipment.

George approached Masumi and gestured in the direction of the newcomers.

"Father, these are the people from the television station. They would like to do the interview with you that we talked about. They are interested in hearing your story about World War I."

"I hope they have lots of time," Masumi grunted. "And I hope they want to hear about how the Japanese Canadians were at first refused and then fought bravely alongside their fellow Canadians. Because that's the story I want to tell."

"Hello Mister Mitsui. It is an honor to meet you," said one of the men from the local TV news station. "My name is Walter Findlay from CBC. I would like to ask you some questions about your recollections of World War I for our evening news story."

"Hello Mr. Findlay," said Masumi. "Welcome to my home."

Findlay was a thin man with gray hair that was losing its territorial battle with his central bald patch. He had a kind face and a gentle manner, helping put Masumi at ease. He was confident and at the same time respectful of the people in the house, recognizing the imposition he made with the camera and equipment. Once everything was ready, he turned to Masumi.

"Mr. Mitsui, may we begin the interview?"

Looking around the room, Masumi said, "I don't see myself going anywhere anytime soon. Fire away!"

The inferred suggestion of a military action was not lost on Findlay. He grinned and proceeded enthusiastically.

"My plan is to finish this segment for the evening news Mr. Mitsui so let's get started. We will try to be as brief as possible and not interrupt too much of your day. Let's start at the beginning of your World War I story Mr. Mitsui," suggested Findlay, offering the same level of respect accorded to him. "How did you, as a Japanese immigrant to Canada, find yourself battling in a war in Europe as part of the Canadian Expeditionary Force?"

"That was over fifty years ago, Mr. Findlay. My memory isn't as good as it once was. I can tell you though, my story starts long before we set foot on European soil. Some things I remember very well and that part of my life, the part where I truly felt Canadian is as clear as if it were only yesterday. And it's all because of the efforts of one man. He was strong willed and principled. He fought for the Japanese people in Canada and was a great leader in our community. Thanks to his efforts, I and over two hundred other Japanese Canadians were able to join the war effort and serve our country.

"His name was Yasushi Yamazaki. When I met him in 1915, he was forty-six years old. Too old to fight in a war, but not too old to fight for the rights of Japanese Canadians. He was president of the Canadian Japanese Association in Vancouver. Yamazaki had seen the ugliest times in Vancouver during the riots of 1907. He helped the Japanese Canadian community stay focused on the cause for fair treatment. He worked at the government level and he made a real difference for Japanese immigrants."

One by one Masumi's family members put aside other distractions and started listening to him speak. This was unusual for Grandfather to relate war stories of any kind. The name Yamazaki was familiar to some of Masumi's children, but not all, and none of his grandchildren had heard him speak of his time in the war.

"While I was still in Victoria, I learned that Mr. Yamazaki was the man in charge of recruiting and training Japanese Canadian troops to join the fight for Canada in Europe. I knew in my heart that this was my call to arms. I needed to show my loyalty to Canada by joining in this fight. I knew this was the path for me. It was my destiny to be a warrior just like all my ancestors before me. Yasushi and I shared a common story. Our grandfathers had both been samurai warriors in Japan. We shared family traditions and an instinct to fight to defend our homeland. This deeply rooted belief in both of us was the driving force directing him to lead and me to join the fight for Canada. As it turned out, the samurai spirit was also the source that guided me and drove me to keep moving forward during the darkest times of the war.

"I left my job at the Empress Hotel, put my few possessions in storage in Victoria at a friend's house and traveled by ferry to Vancouver in search of Yasushi Yamazaki. I had no idea of the influence he would have on me or the direction my life would take before, during and after the war. He wasn't hard to find.

"I found him the day I arrived in Vancouver, hard at work at his newspaper, the *Tairiku Nippo Sha*, in the center of the Japanese community. I soon learned that he always worked this way. He was focused, relentless and dedicated—characteristics I have since tried to copy as a man.

"Yamazaki was larger than life. Once he set himself on a course, nothing could change his mind."

With this memory of time and place returning to him, Masumi related the story of his first meeting with Yamazaki, a meeting which would influence him for the rest of his life.

Vancouver, BC, April 15, 1916

The Japanese section of Vancouver was an exciting and vibrant community. Masumi was surprised and happy to see signage in his native language and so many Japanese Canadians all in one place, living and working in harmony. The streets were bustling with activity, merchants negotiating, delivery boys bicycling and women and children shopping in the food markets.

The race riots of a decade ago were history, but the scars on buildings from fires and thrown rocks were vivid reminders of those incidents. The boarded windows and large locks on all the doors showed the impact they still had on these people. The area was referred to as "Jap Town" by many in the white community. Racial discrimination against Asians in Canada was still prevalent even though Japanese had been immigrating to Canada for the past thirty years.

Masumi opened the front door of the Tairiku Nippo newspaper office releasing the hum and clatter of printing presses and half a dozen people all speaking Japanese at the same time. The collective noise was overwhelming, not at all like the peace and quiet he experienced working in the lounges and hotel restaurant. This was stimulating and exciting. It was tremendous. He was frozen on the spot, taking it all in as a symphony of sound.

"What do you want?" came a call from the other side of the counter, startling Masumi out of his trance.

"Huh? Oh...yes...I would like to speak with Mr. Yamazaki. I want to volunteer to fight in the war. I want to serve my country."

"You have come to the right place tiger!" replied the same fellow. "One second and I'll call the boss."

Masumi still wasn't sure which one of the many people on the other side of the counter was speaking to him, but he was encouraged by the reply. The mayhem continued from the clusters of desks where men and women pounded away on typewriters while others carried on animated telephone conversations. Farther in the back, the large printing press rolled out page after page of newsprint. It was all very fascinating—another world Masumi knew nothing about.

Yasushi Yamazaki emerged from an office in the rear and approached. He was similar in height to Masumi, but certainly stockier and roughly twenty years older. His face was wide, and his square chin reinforced his intensity and air of confidence. This was a man who got things done. Yamazaki's most outstanding feature was his impressive handlebar mustache, a trademark that Masumi was familiar with, having seen a photo of him already.

Yamazaki was born in 1867, a pivotal year for both Japan and Canada as a result of the Meiji Restoration and Confederation respectively. Although unconnected, these events concurrently changed the direction and faces of these two nations. He immigrated to San Francisco in 1888 and traveled the Pacific as a cabin boy on an American war ship. As a ship's cook in the Alaskan waters and a logger and fisherman off the west coast of Canada, he evolved as a knowledgeable and tough individual and businessman. He organized fishermen's unions in Seattle and Vancouver and published newspapers in both cities. He was widely respected in both the Japanese Canadian and Japanese American communities. Was Masumi a little intimidated in meeting Yamazaki? Damned right he was!

"Hello, young man." Yamazaki greeted Masumi with a firm handshake and a smile. "So, you want to fight in the war, do you? Tell me why. What's your story and what makes you want to fight in a war so many miles from here for people who don't even like you?"

Yamazaki's question startled Masumi. This man didn't skirt around the issue; he got right to it. That was clear. It was a good question but one that Masumi had pondered at length. He knew what motivated him. For twenty minutes Masumi shared his path with Yamazaki over the din of the newspaper symphony. When finished, Yamazaki knew all about Masumi's family legacy, his rejection by the Japanese navy and his decision to come to Canada for a fresh start. A great smile spread across Yamazaki's broad chin as he considered Masumi's story.

"We have a lot in common," said Yamazaki. "My father and grandfather were also samurai. I have to say, when I first laid eyes on you, I had my doubts that you would have the physical strength and fortitude required to become a soldier. But your story and your passion tell me otherwise. I think you and I will become good friends.

"But you must understand something important, Masumi." Yamazaki continued, "The work we do here is more than just fighting for Canada and the honor of battle. We fight for civil liberties and against racism, for the rights and equal treatment of Japanese Canadians living in Canada! I'll tell you what I told the Canadian Japanese Association last month. 'We are not fighting for whites, we are fighting for peace and for Canada. But most importantly we are fighting for ourselves, for Japanese immigrants in Canada. When you fight, the whites will admire and respect you. They may not like you, but they will respect you. The riots of 1907 taught us that.' If you still want to join us, you are welcome."

"Yes, Mr. Yamazaki" said Masumi. "I still want to join. I believe in the same things, that Japanese Canadians have our own battle to win and we can do that by showing we are loyal Canadians!"

"Excellent!" Yamazaki replied. "Come, I'll arrange for a place for you to stay and then we will get started making a soldier out of you, okay?"

"Thank you, Mr. Yamazaki. This is what I want more than anything right now."

Hamilton, Ontario, November 11, 1967

"So you see Mr. Findlay, enlisting was the easy part. Preparing the troops for war and then being accepted into the Canadian Forces was a much bigger challenge," recalled Masumi.

Findlay urged Masumi on. "Tell me more about that Mr. Mitsui. I don't understand what you mean."

"We were lucky enough to have recruited the services of Lieutenant Robert Colquhoun of #9 Company of the Canadian Army Services Corp in Vancouver to oversee our basic training. He was a monster of a man towering over all of the Japanese recruits, but he believed in us, in our spirit and in our ability to become excellent soldiers. Over 220 Japanese Canadians trained and marched for five months in preparation to join the fighting in Europe. He trained us well and marched us often. Privately we hated him for that, but he knew what it would take for us to endure war far better than we did. Later, from the trenches of France, I said a silent thank you to him for pushing us so hard. But his work and our willingness were not enough for either the B.C. military or the Canadian forces to accept Japanese Canadians into their units. We were told time and time again that there was no room for people of Japanese descent in the Canadian military."

"But by 1916 didn't the war effort need more men to fight?"

"Yes, that's true. But Japanese Canadians were not welcome. It was still the view of the B.C. government that if they allowed Japanese Canadians to fight for our country that would bring us one step closer to the voting franchise. On that matter we were in agreement."

"Then how were you able to enlist?"

"In May of 1916, Yasushi Yamazaki gathered the entire Canadian Japanese Volunteer Corp in front of Cordova Hall for a troop photo. He told us of his many travels and futile attempts to have our troop accepted by Canadian forces. And he read the final letter of rejection from the federal government. Our troop was ordered to be disbanded. At the same time, the government was trying to recruit 25,000 men per month to join the war effort. We were all angry, confused, frustrated and devastated."

"Later that month," Masumi continued, "Major General E.A. Cruickshank from Alberta got wind of the Japanese troop circumstance and made it known that if Japanese Canadians who fit the enlisting requirements came to Alberta they would be accepted. The Albertans even came to Vancouver to get us to join! I contacted Oura and shared the good news with him and he came to Vancouver immediately. His English was better than mine so he was hired to recruit Japanese volunteers. By August of that year about two-hundred of us got on trains headed for Calgary at our own expense and we went to enlist. We were not permitted to join as a single unit or cultural group. We were required to enlist as individuals. This didn't matter to us because we would be serving in many of the same units and we were finally going to be accepted as Canadians serving in a great cause."

"Maybe you could tell me a bit about some of the other men who traveled with you to Calgary and enlisted like you did," suggested Findlay.

"Definitely," said Masumi, eager to share the attention with his fellow soldiers. "I was friendly with all the Japanese Canadians serving in Europe—every one. But I was probably closest to three men. They would be my closest friend Kumakichi "Joe" Oura as well as Sainosuke Kubota and Masajiro Shishido.

"Oura was a large man, also very strong and athletic. He could do anything, which made him a very good soldier. He was so kind and friendly, everyone wanted to be Joe's friend. But the first thing you noticed about Joe was his smile. It was big, like he was, and he always made you feel like he was really pleased to see you.

"Kubota was the smart one of the group. He was courageous. I think we all were, but he also had a good mind for war strategy. I relied on his judgment on more than one occasion and am here to talk about it because of Kubota.

"Masa reminded me of my brother Tomo. With our mustaches, we looked a bit alike. He had a soft heart and thought of his family back home in Canada often. He didn't do well on ships as I recall," Masumi added with a devilish gleam in his eye. "We were all like family in the forces, the JCs had another level of loyalty and caring, I think. These men really did feel like my brothers. We watched out for each other during all the dangerous raids and campaigns across Europe. But war is a treacherous place and, sadly, one of us didn't return home."

"I'm very sorry to hear that Mr. Mitsui," said Findlay. "I know many of your fellow soldiers sacrificed their lives during that war. I'm just going to stop for a minute while we change the camera angle if that's okay with you." With that, and a nod to the camera man, the tripod was collapsed and family members shuffled around to set up a different angle and background for the rest of the interview.

"Back to your question of how we enlisted, I joined the 192nd Canadian Infantry Battalion at the Sarcee Camp in Calgary in September 1916. I took basic training there, traveled east by train to Halifax and left for Liverpool in November on the Empress of Britain. I was finally going to fulfill my destiny to defend my country in battle."

"How did that make you feel Mr. Mitsui?"

"Exhilarated and terrified at the same time. This had been my dream since I was a small child playing samurai battles with my brother. But now, actually doing it, actually heading off to fight and risk my life made it all very real. I was anxious, but I had no regrets, only pride and determination to be the best I could be and serve with honor and courage.

"I imagined it was how my grandfather would have felt as a samurai fighting for his feudal lord in Japan sixty years ago, drawing on all his courage and preparation and led by noble intentions. It was a call to battle, an opportunity to fulfill his commitment, his duty. This was now my time to follow in the footsteps of my ancestors."

"Please continue, Mr. Mitsui," urged Findlay, as he made eye contact with Masumi and leaned more intimately into the conversation. "What happened after you arrived in England? What happened at Vimy Ridge from your perspective? And tell me about this Battle of Hill 70. They tell me you received medals for your actions and bravery in that particular battle." Findlay glanced at the three medals on Masumi's jacket.

"I'll get to all of that," assured Masumi. "But I have to tell it in the order things happened, so I don't miss anything. There was danger at every turn you see. Men died before we even got to the front. It was a terrible experience."

"The trip across the Atlantic was on a troop carrier out of Halifax. It was a vivid recollection of my voyage across the Pacific Ocean, where I was reminded Masumi was meant to be on land, not on water." Masumi grinned. "The battalion was nervous and excited at the same time. We were going to war and some of us probably wouldn't return home. It was a sobering experience, but we shared it together and where we came from suddenly didn't matter quite so much.

"We continued our journey to the front lines, but the first stop was the training barracks on Saint Martin's Plain in southeastern England. This is where we acclimatized ourselves to the geography, climate and time zones. It was a preparation stage for what was to come."

"We celebrated Christmas as a unit in a small British pub in Cheriton near our base. It was the first Christmas away from family for many of the men. Emotions were mixed between thankfulness, excitement and just plain fear. No one spoke of it, but we all wondered if this would be our last Christmas. Sadly, for some men in the room it was."

"On December 28th, after six weeks of arduous training, lectures and equipment preparation, the 9th Reserve Battalion was assigned to the Canadian 10th Battalion. We were loaded on a cross-channel ferry and headed for France.

"The war was into its third year by then. The battalion had been elevated from a re-enforcement unit to a combat unit, so we knew we would be on the front line somewhere."

"Take me back there," Findlay encouraged Masumi, "to the sights and sounds and smells of your experience. What were your feelings and those of the others as you all prepared for war?"

Looking up, as if his next words were written on the ceiling, Masumi dived deep into his memories, to the British countryside, to the coastal plains of southeast England and the white cliffs of Dover, to a company of men in military uniforms feverishly preparing for war by digging a trench to nowhere.

CHAPTER FIVE

World War 1

Benevolence and Mercy
...love, magnanimity, affection for others, sympathy and nobility are traits of benevolence, the highest attribute of the human soul.

St Martin's Plain, England, November 12, 1916

St Martin's Plain was located on the southeast corner of England on the same general heading from London as the popular beach towns of Brighton, Hastings and Folkestone and forty kilometers from the French coast; close enough to hear the battle explosions across the English Channel. Also close enough to know that their next trip across that channel would take them to the front lines. But the events of this day were anything but a day at the beach for the fresh troop arrivals of the Canadian 192nd Infantry.

St Martin's Plain served as the base for troops destined for the European front during World War 1. They were designated to the 9th Reserve Battalion and to their new quarters just west of Cheriton. It didn't take long to get into the routine of troop preparation.

"Dig deeper, dig faster you sorry Canucks!" yelled the British drill sergeant. "The faster you get your hole dug the better your chances of not getting your bloody head shot off! This is trench warfare. Where you're headed, the better your trenches, the better your chances are to live to tell your grandchildren about fighting in this damnable war." The sergeant might have been impressed with the Canadians work ethic, but their lives would depend on the skills he would develop in them over the next month, so he drove them like they were hapless, inept rookies. Their lives depended on it.

"When we're done here, we go back to the range for shooting practice and then a nice brisk ten-mile hike!" he bellowed. And then, with extra emphasis "WITH FULL PACKS!!!! Who's the lucky wanker carrying the Lewis gun today?" he barked.

"More marching!" Masumi moaned to Joe, digging nearby. "I thought when we saw the last of Colquhoun our marching days would be behind us. What is it with the infantry and marching?" he half asked to Joe and half to the universe at large. Neither answered him.

At the end of another nondescript meal, which included some kind of meat from a can that bore no resemblance to any form of livestock familiar to the soldiers, Masumi and Joe returned to their barracks. Joe lay on his bunk while Masumi tidied his. The sleeping quarters were spartan. Row on row of bunks lined the inside of the shack which had been haphazardly assembled from clapboard and corrugated iron for housing the troops. The lighting flickered from a string of single bulbs running the center of the room. A bathroom shower was situated on the end of the rows of bunks. It was only large enough for ten of the thirty men assigned to each building. Heating the metal and wood shack was also a challenge with a centrally located, over-sized, pot belly stove that burned coal. Beds closest to the heat source were in high demand.

Masumi never stopped working. He was folding his uniform just so when Joe interrupted him.

"How did they ever find a uniform small enough to fit you Masumi?" Oura delighted in teasing him. He thought Masumi was too serious and needed a little ribbing now and again.

"What do you mean?" Masumi replied defensively. "I made the minimum height by two inches!"

"You're lucky there wasn't a minimum weight requirement. That's what I'm talking about."

After a short pause, Masumi returned to his cleaning and replied to Joe without lifting his head, "Have you ever read stories by Mark Twain, Joe? He explains it like this: *It's not the size of the dog in the fight, it's the size of the fight in the dog.* I like Mark Twain. He understands Masumi." He emphasized his point by jabbing his finger in Joe's general direction.

"I think he meant *It's not the size of the Mitsui in the uniform,*" Joe chuckled and feigned a cover-up of his laughter. Several of the men joined in, laughing at Masumi's expense but it was friendly banter that helped distract their attention from the more serious matters of their pending deployment.

Training intensified in the ensuing weeks. Most of the men had little to no military training. Neither did the enemy, but the Allies didn't know that. Better preparation saved lives, and that was what they intended to do with these troops—train the hell out of them.

The days were full of preparation, both physical and mental. The army hoped to increase Allied chances of victory and survival by teaching raw recruits the craft of warfare. Through formal classroom sessions, the men learned about Duties, Night Operations, Discipline, Trench Warfare and Care of Their Rifles. They could disassemble and reassemble their rifles in under one minute and they could attach a bayonet in three seconds. It could save a life, theirs or a fellow soldier's.

After more than a month in the British training camp at Saint Martin's Plain, the men of the 9th Battalion earned a break. One week's leave was granted, and many took the train to local villages or cities to unwind and have some fun.

Four Japanese Canadian soldiers from the unit, Masumi, Joe Oura, Taisuke Tanaka and Masa Shishido, decided to enjoy their leave by boarding the train and heading to London for a couple of nights. Once there, they toured famous landmarks and enjoyed the celebrity that went with being a Canadian soldier in England. At first, the British were confused to see Japanese people wearing Canadian uniforms, but it really didn't matter to the Brits because they were Canadians.

At Westminster Abbey a guide asked, "How is it that Japanese are fighting for Canada, mate?"

"We are Canadians fighting for Canada!" declared Taisuke Tanaka. And that was how they responded when anyone asked thereafter.

They visited the famous and ancient buildings of London. Masumi, a student of ancient warriors, was most fascinated by Roman history in London. He held gladiators in the same high regard as samurai and was surprised to learn that the Roman Empire at one time reached as far as England. He was impressed by the design of Nelson's Column at Trafalgar Square.

"I think we should have one of those in British Columbia," Masumi suggested admiring the tall spire honoring Admiral Horatio Nelson.

Hunger and thirst finally overcame their tourist curiosities and the search began for a fine establishment to cap off the evening with dinner and a few local drinks.

"I think we should try a pint of Guinness," suggested Shishido.

"I think we should try a few of them," responded Oura with a big grin on his face.

After seeking advice from some locals, the men headed north on Charing Cross Road to an establishment known as the Bear and Staff. It had been operating at this location since 1714.

"If it's been here since then, the food and drink must be good," said Masumi jokingly. "I don't think we can get into too much trouble here, can we *mates*?" He tried out the local vernacular.

The men were well received by the pub staff and were furnished with local beverages that the waiters assured them would be tasty and not terribly dangerous to consume. The results proved otherwise.

To the men's surprise, they became the center of attention in the pub that evening. Japanese Canadians were an oddity for the Brits and they welcomed them with a warmth these men had not experienced for many years. Drinks were shared, stories were told and singing and dancing carried on late into the night.

Masumi loosened up under the influence of more beer and whisky than he had ever consumed in his life. He shared his samurai legacy which drew the interest and respect of many of the locals sitting nearby. The British history of knights and castles was a proud legacy of the Englishmen, so even though the stories of samurai and shoguns differed, they understood why they were important to Masumi and honored him with all due respect. He moved up a notch in the eyes of his fellow partiers and earned a few more free drinks in the process, not that he needed more.

The next morning, the four men awoke with outrageous headaches and vague recollections of the preceding evening. Oura had some fuzzy images of awkward dancing by two of the men. He may or may not have been one of them. He wasn't entirely sure. Tanaka recalled some rousing but painfully out of tune singing by all four of them along with the men and women who had gathered to share in the festivities. They learned some very off-color songs which, thankfully, none of them could remember. They had "cheered" with large glasses of ale and then emptied the contents. It seemed like fun at the time until all the food and libations consumed started to act in reverse and one by one the soldiers emptied their stomachs. Other memories of clothing being removed persisted, but most wanted to forget those incidents altogether. The rest of the evening's recollections were blurry for most and a complete blank for others.

The men learned a valuable lesson that evening; Guinness and sake were very different. Also, consumption in large beer glasses versus small sake cups was directly proportional to the ache in your head the following morning.

The train ride back to the barracks was subdued, in part because loud noises and thinking brought pain to the remaining active parts of their brains and because the men knew this was their last hurrah for some time to come. The thoughts of what lay ahead put everyone in a pensive mood. Their next trip would put them directly in harm's way.

On December 28th, the 9th Battalion was transferred to the 10th Battalion, by then, an esteemed military fighting unit in the war effort. The 10th Battalion had distinguished themselves as an elite Canadian combat unit taking part in all major Canadian initiatives as well as numerous small ones. The men of the 10th Battalion came primarily from Canada's prairie provinces. They weren't military; they were ranchers and farm hands, lawyers and accountants; average, hardworking Canadians who dedicated themselves to fight for their country. On one occasion a captured German soldier was heard to say, "You fellows fight like hell!"

Masumi and the other JCs were honored to be assigned to this troop but even more terrified by the future assignments they would face.

Their next phase of the journey began as they embarked on a ferry destined for France, a short hop across the English Channel. The trip took them one step closer to the fight. The bright reflection of morning sun off the white cliffs of Dover faded as they journeyed eastward. Upon arrival in the makeshift port of Calais, they disembarked and received orders that they would be joining the Calgary 10th Battalion's reserve troops. A buildup of Canadian troops in the area signaled a pending offensive and it was very likely they would be a part of that battle very soon. That thought brought chills to Masumi.

From the port, the troops were transferred to (or more accurately herded to) boxcars for transfer to the front. A quick lesson in the French language, courtesy of the words stenciled on the side of the boxcars, "8 chevaux/40 hommes," helped them decipher that the smell escaping from the doors of the boxcars was due to sharing this mode of transport with cavalry horses.

"Well boys," hollered one of the troops, "now we know where we stand—as an equal with a horse! Next thing you know they will have us shoveling their shit, another new training exercise!"

Masumi climbed into the boxcar and tried without success to ignore the stench.

The first ten weeks of their deployment did not involve front line action. Instead, the troop built roads, dug trenches, practiced firearms training and, of course, marched. This troop had an instrumental band which offered some additional entertainment, but Masumi felt that, when the battle began, he would be happier holding a rifle in his hand than a trumpet.

Ecoivres, France, (Battalion billet location), March 19, 1917

Along with Masumi, twenty-one other JCs were assigned to the 10th Battalion that week. The troop already had eleven JCs who had joined in December 1916. Canadians with names like Tosaku, Kichimatsu, Heikichi and Toraki had preceded him. Men who had endured the same feelings of racism at home and an unwelcomed presence in the military until Alberta said "Welcome."

Here in France the commander of the 10th Battalion, Colonel Dan Ormond, was vocal in his dissatisfaction with JCs joining his unit. "The extra work entailed in handling these men is much more than should be expected from a Company Commander. From three month's experience with eleven Japanese, I do not consider them to be satisfactory reinforcements and ask for them to be transferred." He didn't say where. He just didn't want them in his troop. Prejudice and racism had followed these thirty-three men halfway around the world to Europe.

Masumi learned from Sugimoto Tanaka who had been in the troop since December, that Colonel Ormond's request had been denied.

"He is not friendly to us, Mitsui san," confided Tanaka. "We have some language difficulties, and this frustrates the Colonel. Maybe you can act as a contact person for the JCs and smooth out this difference because your English is better than the rest of us here."

Ormond, a career military man, had little patience for anyone he felt was not fully prepared for armed conflict. Most of the soldiers within the troop felt differently than Ormond. While some harbored negative feelings towards Asians, the vast majority of the men viewed them as equals. They respected their courage to fight for the British war effort as Canadians. In circumstances of life and death and reliance on fellow soldiers, the color of one's skin meant less and less as time passed and bonds of trust were built.

Masumi's English language skills did help bridge the gap between the commanders and the other non-Japanese troops. His value to the battalion grew as an intermediary and translator for the other Japanese soldiers. Many of these soldiers came to Masumi in the weeks and months following, looking to him as a leader among their faction.

One condition that no one prepared Masumi and the other soldiers for was the waiting. Life in the army was often about waiting. From the time he enlisted in Calgary, to the plains of Saint Martin, to the billets in France, they waited. Waited to be called into battle. For many, this created stress and anxiety. For others it was simply boredom and an anxiousness to get into action. For Masumi it was a time to reflect, a time to go back to those many conversations with his samurai hero, a time to revisit his own thoughts on bushido. During these times Masumi built his inner strength, his mental fortitude, his patience and his tolerance. He internalized this learning opportunity and character building into self-control. While others complained, Masumi learned.

In addition to self-control, another of the attributes of bushido that came to his mind surprised him. It wasn't courage or loyalty or even justice that seemed ultimately important and appropriate at this point in his life. The trait that came into his mind frequently was benevolence. His grandfather had spoken to him about a man having the power to command, the power to kill and the need to demonstrate compassion and mercy. Most men never reached a point in their lives where they'd possess the power (or need) to kill another man. Could he do that? Would he know when to choose between killing and being compassionate? Masumi was not a barbarian; he could not kill for pleasure or hate. He saw his role and that of his fellow troops as defenders. And, in that capacity, he would have to decide who lived and who died.

Masumi thought back to the time, many years ago, when he'd asked his grandfather if he had ever killed anyone. Of course he had, Masumi now realized. But he had framed the answer very well to his grandson. There were times in a soldier's life when that was the only choice, but he must not make that choice without the consideration of benevolence. Most importantly he had to make sure he and his men were as safe as they could be. Masumi undertook this responsibility to communicate the safety lessons and risks to his fellow Japanese Canadians since they did not always understand the rapid-fire instructions given in training. The ever-expanding numbers of casualties in this war suggested that keeping his fellow troops alive was going to be a mighty challenge.

Masumi and the other soldiers joining the 10th Battalion on March 19th, 1917, were placed as active reserves. They were expected to remain there and be available as needed during the next planned offensive, a site of high ground known as Vimy Ridge. Nevertheless, they trained with the regular troops on a mock battlefield replicating the Vimy Ridge countryside, distances and topography.

The 10th Battalion was the most prepared battalion to this date in the war. They would not fail! Masumi embraced the training, preparation, conditioning, shooting, bayonet drills, grenades and trench warfare. He paid particular attention to the drills involving gas masks and chemical warfare. This was new to the troops and posed an exceptional and gruesome threat. He learned how to shoot and load the formidable Lewis Gun, an impressive automatic military assault rifle. The German's had nicknamed it the Belgium Rattlesnake due to its deadly effectiveness. The gun, at twenty-eight pounds plus ammunition and fifty inches in length was, for Masumi (at 120 lbs and 64 inches in height), too much to carry without difficulty, but he learned about it anyway.

During training on the firing range one morning, Masumi offered to return the Lewis Gun to storage so that he could try it out during practice. He was struggling with the beastly thing when a drill sergeant bellowed at him. "Mitsui, are you gonna fire that fuckin' gun or are you gonna marry it?" Masumi just smiled and mumbled something about the "fight in the dog" which no one except the soldiers right beside him even heard. The sergeant's question wasn't too far off the mark though as Masumi began firing the automatic rifle, the vibration and kick from the gun shook Masumi like a small dog in a tug of war with a much bigger one. The big dog was winning this round as Masumi rattled around like a rag doll.

Less than one week later, on March 24th, Masumi and the other new recruits were sent to the front line. Their journey involved a two-hour train ride and a five-hour hike to a small village very close to the front line in Ecoivres, France.

Fellow soldiers had described the front lines for the new troops. Newspapers back home had covered stories about the horrendous conditions for Allied soldiers, but none of that prepared Masumi or his fellow troops for the realities of the world they were about to enter. This was also the first time they experienced the threat of death. In some cases, men with rifles in German trenches as close as thirty yards away would happily put a bullet in their heads if the opportunity presented itself. For the first time in his life Masumi was thankful he was short!

Vimy, France, April 9, 1917

In comparison to many battles fought in World War 1, the battle at Vimy, France was a small offensive. The Ridge, as it became known, was a seven-kilometer escarpment stretching across a small section of northeast France rising 145 meters from the Douai Plains. German forces held the strategic position on Vimy Ridge for over two years. The war had already experienced major battles with huge casualties on both sides. Battles were associated with the names of towns like Mons, Marne, Gallipoli, Jutland and Verdun. These sites became legendary to all the Allied troops and to friends and family at home. Loved ones followed the progress of the war effort by way of the towns and villages named in letters they received from the front. Hundreds of thousands of men had died in these conflicts and yet, by early 1917, the result of the war was far from clear. Nevertheless, the Allies were making progress and a few strategic victories could turn the advantage distinctly in their favor.

To this point in the war, the forces of France and Britain had been unable to unseat the Germans from the high vantage points of Vimy Ridge. The trenches dug by soldiers on both sides demonstrated an enduring battle with little progress made by the Allies or ground lost by the Germans.

On this day, the challenge to take the ridge and hasten the German retreat fell to Canadian troops. In all, thirteen brigades numbering in excess of 30,000 men were configured along a strategic plan of attack that involved meticulously timed artillery barrages of flame and shrapnel. This was followed closely by Canadian foot soldiers advancing across "No Man's Land" and storming German trenches just seconds after the bombing ceased. It was a very dangerous and unexpected assault requiring critical timing. It became know as the "creeping artillery barrage." The danger for the Canadian troops occurred when they "leaned in" as close as possible to the bombing while still managing to avoid being hit themselves by friendly fire from their own artillery.

The coincidence of this battle taking place on Easter Monday was not lost on men of faith in the Canadian forces. For those who believed in God, it was helpful to know they were going into battle on the Day of Resurrection. The symbolism for the Allied forces and those European countries who had been overrun by German forces was meaningful. It was even comforting to have the peace of mind brought about by living a Christian life and believing in a life ever after. For those men who did not have a religious persuasion, the calm before the storm of battle gave them pause for thought.

For most of the Japanese Canadians, their religious beliefs were rooted in the ancient Shinto traditions or "way of the gods." This was their reliance on a higher power. If ever faith was needed in their lives, today was the day.

Easter Monday was frigid with a mixture of rain and snow fortified by a harsh westerly wind. The water in many of the trenches and shell holes had a thin layer of ice forming and fog clung to the ground, making for an eerily silent, still tapestry. That was about to change.

The Allied attack on Vimy Ridge began at 5:30 a.m. on the morning of April 9, 1917. Biting wind and frozen mist engulfed each soldier. The eerie silence belied the turmoil that was about to be unleashed. It began with a thundering barrage of explosions unlike any the men on either side had ever witnessed. The Allied foot soldiers began their assault on the German trenches while the last bombs exploded right in front of them. The Germans were not prepared for the fury of that morning, while the Canadians had prepared for weeks for this exact moment. They had practiced on replicated fields and co-ordinated their timing in such a precise manner that it was sure to succeed. At least that's what everyone thought, and believing was half the battle.

The thirteen Canadian Brigades attacked at once, spreading out along the Ridge, starting from south to north. Brigades 1, 2 and 3 formed the 1st Division moving from west to east with the goal of securing an area known as Farbus Wood. The attack was planned in stages to capture progressive north-south lines of demarcation known as the Black Line, Red Line, Blue Line and Brown Line. Each line represented a milestone and the signal for another round of artillery fire to disorient the Germans and weaken their defense against the relentless Canadian ground attack.

Each division had an objective, as did each brigade, each battalion and, in fact, each man. The 1st Division's goal was to advance their troops four-thousand yards into an area stronghold of German heavy artillery by early afternoon that day. They reached their goal by 1:30 p.m. as planned.

The 2nd Division, consisting of the 4th, 5th and 6th Brigades had a slightly shorter distance of land to travel to their destination of the line between the town of Farbus and Vimy, some three kilometers east.

The 3rd Division, Brigades 7 and 8 had the shortest distance to travel of all divisions needing only to capture the Red Line below the steep eastern slope of Vimy Ridge, a distance of approximately twelve hundred yards. They were to take the ground between Vimy and La Folie Wood.

Once again Masumi's Battalion, the 10th, was held in reserve, ready to support the assault led by Brigades 11 and 12 in the 4th Division. This was the final assault team assigned to capture the stretch of land between Hill 145 near La Folie's Wood and a high point of ground known as "The Pimple."

Masumi and his fellow soldiers from the 10th Battalion began this mission at 4:00 a.m. with a hearty hot meal and a prayer. They all knew many Canadians would die in this battle, but their loyalty and bravery gave them the courage to take their positions. Masumi and his division were in the second wave of the assault. He knew what that meant; he and his troops would be advancing over the bodies of their fallen comrades. The thought turned his stomach.

"Let's go men," ordered Company C Major Sparling. "We have to reach our starting positions by 5:30."

Many of the men in Company C were Japanese Canadians. Masumi felt proud to be going into war with all of the men in his Company but even more proud to be shoulder to shoulder with those of Japanese descent. Yamamoto, Tanaka, Matsumoto, all taking their places on the line and in history, showing their loyalty to Canada.

"Kubota san, are you okay?"

"Yes Masumi. I'm ready, but I'm scared."

"Me too. But we both have the warrior spirit. We will be okay. But be careful today, okay"

"I will. I have a family to go home to. But I will not let my country down!"

"Oura? You ready?" asked Masumi.

"This is what we came here for isn't it? Yes, I am ready," said Oura.

As the four Canadian Companies from the 10th Battalion quietly maneuvered into position, Major Sparling reminded the men, "No talking and no cigarettes from this point! We don't want to alert the enemy that we're moving closer."

As the predetermined assault launch loomed closer, the weather turned even harsher. The winds increased, the temperature dropped, and the cloud cover closed in even more. The flooded trenches and shell holes the Canadians were using for cover were already filled with icy water which was now below freezing. Between the mud, wind, rain and snow, it was the most miserable of conditions one could possibly imagine. They would soon be waist deep in the frigid water of those shell holes.

"Send the signal wireman," whispered Spalding. "Kamloops." The code word informing headquarters that they were in position.

At 6:30 a.m., precisely as scheduled, the barrage began. This wasn't typical artillery gun fire or even a routine aerial assault. This was a deafening roar and a blazing flare of light meant to intimidate and disorientate. It was later described as a "pyrotechnical display" and a "sheet of flame." In total, 983 guns fired simultaneously and relentlessly on predetermined German targets. The German troops were caught completely off guard and hunkered down to survive the assault. The Canadian troops waited. After three minutes of bombing, the creeping barrage of gunfire was scheduled to advance, clearing the way for ground troops to move in on the disoriented Germans and capture the ridge foot by foot.

The long-range guns lowered their angle of fire for the next round, enabling greater distance. After fifteen minutes, they commenced their second round of firing, sending German soldiers fleeing or to their ultimate demise. After three minutes the explosive assault ended and Canadian troops advanced once again upon the injured and confused Germans.

By 6:47 a.m. the first German trench had been captured. In the first fifteen minutes of the battle, the loss of human life was unimaginable. Company leaders and soldiers alike fell in the face of rifle and automatic gunfire as the Germans defended their strong positions with vigor.

The advancing troops in all four divisions encountered heavy resistance at first, but the relentless pounding of artillery and the pressure from Canadian troops, including well thrown hand grenades, ultimately exhausted the German troops.

Oura had a particular talent for throwing hand grenades. He was spot on target for distance and accuracy and blazed a trail for a group of the 10th Battalion to advance deep into enemy lines on the ridge.

"Nice throw, Oura," said Kubota. "There's another machine gun on our left. Can you throw it that far?"

"I'll drop one right in their laps," he replied.

The target was further than Oura expected. The throw was on target, but the grenade exploded before it even landed.

"Duck," yelled Oura as he realized the explosion could return grenade shrapnel back on his fellow troops. The result was a complete annihilation of the gun position and the men in the bunker. The munitions for the machine gun also exploded, creating one of the larger explosions on the ridge save for the bombing of the creeping barrage.

"Nice work!" yelled Masumi over the deafening roar that was increasing in volume as the assault continued.

The plan was working to perfection, and after three repetitions of the creeping barrage strategy, the Canadians had accomplished more in fewer than thirty minutes than the French and English had been able to do in weeks and even months. The deeper the Canadians advanced on their targets, the more readily German troops began surrendering. It was clear these men were tired, hungry and low on supplies—including ammunition. Those who didn't surrender started to retreat in a quick exit to the East, towards Germany. The strong positions they held in France for so long were gradually being liberated by the Canadian troops.

As the day progressed, the weather conditions worsened. The addition of a relentless sleet storm was an aid to the Canadian troops, however, as it blew in the face of the German troops providing strategic cover for the advancing Canadian infantry.

For the 10th Battalion, the progress was not going as well as the other three Divisions. Their troops had been weakened by a previous conflict and the resistance from the Germans exceeded expectations. They had more guns and ammunition held in reserve along the high ground known as The Pimple, and the Canadians were under siege at one point.

"What should we do now?" asked Kubota, clearly looking to Masumi as an unofficial leader of the Company.

"Keep your head down!" he replied. "Reinforcements are coming."

Masumi didn't know that for sure, but he trusted in the planning of the attack and just hoped they hadn't underestimated their opponent or advanced too quickly. In due course, British troops aided in the assault on Company C's left and the 7th Brigade moved in on their right. Together they caught up to the barrage and continued the assault on The Pimple, the highest point on the ridge.

Working their way up the steepest incline across all of Vimy

Ridge, Masumi and his men encountered an elaborate trench and tunnel system that was unknown to the Allied forces. As they crept into the trench, they could hear Germans speaking somewhere in the distance. Not knowing how many men might be hiding deep in this catacomb of tunnels, Masumi advanced cautiously. As he and Kubota and four others from their troop entered a larger, dimly lit underground room they came face to face with a small party of enemy soldiers. Kubota reared, raising his rifle in preparation to fire.

"Wait!" Masumi ordered as he looked into the eyes of these men—tired, malnourished, afraid. These weren't men but just boys. Masumi's instincts took over. They did not have to kill them. It was clear the Germans were more than willing to end this fight and surrender.

"These men are our prisoners," Masumi stated. "We will disarm them and move them into the prison barracks. Enough people have died today."

"Drop your weapons!" Masumi yelled as he motioned to the Germans with a wave of his gun towards the ground. They grasped the intention of Masumi's gestures without understanding his words. They were obeying the orders of a Canadian soldier who looked Japanese, but to the Germans there was no doubt. They had been bested by Canadians this day. Luckily for them, their defeat was led by a Canadian with a heart and compassion for people when it mattered, even for sworn enemies.

Tens of thousands of men lost their lives during the Battle of Vimy Ridge, over 10,000 Canadians alone. This stronghold never reverted back to German control during the remainder of the war and has since become known as a defining turning point in the conflict. The local French countrymen and women were exuberant in their delight with their liberation by Canadian troops as the tyranny of German rule was lifted.

The 10th Battalion held the line at Vimy Ridge in the muck and the mire and freezing conditions for two full days. They were called into action for two small skirmishes on April 11th and again on April 14th and then a major assault on Arleux-en-Gohelle on April 28th and 29th. After a grueling month of battle, the 10th Brigade was granted a two-month reprieve before they were involved in a front-line combat again.

During the battle in Arleux, Masumi and a farmer from Maple Creek, Saskatchewan named Peter huddled in a bunker directly in the line of fire with German troops in similar bunkers a short distance away. These two men, along with another ten, represented a preliminary assault team assigned to provide cover fire for advancing Allied troops. They persisted in an intense exchange, firing on enemy positions during the attack. The Germans replied with an equally intense defense, and the lines were drawn with neither side advancing or retreating.

The offensive stagnated as the men in bunkers became snipers waiting patiently for a movement from either side in an effort to pick off the enemy one at a time. It was a stressful, gut wrenching time.

Huddled in the trench with Peter, Masumi was miserable. Peter looked worn and beaten with a dirt covered face smeared with sweat, rain or tears. In his early twenties, Masumi had learned Peter worked on the family farm. They grew wheat, and he was proud of it. "I'm really scared Masumi," whispered Peter.

"Me too," confided Masumi. "We've been driving the Germans east for almost a month now, but so many men are dying on both sides. I don't know how we are managing to stay alive."

Peter kept poking his head up to "take a peek" as he described it. His anxiety was getting the best of him as he fidgeted in the bunker struggling to keep out of the water pooling at the bottom.

"Stay down, Peter."

"I just want to..." were the last words Peter ever spoke. The horrific sound of a large caliber rifle bullet bursting through flesh and bone told Masumi Peter had been shot. He instinctively ducked and shifted in the bunker to see if he could help Peter but half of his skull was gone. He had died instantly.

With Peter's body laying beside him, Masumi felt the need for revenge and a will to end the stalemate. He reloaded his gun, popped his head up to sight a target and fired as many rounds as possible before attracting new counter fire. Perhaps the same

German rifleman who had killed Peter fired an equally deadly shot at Masumi. The bullet headed straight for his head but took a slight detour as it deflected off the bayonet blade on his rifle. That small piece of metal meant the difference between life and death to Masumi that day. The bullet split into fragments and one of those pieces of hot metal struck Masumi's forefinger of his right hand. The damage was severe enough to send him to the hospital. As the troops were relieved later that day Masumi went to the hospital while his battalion returned to their billet. Ironically, the real luck from this incident was yet to occur.

The battalion traveled westward to begin a renewal of their mental and physical strength, drained from them on the front lines. They spent two days and nights at their previous billet location in Mont Saint-Eloi. In the early hours of May 1st, 1917, a single long-range shell exploded on the chateau that housed many of the men from the 10th. Fifteen Canadians from the 10th died in the single explosion and another thirty-eight were injured. Masumi was safe in a military hospital in a nearby village attending to his wounded finger and avoided another life-threatening incident. He returned to his unit on May 5th, finding a sorrowful and grieving group who were glad to reunite with one of their own. These were men who shared a common brotherhood where race meant absolutely nothing. Masumi finally felt like he belonged.

Maisnil-les-Ruitz, France, May 5, 1917

Returning to the battalion six days after he was wounded, Kubota and Oura greeted Masumi. He was glad to be back with his men.

"Tell me what happened when the shell hit the billet chateau," Masumi asked, trying to understand how this tragedy was possible.

"It was 6:30 in the morning," replied Oura. "Most of the men were awake but just getting ready for morning mess. It came out of nowhere. We thought we were safe this far from the front line, but it must have been a large naval gun mounted on a rail car or transport."

"How could they have targeted the chateau with such accuracy from a great distance?" Masumi asked.

"We don't know. A lucky hit maybe? Not lucky for us though."

"Fujita and Onishi were killed and five others injured," Oura continued. "Most of the band members were killed in the explosion. It's a terrible thing. Those guys weren't even fighting. They were just here to boost morale. You were lucky again, not being here when this bomb exploded. You can kiss your bayonet for saving your life, twice!"

"I heard about the explosion, and then wounded men from the 10th started arriving at the hospital last week," said Masumi. "Being around all this dying and suffering is harder than I expected."

Masumi headed to the billet location assigned to him upon his return. On his way, he noticed a familiar sight from his life in Japan, but something new at camp. Some of the Japanese soldiers had built a small Shinto shrine in order to connect with their gods and deal with the enormous stress of this war. Masumi knew something of Shinto or "the way of the gods" from his years in Japan. It didn't conflict with samurai or bushido. It was another way he could incorporate Japanese culture into his spiritual life, and he planned to learn more about the religion when he returned to Canada.

Arriving at the temporary accommodations he had been assigned to, he saw some familiar faces.

"Hey Mitsui, welcome back! You missed some fireworks last week."

"I am happy to miss fireworks like that," Masumi replied to the men, not knowing who had yelled out. "It's bad enough to expect people to try and kill you in battle, never mind while you are sleeping."

"Who are you kidding Mitsui? You never sleep anyway," came the reply from another soldier in the room.

It was true; Masumi slept only four or five hours every night. He was last to sleep and first awake most days. That was just how his energy level worked. He didn't need much sleep and his brain was always busy.

Back in the relative safety of camp, Masumi reconnected with his men, got back into the swing of the daily life of a military unit away from the front lines, and filled some idle time pondering his life:

past present and future. He had been very lucky at Vimy Ridge and especially at Arleux. He'd watched his fellow soldiers fall in the line of fulfilling their duty. That was the hardest thing of all for him. But here, he could escape the atrocities of war and the extreme cold and discomfort of life in the trenches. He could heal his body and his soul and look for ways to reset his troubled heart and mind.

Most of all, Masumi thought of his grandfather's lessons about benevolence in the heart of a samurai. He was proud of not killing those German soldiers they had taken prisoner. But benevolence was more than showing mercy to his enemy. It was also about compassion for his comrades, and he vowed to do the best he could to help ease their pain and suffering wherever that occurred. Fighting in a battle was only half the job. The other half was caring for the wounded and acknowledging the men who had died in service to their country. This was the highest price a man could pay, and Masumi steeled himself to be respectful of this sacrifice whenever it was made by any soldier. He knew that war was taking a toll on his fellow soldiers and, as a good leader, he should help build troop morale.

Masumi also thought about how the war experience was affecting him as a person. This introspective discovery took place on an ongoing basis. It happened while they hunkered down in a mud hole a hundred feet from a German suffering the same inhuman conditions in his mud hole. It happened back in the safety of camp, in the quiet of his bunk at night. And it came to him as he was helping his fellow soldiers deal with the death and destruction happening all around them every day.

It occurred to him that, just as Canada was evolving as a nation in the eyes of the world, so too was Masumi evolving as a man. Even at thirty years old he could look back on the bright-eyed dreamer who arrived at Yamazaki's newspaper office in Vancouver just one year ago. This experience had changed who he was. He was also thankful for the guidance and personal instruction he had received from his grandfather. Without that he would most assuredly have failed. Maybe he wouldn't even have enlisted to fight. But here he was becoming a leader, becoming a man.

With the improving weather and rest for the troops, the dark cloud of the battle at Vimy Ridge began to lift. Gradually the men recovered from their wounds, the physical ones first and then, slowly, the mental ones. The armed forces could take a count of the injuries and deaths but it's hard, and maybe even impossible, to measure the mental damage caused by the atrocities of war. Seeing a friend's head blown off, three feet away, leaves a mark on the soul. First from the visual impact and then the mental one. *That could have been me!* was a soldier's first discernible thought after witnessing something horrible in battle. What followed was guilt for surviving and wondering what you did to deserve life as others perish.

After breakfast on the second morning in Maisnil-les-Ruitz, Masumi felt like enjoying the refreshing revitalization of spring in France. The harsh weather they had encountered during the recent battles had been replaced by sunshine and warmth. Leaves were returning to the trees and daffodils were blooming randomly around camp. He wandered over to the Shinto shrine in response to an internal urging to take some time and think about God. Masumi knew something of the Shinto beliefs and rituals from his family, but that was when he was very young then and he had not pursued that path in Canada. He remembered seeing some of the glorious temples in Kyoto as he passed through there in 1908 on the train. He had certainly found himself praying in the trenches, so he must have been speaking to someone. Was it God? Did this curiosity with religion have anything to do with his bushido path or in living his life by a samurai code? He was beginning to understand the teachings of his grandfather, but religion was something else, wasn't it?

These feelings of mortality and vulnerability were not uncommon for soldiers, especially ones faced with the reality of "kill or be killed."

He encountered Taisuke Tanaka at the shrine. It was obvious he was in a personal, spiritual space so Masumi waited patiently, respecting his privacy and personal needs. Masumi watched as Tanaka washed his hands in a bowl of water and then placed a piece of paper with writing in a small compartment of the shrine.

"Good morning, Masumi san," greeted Taisuke. "This is a most glorious morning to celebrate being alive, is it not?"

"I think any day is a good day to celebrate that, my friend, but yes, today is a wonderful relief from those horrible days in April." After a brief pause Masumi asked, "Can you tell me a little bit about this shrine and Shinto, please."

"Well this is hardly a shrine I would say, but it is a place where we can respect our gods and pray for our safety and deliverance here and in the afterlife. I'm not an expert in the ancient religion, but I can tell you it has been a part of Japanese culture for hundreds of years. It is part of who we are as a people, you know," Taisuke explained. "You do not need to call yourself Shinto to be able to do this. You just need to be respectful of the place and the people in it."

"That is part of bushido," said Masumi.

"Indeed. There are similarities, but Shinto focuses more on purification and prayer. For me this is about achieving inner peace and respecting others. There is also a ceremony for the dead and this is what I have just been doing. Giving respect for our fallen comrades."

"I like that," said Masumi. "Perhaps you can show me."

"I would be happy to. Do you know that dance is a part of Shinto? Would you like to dance with me?" he said with a wide grin.

Masumi had a flashback to the pub in England he and his comrades had visited just a few months back, though it felt like years ago now.

With a sheepish grin Masumi said, "Maybe another time, Taisuke. Dancing is maybe not for Masumi." And both men had a good chuckle. It was good to laugh a little. There hadn't been much to smile about lately.

Later that night, in the quiet and solitude of his bed, Masumi's thoughts returned to Taisuke and the Shinto shrine. So many men in his company had died in battle and even in the presumed safety of their billet home in rural France. He felt very lucky to be alive and only suffering from minor wounds to his knee and finger. Somebody must be watching over him and protecting him. How else could it be explained?

As his mind wandered, he mentally reviewed the bushido code—justice, benevolence, respect, honesty, duty, courage, self-control and honor. These were powerful words to Masumi but they didn't include some of the words and ideas he discussed today with Taisuke. Words like faith and forgiveness were part of religion and belief.

As a man faces death on the battlefield, he needs inner strength, in some cases a lot. Where it comes from is far less important than merely having it present. "If religion is the source of that inner strength, then who am I to decide if one man's religion and beliefs are superior or inferior to mine?" he asked himself. "That's no different than skin color really. That doesn't define the man. It's his character and humanity that does."

As he nodded off to sleep Masumi committed to himself that he would become more knowledgeable about God.

The Baseball Game

The planned relief from combat for the battalion after the battle at Arleux extended for ten full weeks. They enjoyed an extended and much-needed, physical and mental respite many miles from the front lines of combat. Fitness and recreation were encouraged as part of the rehabilitation regimen. During this hiatus, a crate from Canada arrived in camp with the label "For Recreational Purposes." Two of the men tore into the parcel, discovering sports equipment—two genuine Louisville Slugger baseball bats, a box of one dozen baseballs and twelve gloves in both medium and large sizes. There was also a book entitled, *The Knickerbocker Rules and Play of Baseball.*

Popular in the United States, baseball was familiar to Canadians who had also taken interest in this North American pastime. But, unbeknownst to the Canadian soldiers, baseball was very popular in Japan as an amateur sport played in colleges and universities.

American baseball leagues continued to entertain fans across the United States during the Great War, mostly because their country wasn't involved until 1917. But Canadian troops overseas were hungry to hear of the exploits of modern-day sports heroes like Babe Ruth, Ty Cobb and Shoeless Joe Jackson. The army felt that allowing the troops to play the game and blow off steam while having some fun would be a great tonic.

It didn't take long for the battalion to schedule their first baseball game. Surprisingly, to the rest of the battalion, the Japanese Canadians were keen to field their own team. The rest of the Canadian corps saw this as quite amusing. Even though most of them had only ever played the game in the schoolyard, they felt their brawn would reign supreme over the upstart Japanese contingent.

"Let 'em try!" was one response. "They won't stand a chance!" offered another. "Crazy little bastards!"

Masumi was chosen as team captain, and he opted to play first base. There were a lot more people on both teams who wanted to play than spots to fill, but a final roster was determined and the JCs set about to strategize their game plan. Oura would be the starting pitcher for the Nippons. He was a natural for the position after displaying his skills in tossing hand grenades. Pitching a baseball couldn't be much different, could it?

The other team was led by Sergeant Ian McDougall. They called themselves the All-Stars, a less than humble team name selection fueled by ego and overconfidence. The players were certain their strength and endurance would be a ticket to victory. McDougall was a crusty army veteran, as tough as nails, and he picked a team of similarly brawny, grizzled soldiers who could probably throw some of the smaller Japanese players twenty feet if they were given the opportunity. This example of optimal characteristics worked in the army, so it would definitely work in baseball…they assumed.

On game day, the two teams gathered on their respective sides of the newly constructed playing field. The practice shooting range had been converted to a ball diamond with sand-filled hemp gunnysacks for bases and a home plate fashioned from a single piece of wood. The men paced out the distances to bases to conform to major league standards. The pitcher's mound was located at the intersection of two imaginary lines, one from home plate to second base and the other from first base to third base, exactly sixty feet from home plate. When complete, the diamond was a thing of beauty. The teams agreed to play an abbreviated six inning contest with sandlot rules, and two enlisted men who claimed to have a good understanding of the rules of the game volunteered to be umpires.

Game day was one of those special sunny days, where the men could forget the brutality of war. Instead, they enjoyed the magic of this foreign country and the beauty and simplicity of the game of baseball.

All the players mustered at the ball diamond at 10:00 a.m. wearing T-shirts or singlets along with military issue pants and footwear. But just before the game began, the Japanese stripped to long-john underwear and bare feet. This drew great guffaws and finger pointing from the All-Stars and the rest of the troops who came out to watch the game. What were these crazy guys doing? How could these puny Japanese soldiers even dream of overcoming the obvious advantage of a bunch of rugged farmers, miners and outdoorsman? But it didn't take long to understand the strategy behind their plan.

"Ever hear of a guy named Shoeless Joe Jackson?" asked one of the Japanese players. "He did okay without his cleats."

"Ready? Play ball!" yelled the home plate umpire with his new-found air of authority. And with that, the game was on.

Sergeant James Shaw was the first at bat for the All-Stars. Shaw anticipated the offering by Oura, ready to rip the skin off the ball and send the innards into a small forest deep in left field. He had seen some professional baseball in New York state before the war and imagined this would be as easy as digging a hole. As the pitch arched towards him, he waited…waited…and then whoosh! He spun himself fully around just in time to see the ball landing untouched in the catcher's mitt.

And so it began. Shaw struck out with two more similarly charged, but misguided swings and he returned to the bench equally confused and embarrassed.

Oura, a student of the game, kept his pitches low, forcing either strikeouts or ground balls.

"Nice pitching Joe!" yelled one of the Nippon infielders. "You can strike out all of these guys!"

The speed of the Japanese infield was astounding, and they played flawlessly. Their ability to move without the heavy boots and pants gave them a clear edge on their opponents. Their game was all about quickness. The same was true when they came to bat as they outran throws and stole bases almost uncontested. Once on base, they could steal the next one with ease, taunting the All-Stars to throw the ball into the outfield in an attempt to catch them stealing at second or third base.

And all the while the JCs grinned. They were enjoying their success.

After each inning, the outfield would leave the gloves at the position so the other team could use them. Fortunately, no bats were broken, or balls lost, so the future of baseball in the 10th battalion camp was assured.

Occasionally, one of the All-Star batters got hold of a pitch sending it deep into the bush in the outfield. The batter trotted around the bases with a wide, triumphant grin on his face, his hands in the air in jubilation. But the Nippons unleashed a barrage of singles, bunts and base-stealing that mesmerized and confused the All-Stars. They even turned a couple of double plays to add insult to the drubbing the All-Stars were already enduring.

In the sixth inning, with the All-Stars at bat, Private George Brooks managed to hit a single between the short-stop and third baseman and found himself safe at first base. Having seen the Nippons stealing bases time and time again Brooks was determined to match their technique. Taking a lead off first base, he waited for Oura to throw the ball and then he started his charge to second base. As he closed in on his destination, he looked to see the second baseman catching the ball thrown from the catcher. He hadn't run fast enough to beat the throw. He stopped and instinctively turned to go back to first base looking over his shoulder and realizing the second baseman was now in hot pursuit. As he hastily retreated towards first base, he saw the first baseman catch the ball thrown from second, so he pivoted, reversing his direction in an effort to try for second base again.

This "hot box" continued for several rounds back and forth exhausting Brooks in the process. He could have been tagged out a couple of different times, but the JCs played with him like a cat toys with a mouse. Eventually he collapsed with a thud, creating a cloud of dust from the field. The second baseman crouched beside him with the ball between his thumb and two forefingers and lightly tapped him on the forehead, grinning with delight in their mastery of every aspect of the game.

The base umpire dramatically thrust his arm in the air, thumb extended and hollered, "You're out!"

Behind by a dozen runs, the All-Stars realized they had sorely misjudged the Japanese. These little guys were unbeatable.

The logical reaction to this surprisingly lopsided and unpredictable outcome of the game would be an angry and humiliated All-Stars squad. But the smiles and camaraderie of the JCs was contagious even across team lines. And the grins on the faces of the Nippon players were infectious. The All-Stars just had to laugh at them or rather, with them.

Masumi lasted for two innings at first base before turning the position over to a younger player and focusing his full attention to his duties as manager. It became very clear to the All-Stars that they had been out-maneuvered by strategy and execution. There was no escaping the fact that these Japanese Canadians had demonstrated an ability to play to their strengths and capitalize on their opponents' weaknesses. Respect was due.

By the end of the game the All-Stars were almost happy they were losing because their opponents were having so much fun without ever taunting or demeaning their opponent. *Benevolence and respect,* Masumi thought, *even in a game.* The final score was 24-8 for the Nippons, but no one cared. The All-Stars announced that any future games would include a mix of Japanese on both teams, "Just to keep it fair."

It had been a memorable team-building day with a lot of laughs, just what the battalion needed. It was a cathartic experience for the whole troop. Later, when they returned to battle the real enemy, they would do so as a closer union, a single unit watching out for each other through all they still had to face, with a realization that men brought different skills to the front. Each was a valuable team member is his own right.

For the JCs this day delivered a deeper realization that they had succeeded in gaining respect from their fellow Canadians. More than that, they'd achieved a level of acceptance and inclusion that had been missing here and back at home. Here and now, men from across Canada embraced their fellow soldiers of Japanese descent and chose to treat them as equals.

For the first time they felt a real sense of belonging as Canadians in this most hostile environment of war. Through the simplest of actions, a simple game of baseball, they had earned it.

Hamilton, Ontario, November 11, 1967

Masumi was clearly emotional during his recollection of the events of Vimy Ridge. He wiped tears from his eyes half-way through the story and was only able to get a grip on himself by relating the lighter recollections of the baseball game.

"That's a wonderful story, Mr. Mitsui," said the CBC writer. "The baseball one at least. The recollection of your part in the assault on Vimy Ridge is heart wrenching, but still very inspiring. So much individual courage and sacrifice that most people today just don't understand. It's terribly heartbreaking. This would have been the first real encounter with the enemy at the front lines for most of the Japanese Canadians, am I right?"

"It was," said Masumi. "We had only been there a few months and spent most of that time training and traveling. To be thrown into such a major offensive was difficult. Losing many of the men we had come to know during our preparation for battle was the hardest part. We knew that death would be a part of the battle, but you are never ready for it to happen.

"The Japanese Canadians performed with courage and bravery. Oura once said that some British officers asked him if the Japanese soldiers fighting for the 50th Battalion were veterans of the Russo-Japanese war because we fought with such skill and bravery. They were astounded by our courage and our resilience," added Masumi. "The mud, the rain and snow, the rats, the lice and the cold were all horrible. The food was inedible, and the waiting was agony. But none of that compared to the gut-wrenching terror and anguish of the dead and dying. So many men died. I don't know how I survived really. I was lucky." Masumi looked around the room at his loving family.

"This is why most veterans like me don't talk about the war. The memories are too difficult to recall. They are too painful."

"That makes sense to me now as I listen to your story Mr. Mitsui. The sharing of your experience brings tears to my eyes," said Findlay. "This story and others like it are important to share with Canadians today. Like you said, this is about the birth of our nation, about the great sacrifice made by many brave men so that we can live as free people of the Commonwealth today.

"Three generations of Canadians have been born since the end of World War 1 and most people alive really have no knowledge or appreciation for what happened in the trenches of Europe fifty years ago. It's especially important to hear it from someone who was there and is alive to tell about it," explained Findlay as he looked straight into Masumi's eyes.

Findlay turned to face the camera to capture his comments. "As we celebrate Canada's centennial this year, we are focusing on stories of confederation, the building of the railways across Canada, our bilingual heritage and the positive events in history that helped make us who we are as Canadians. But there's another side to the story, the dark and tarnished side of who we are and how we got here. We need to look at our successes and our failures as we move through the journey of life, and experiences like those of Sergeant Masumi Mitsui can help us do that. Vimy Ridge, and the whole First World War for that matter, can be characterized as both successes and failures. We won the war, but at what cost? And more importantly, what have we accomplished with respect to immigration and acceptance of all races as new Canadians?"

Returning to Masumi, Findlay asked "Have you been to the memorial at Vimy Ridge, Mr. Mitsui? It's really an amazing tribute to the men who fought and died there."

"No, I haven't," Masumi shook his head. "It is just far too painful for me to relive those days. I lost so many good friends and comrades over there. I want to forget the experience. But I don't want to forget my fellow soldiers, which is why I pay tribute to them every year, to the soldiers but not to my country. That is another story," he said, emphatically putting an end to the discussion with a dismissive wave.

"I know this is very difficult for you, Mr. Mitsui, and I am grateful that you are sharing your experiences with me. I promise to tell this story accurately and compassionately from your perspective. But I have one more request for you. Can you please tell me about the battle that earned you these?" He pointed to the medals pinned to Masumi's jacket. "Tell me what happened four months after Vimy Ridge, at the battle of Hill 70? Why was it even called Hill 70?"

"Because it was seventy meters above sea level. That doesn't sound like much and it's an unusual statistic to describe a point on the map because that's all it was," Masumi responded. "But, like Vimy Ridge, it was the highest point in the area around a village called Lens so that made it important strategically. Tactically, it was the next most important piece of real estate, good for military dominance and a stronghold of the Germans. We had orders to take it at all cost, and the cost to our unit was so very high, worse even than Vimy Ridge. At Hill 70, I gathered the strength and conviction I needed from my warrior spirit, from my samurai heritage, and from the lessons I learned from my grandfather.

"Lieutenant-General Arthur Currie was named commander of the Canadian troops after he led the successful battle at Vimy Ridge. He was a great leader, a great Canadian and the men followed his command because we believed in him."

Le Brebis, France, July 29, 1917

"We can't take Lens from the Germans with a frontal assault," declared Currie. "Their entrenchment is too strong. We would lose all of our men in the attack and fail in the process." He spoke to the High Command of the Allied forces during a strategy meeting at Les Brebis, France. This group of men formed the brain trust of the Allied land assault in Europe. But everyone knew who was in charge and no one interrupted General Currie as he laid out his plan.

Private Masumi Mitsui stood quietly behind the officers listening to the strategy session. Lieutenant-General Currie had come to the barracks and made a point of personally inviting Masumi, in front of all the other men, to attend the strategic planning session after dinner.

"Just like Vimy, timing of the attack will be critical. I invited Private Mitsui to be part of this plan so that he could translate everything to the other Japanese soldiers under my command.

Six battalion commanders and General Currie clustered around a table strewn with maps and photos from their reconnaissance efforts. Lights were dim and the smoke was thick. Arthur Currie stood at the center of the table commanding the attention of all the officers present. Other senior officers from the battalions formed a wider circle behind the commanders. It was imperative that everyone understood the plan in order to be effective leaders.

"We must draw German forces away from Passchendaele if we are to advance."

General Loomis pointed to a talisman on the map identifying Passchendaele. "What do you suggest, General?"

"My recommendation is to attack here." Currie pointed at another spot on the contour map. "At Hill 70. It's a strategic stronghold for the Germans and vital to our ultimate capture of Lens and the surrounding area."

"We use the same creeping barrage tactic that served us well at Vimy. The 1st and 2nd Canadian Divisions advance in parallel across this three-mile front," he continued, once again pointing to the map. "We will take Hill 70 and the northern suburbs of Lens."

"I am concerned about the commitment of recent additions to the battalion since April," said Colonel Ormond. "These new recruits seem to lack keenness and the spirit necessary to win. They are not here out of duty to their country like the early recruits and that makes me think they might let us down."

"If you recall, Ormond, you said the same thing about the Japanese Canadians who joined our ranks in December," said Currie. "They didn't let us down and neither will the new recruits. I'm confident in their preparedness and their will. Isn't that right Mitsui?"

"Absolutely General. You can count on everyone in the 10th Battallion."

Following this tactical session, the Canadian Battalion, new recruits and veterans alike, practiced on a re-creation of the Hill 70 terrain near Les Brebis for the first two weeks of August. The attack was set for August 15th, 1917.

Hill 70, France, August 15, 1917

Hill 70 was a longer, more gradual slope than Vimy Ridge with a shorter distance from bottom to top. But it was a hill nonetheless and critical from a strategic point of view. One of the predominant features of the area was a huge chalk pit, and the dusty whitish soil clung to clothes and boots regardless of whether conditions were wet or dry.

Masumi's brigade, the Second Canadian Infantry Brigade, was part of the 1st Canadian Division, assigned to take Hill 70 with support from the First Brigade on their left. The Second Division would move on Lens itself. Their goal was to "walk, not run" to the Hill and beyond to the chalk quarry. If they ran, they were at risk of being killed by their own creeping barrage mortar fire. Their preparation was critical to both their survival and their success. They had done this before at Vimy Ridge. They knew what they were doing.

The assault started at 12:30 a.m. on August 15th with the positioning of the various divisions. By 4:25 a.m. all troops had reported in as planned and were ready to proceed. The code word "Aberdeen" was dispatched by Colonel Ormond and precisely two minutes later the barrage began.

Masumi shared a trench with Private Tokutaro Iwamoto and Private Joe Oura, as they waited for the cover fire to begin. They attached their bayonets in preparation and waited to act on their orders. Masumi took note of the small crease in his bayonet, created by the bullet that was redirected from his head to his finger. Perhaps it would bring him luck again this day.

As part of A Company, Second Brigade, their role, along with D Company, was to make the first assault on enemy trenches and establish cover for Companies B and C to follow in leapfrog fashion. They couldn't help but remember the fallen soldiers from the first assault at Vimy Ridge they had to leap over. Now Masumi and his fellow soldiers were at the front of the assault.

As the mortar shelling reached its scheduled conclusion, Masumi yelled, "Let's go!"

Without words, Iwamoto and Oura followed him as they rushed forward. They progressed about a hundred yards before encountering enemy fire. That was how long it took for the Germans to realize this was going to be another bad day for them. The retaliation from the Germans was swift and powerful. Heavy counter fire engulfed them, and the Germans fired gas canisters into the advancing Canadian lines.

"Dig in to your position men," yelled Masumi as he took on a leadership role. A Company's Captain Stephenson had been severely wounded earlier in the day's conflict after taking a hit in the shoulder and neck. "Let's open the way for B and C."

After Companies B and C leaped-frogged over Masumi's men, the German resistance intensified. Over half of C Company was killed. B Company suffered even greater losses as two thirds of their men fell to enemy fire and the gas. Still, the ferocity of the battle intensified with explosions from grenades and Mills bombs along with the constant creeping barrage from the Allied mortars. It was a chaotic scene of explosions, flying debris and the worst loss of life Masumi and his cohorts had experienced in the war so far.

Masumi's Company A advanced further, leap-frogging B and C Companies, giving them time to collect themselves and aid the injured. Masumi and his men were right on the edge of the German line, but still behind the barrage. Masumi, Oura, Iwamoto and three other soldiers jumped into a German trench and were immediately entangled in hand-to-hand combat in very close quarters. The Canadians overwhelmed the Germans who were weak and demoralized. They took four Germans as prisoners and then proceeded along the trench.

During this confrontation, Masumi's left foot got stuck in a mud hole and the force of combat twisted his body causing an agonizing pain in his knee. It wasn't a fatal wound and it wouldn't stop him from fulfilling his duty, but he knew something had torn as the pain persisted.

Creeping deeper into the trench through mud and corpses, Tokutaro found three more Germans hiding in an alcove and quickly realized these soldiers were not fighters; they were communications men. He ordered them to raise their hands and they complied, not understanding the orders but recognizing his gestures and the futility of resisting. Wisely, Toku searched the pockets of the signal sergeant and found a small book in his possession.

"Look Masumi, I think I found a German code book," he called waving the book in the air.

"Get that to Lieutenant MacEachern right away, Toku," Masumi advised. "It could help save lives." Toku gladly retreated to base camp with the book stowed safely in his pocket.

In all, the Fighting Tenth captured more than one hundred prisoners, including three German officers, in the early hours of the day. Fatal skirmishes continued across the entire slope of Hill 70 as key machine gun posts were won and lost. As the Canadians captured gun placements, they turned the guns towards the retreating Germans. Occasionally, the Germans would recapture placements and reverse the direction of fire. Poison gas circulated in the wind bringing some to their knees while bypassing others. As the winds shifted, the gas flowed back towards the Germans, making their weapon unpredictable and lethal to both sides.

The gunfire and bombardment abated by mid-afternoon, and the Germans showed little interest in trying to recover the ground they lost at Hill 70 earlier that day. But they still held strong at the chalk quarry and the Canadians failed to achieve that final goal according to plan. A subsequent attack was developed for an assault on the quarry at 4:00 p.m. the next day. They would not lead with the heavy bombardment as before. That would act as a signal of another pending assault to the Germans. Instead, the final charge would be a quick blast from the creeping barrage and an aggressive push by the Canadian foot soldiers. Losses were expected to be high again.

At the designated hour, the charge began. The battle was brief but bloody. During the attack, Masumi realized one of the Lewis gunmen had been taken out by German fire and they were making their way to capture the Canadian gun.

"Cover me, men. We have to get that Lewis Gun into action or we will lose it to the Germans," he barked.

"We'll pin them down, Masumi. Hurry!" said Oura.

Masumi stood and ran to the gun, reaching it before the Germans. Sprinting on the steep slope sent a sharp pain through the middle of his injured knee but this was no time to hesitate. He felt pangs of guilt as he shoved the dead Canadian gunner aside so he could reposition and fire the heavy gun. Callous as it was, he acted fast to save other lives. He managed to load and position the gun and provide the critical cover fire. As he held down the trigger, the gun fired repeatedly. Masumi was shaken and battered around by the sheer power of the weapon. The roar of the bullets exploding, rang in his ears and his vision was blurred as he hung on to the rifle stock. He thought back to those days on St Martin's Plain and the time he had taken to learn about this weapon. It paid off today.

Oura joined Masumi to help man the Lewis gun, and together they killed a dozen or more German soldiers including a key gun installation that had been massacring many Canadian soldiers.

"Nice shot. That machine gun was hurting us badly."

"I think they are retreating now." Masumi stopped firing.

"Not everyone," Oura yelled. "Over there!" He pointed to a charge of Germans trying to regain some lost ground. Masumi and Oura were the focal point of the German attack as they attempted to silence the Lewis Gun that was their greatest problem right now.

Oura gathered the last of the munitions and loaded the gun for a final round. Masumi fired in the direction Oura pointed. Many more of the German regiment fell to his relentless attack. They dropped to the ground and crawled back to cover. Masumi and Oura never saw them again.

They abandoned the Lewis Gun when they ran out of ammunition, but by then the Canadians had captured the chalk quarry and dug in on the far east side. The First and Second Divisions held the line during numerous counter-attacks by the Germans. Masumi lost track of how many times they tried to regain the chalk quarry but the Canadians in general, and the Fighting Tenth specifically, held their ground.

The battle on Hill 70 was the bloodiest and greatest loss of human lives the battalion had experienced since Masumi arrived. C Section started the day with thirty-five men and ended with only five survivors. Masumi was one of the men who had survived to claim victory and his close friend Oura was another. While it was important to the war effort, the cost of lives lost was very upsetting for Masumi. He found himself sitting on a dry mound of dirt staring aimlessly into the horizon as images of the day flashed across his memory—images he would never be able to erase.

During lulls in the action Masumi returned to the battlefield to care for the wounded. He dressed wounds, applied splints and provided moral support where he could. Despite his own injured knee, he carried wounded men on stretchers back to the hospital at base camp and brought water back to those waiting to be evacuated. His energy seemed boundless and his dedication to his men and his battalion was unmatched that day.

There were some uplifting moments in the day. One was the simple fact that he and some of his fellow soldiers had survived.

Another was their triumphant liberation of the villagers in a small community in France. He had no way of knowing at the time, that the soldiers in the Canadian Expeditionary Force would be remembered as heroes in this small village for decades to come.

In the quiet of the night following the successful assault on Hill 70, Masumi compared the battle conflict with the samurai stories his grandfather had shared with him. Somehow those stories seemed exciting and even glamorous. The reality of war and killing was neither of those things. Instead, he felt emotionally exhausted and heartsick. So many men had died. Men from all countries on both sides of the battle lines. Personally, Masumi felt many parts of bushido had been present today providing him with guidance and inner strength. The traits of respect, honor, duty and most of all courage were all part of his actions on Hill 70. In spite of that, this was by a far measure, the saddest day in his life.

Hamilton, Ontario, November 11, 1967

Reaching for a tissue to wipe his eyes, Masumi took a break from his memories. He was emotionally drained from reliving them and the pain and suffering endured by so many during that terrible time.

"I'm sorry," admitted Masumi. "This is a very difficult and personally painful experience for me to share with you. I lost many friends and saw many horrible things that are burned into my memory. Things I wish never happened. But they did, and I can't ever change that. Going back and recalling them makes me very sad."

"Don't apologize, Mr. Mitsui," replied Walter Findlay. "The bravery you and the Canadian forces showed and the personal sacrifices you and others made for your country are the kinds of things people really need to learn about from these horrendous events that happened fifty years ago."

As Masumi regained his composure, he scanned the room discovering nearly a dozen people looking at him in complete silence. Findlay and his camera man were the closest to him but as he looked around, he saw all four of his children. Amy and Lucy were crying. George and Harry's eyes were transfixed on their father. No one in the family had heard these stories before. They weren't the stories he ever wanted to share with his children. Admitting he had killed people was nothing to be proud of, and a killer was not the kind of person he wanted to portray to his children and grandchildren. But, they were getting older and could understand that a man's actions in war did not define him. So he reasoned they were ready to hear the stories.

Hiro made eye contact with Masumi as he continued to look at the faces surrounding him. Hiro could only manage a smile and an admiring nod as he choked back his emotions.

"Can you continue Mr. Mitsui?" inquired Findlay. "This was August of 1917, but the war lasted for another year after that. What happened to you and the men of the Tenth Battalion after Hill 70?"

"I'm okay," said Masumi. "As hard as this is, it feels kind of good to share these memories. Like releasing secrets I've held inside for most of my life.

"The loss of so many men in the battle on Hill 70 meant others needed to be promoted. I was awarded a field promotion to Lance Corporal on September 25th, 1917 and officially held the role as a leader among my fellow soldiers, not just the Japanese Canadians but all the men in the 10th battalion. This was a proud moment for me as it confirmed in my heart and my mind that I truly was a leader as recognized by my senior officers. I took this responsibility seriously.

"Later in October I was appointed to full Corporal and awarded the Military Medal for bravery. It's this one right here." Masumi pointed to the first silver medal pinned to his lapel with a ribbon of red and white stripes on a blue background.

Findlay examined the medal which had printed on it the words *For Bravery in the Field.*

"It sounds like you deserved this award for your courage on Hill 70, Mr. Mitsui," said Findlay with solemn respect.

"Thank you." An image flashed back to Masumi of the day Lieutenant-General Currie had given him this medal.

"The battle for supremacy in Europe was far from over and the 10th Battalion played a major role in defending and capturing new ground. Before the end of 1917, the battalion encountered action in and around the villages of Lens and Loos in France and then moved on to harrowing battles at Passchendaele and Wieltje, Belgium. You've heard of the battle in Passchendaele, haven't you?" Masumi asked looking right at Findlay.

"Yes, of course," replied the CBC correspondent. "It was reported to be one of the bloodiest and most difficult battles of the whole war."

"That doesn't even come close to describing it," recalled Masumi.

Passchendaele, Belgium, October 30, 1917

The territorial battle for control of the flat Belgian plain known as Passchendaele waged on for over two months through August and September of 1917. For most of that time it rained. More accurately, it poured. While the offensives, defenses and counter-offensives would be difficult under any circumstances, the greater enemy was the weather and the mud. The rain and potholes from shelling turned into enormous pools of waist deep mud, making it difficult to do anything. Recovering wounded soldiers and dead bodies required as many as sixteen men on a single stretcher to carry them back to the hospital or the morgue. Traveling back and forth to the front line—which was just an imaginary location at this point—meant slogging through heavy, deep mud full of bloating bodies and dead horses. These were by far the most horrendous, gut wrenching conditions the troops had encountered throughout the entire war.

The British army had failed to take the ridge at Passchendaele by the middle of October and had suffered serious losses in their attempts. The Canadians were called in to do what they had done at Vimy and Hill 70, and that was to take Hill 52, the village of Passchendaele.

"We will be training for the assault of Passchendaele today men," shouted Colonel Ormond of the 10th Battalion. "We are under the command of General Currie once again, the finest tactician and leader in the war!"

"This battle may be our most challenging yet," bellowed Currie. "The Brits have stalled under fierce fire from the Germans. Every man must carry an extra load and dig a little deeper in preparation and execution of this critical mission. I don't mean dig a deeper hole. I mean dig deeper into your personal reserves and push forward. If we can send the Germans packing from this point, we will have them on the run. It could be a turning point in the war, men. It's on us Canadians to lead the way!"

Before the next series of attacks were scheduled on Passchendaele, the Duke of Connaught inspected the Allied troops. Roughly a week after that, General Currie gathered the troops for presentations of medals for recent acts of heroism and bravery under fire.

He called the name Lance Corporal Masumi Mitsui.

"For conspicuous bravery and distinguished conduct in action. For showing marked ability and spirit. And for splendid work dressing and evacuating the wounded. It is my honor to award you the Military Medal for bravery. Congratulations soldier!" Currie continued with all the military ceremony and seriousness he could muster: "It pleases me to be honoring some of the Japanese Canadian troops here today," which was an obvious jab at Ormond. He smiled as he handed the medal to Masumi.

During the first half of November, the Canadians moved back and forth between Passchendaele and Ypres, from the front line to reserve and back again. On several sorties Masumi found himself paired with Masajiro Shishido, a solid and intense fighter who often spoke of his wife and son back home in British Columbia.

Hunkered down on the front line, close to the Germans, in the early hours of the morning they shared a quiet conversation.

"It must be hard for you to be here with a wife and child back home, Masa," said Masumi.

"More difficult than I ever imagined, and it doesn't look like we will be going home any time soon," said Masa. "But I know what we are doing here is right for Canada and for the Japanese Canadians who pray for us every day. My biggest fear is that I will be killed and leave my wife and daughter on their own."

Suddenly, the peaceful morning was shattered by small and medium arms fire bombarding the Canadians, forcing them to keep their heads low. Masumi and Masajiro knew this meant the Germans were attacking, but they had a plan. As bullets flew over their heads, the noise of the advancing Germans grew louder.

The attacks by the Germans had been fewer and fewer after the losses of men and military power they had experienced lately. They seemed content to try and hold their ground rather than recapture lost positions. But Currie had prepared his troops for all possible scenarios, so the men were ready to react.

"Remember Masa, stay low and wait until they are close before we return fire," counseled Masumi. The strategy was to let the Germans approach the Allied front line and then flank them, so they could attack from the side. It worked to perfection.

The Canadians returned fire, forcing the Germans to take cover. During the confusion, a handful of Canadian troops managed to slip around their flank and inflict serious casualties on the enemy. Masa was ready to attack and kill the remaining German soldiers, but Masumi held him back.

"Let them go," Masumi urged. "The ones who aren't killed or wounded are busy helping the others back to where they came from. Enough people have died here today," he said, repeating that familiar phrase. "The town of Passchendaele will be in our control by the end of today," he predicted. And he was right.

Once again, the Canadian troops led a successful mission where others failed. Maybe the Brits, French and Dutch had softened the Germans for Canada or maybe the intensity of the Canadian troops finally broke the back of the German lines. Whatever the case, victory was at hand and the Canadians, including a strong contingent of Japanese Canadians, were the reason why.

Many people questioned the wisdom of trying to take Passchendaele under such gruesome and difficult conditions. And the ultimate gains compared to the cost of human lives made the battle a difficult one to justify. But for Masumi, this was just another battle in a war that was as much about his fight for Japanese Canadian recognition as it was for Allied supremacy.

⁓

December 17th, 1917 was a memorable day for Masumi and the other Japanese Canadians in the war in Europe. On this day, the soldiers cast their votes for the federal election back home. Here, on foreign soil, Masumi and other Japanese Canadians were given the right to cast their ballots for the first time. Here, they were equals among their fellow Canadians, most of them at least. Even after the sacrifices made by the Japanese Canadian soldiers, some of the white Canadians—the ones from British Columbia in particular—voiced their disapproval. As Masumi and Oura waited in line for their turn to vote a nearby conversation, loud enough for them to hear, typified the attitude they experienced at home.

"They aren't allowed to vote at home," protested George McLanders. "It's the law. Why should they be allowed to vote here?"

"I think there's something wrong with that law," said Private William Beggs as he stood in line to cast his ballot.

"What?" asked McLanders.

"These little guys are fighting right along beside us and risking their lives for their country just like the rest of us. Why shouldn't they have a say in who's elected?"

"Because they're Japs."

"And you're a fuckin' Scot, but you get to vote, don't you?"

"It's not the same."

"You're right mate. It ain't the same, but it should be!"

Voting day was a soul-searching day for Lance Corporal Masumi Mitsui. The treatment of some of his fellow soldiers, men he regarded as friends and compatriots, brought back the painful feelings of rejection and hatred directed towards Masumi, his family and his friends back in Canada. It also showed that a divide still existed among the soldiers in the battalion, a divide that he thought had been overcome. It was buried a lot deeper than it used to be, but it was not vanquished. Some were sympathetic and others still harbored raw prejudice toward them despite their allegiance and dependence on each other. He wondered how his life would be different in British Columbia when he returned home. Would their efforts to gain respect by fighting for Canada be recognized? Would he be a celebrated war hero or would he be treated exactly as he had been before he left? Time would tell, assuming he lived to see that day.

"Who are you going to vote for, Masumi?" Oura asked Masumi when they reached the front of the line.

"I have no idea. That doesn't matter nearly as much as the fact I am even able to vote. That's my satisfaction today."

In the end, Masumi found strength in the experience. He found resolve in his mission to gain equality for the Japanese people in Canada. This was, after all, what they were fighting for. And this day had been a little taste of what it was like to exercise his democratic franchise to cast a ballot in an election.

Hamilton, Ontario, November 11, 1967

"It's a real head-scratcher isn't it, Mr. Findlay?" asked Masumi. "You risk your life for your country and you get paid back with rejection. But it was the start of change. Yamazaki had been right. We were gaining respect, one person at a time. As you know, we did get the vote, but not all at once and not without a lot of work. But that's a story for another time. Let's get back to the war. It was coming to an end.

"We fought the Germans back and forth across France and Belgium for the rest of 1918. The attack and retreat scenario continued as we would overtake a German stronghold one day, and they would rally and force us out the next. Many men died on both sides and many more were wounded."

"These sound like extreme conditions, beyond human endurance," said Findlay. "Was there a strong urge to just run away and return home?"

"Every day…for every man," said Masumi. "But the penalty for desertion was death."

"Excuse me?"

"Yes, I'm not joking. Twenty-five Canadians were executed by firing squad during the First World War. It's a fact, you can look it up. The Brits executed over three-hundred of their own men during the war for crimes like desertion, cowardice and even murder. You could leave, but if you got caught you would be shot by firing squad. Your chances were better facing the enemy. There really wasn't anywhere to go."

"This is part of Canadian war history that few of our countrymen know about Mr. Mitsui. It's a black mark on the military for its treatment of its soldiers to say the least," said Findlay.

"Let's talk about something else," requested Masumi. "Christmas in 1917 was a very strange time on the front lines of the war in Europe."

"Why was that?" asked Findlay.

"By then, men on both sides, Allies and the Axis had been away from families and endured unthinkable experiences for two to three years. We were all tired, homesick and wishing we could be anywhere else, but mostly with our friends and families at home.

"I was lucky enough to get leave two weeks before Christmas and I went to Paris. But what happened on Christmas on the front lines was shared with me. It's a story that has been told a hundred times, I'm sure. It was quite unbelievable.

"Men from both sides ceased fire, came out of their trenches to shake hands and wish each other a Merry Christmas. In some cases, small gifts were even exchanged. When the senior officers heard about this, they were angry but, for one brief moment during the war, a sense of peace and goodwill toward men took over, a sense of caring for your enemy as a person who was also missing family on a special day of the year. It didn't last long but it happened."

"I've never heard that story before. It really is unbelievable, as you say. Heart-warming and sad all at the same time. And then the next day you returned to trying to kill each other?"

"Yes, that's how it was."

"Your recollections pique my curiosity in another way, Mr. Mitsui.

What happened in Paris on your leave? Did you visit the infamous Moulin Rouge?" Findlay asked with a slight grin.

"I cannot speak of these things with my children in the room," Masumi grinned, thankful for a lighter moment in the interview. "I was a single man in Paris in 1917, on relief from the war. I will leave the rest to your imagination." He laughed in response.

"Very well." Findlay grinned back at him. "Please continue when you feel up to it."

"Let's keep going," said Masumi. "If we stop now, I'm not sure I would want to do this again, at least not any time soon."

"In 1918 it felt like we were starting to gain the upper hand in the war. We advanced more than we retreated. We progressed through Europe and drove the Germans back, closer and closer to Germany and the end of the war day by day and foot by foot.

"It was difficult to keep troop morale high as we advanced. We were winning but men still died every day. The pressure and fear of knowing that the next guy to die could be you was overwhelming." Masumi paused, deeply affected by the numerous images this narrative was unearthing.

"One thing I did, to give the men a boost in morale, was to fill my canteen with liquor at every village along the way. People had abandoned their homes and possessions, so I didn't think they would mind sharing some wine or brandy with Canadian forces. I would dump out my water and fill my canteen with booze from one of the village homes. In the evening after dinner I passed around the canteen. The men loved this, a little thing that made a difference.

"Here's the very canteen." Masumi reached beside him and pushed back a cabinet door, pulling out a canvas covered canteen that was dented and dirty, a genuine war relic.

"That's fantastic!" said Findlay. "You really did that? Amazing! And you still have it."

"It's important to me." He kept it close to him day in and day out. This battered old remnant from World War 1 had great provenance. It was passed around the room and each person held it with unusual respect and honor as they pictured images of those war weary men enjoying one brief pleasure at the end of a day in the course of a dreadful experience. It was a haunting moment for all. George opened the cap and smelled the contents but quickly jerked his head away with a disgusted look on his face. Masumi grinned at George's reaction knowing all too well the canteen reeked of ancient French brandy which was stale and pungent after fifty years.

"Let's get back to 1918, when you said it felt like the Allies were starting to gain the upper hand," suggested Findlay. "How were the troops able to turn the tide and bring an end to this War to End All Wars, as it became known, even though we now know that wasn't to be?"

"We started the year in Loos, France and worked our way around the area clearing villages of German occupation. I can't remember all the names of the villages, but I can sure remember the faces and gratitude of the French people as we liberated them from the Germans. They were so happy to see us and thank us. It was a wonderful feeling. They shared bread, cheese and wine with us, and the women couldn't stop kissing us. I was shy around women back then and a little embarrassed by the attention. This reminds me, I have another baseball story to tell you," said Masumi.

"Excellent," said Findlay. "I really enjoyed the last one."

"In May 1918 our battalion was stationed in Liencourt, France with other British and Canadian battalions. We were there for a few weeks to rest and recharge. During that time the Second Brigade staged the first ever Military Circus. I know," said Masumi, "it doesn't sound like a baseball story, but I'll get to that.

"So, anyway, we organized a grand circus parade and equestrian events. We also planned baseball, soccer and football games and even had a dance in the evening with the nurses from three different hospitals." He winked in Findlay's direction.

"But the best part of it for me was the baseball tournament. The 10th Battalion went undefeated, eight-zero." He raised a fist in victory. "We put together a team of big hitters and fast runners, Japanese mostly, and we used the same tactics as before. We were unbeatable and finished in first place!" He changed his raised fist to a raised forefinger. "That feeling of being part of the team—a feeling of acceptance—returned. The whole experience was invigorating and it took us away from the war, for a little while at least. It was great!

"The Tenth Battalion had replaced the lost members of their band who were killed in the explosion at Mont Saint-Eloi with men who had recovered from their wounds or new recruits. They also scavenged musical instruments to replace what was lost in the random bombing in May of last year. They provided great entertainment for everyone. I believe this was a boost to the corps' spirit.

"From there, the troop moved to various points of conflict in France during the first part of 1918 but enjoyed extended periods of relief as well. This, along with the onset of spring in France, brightened spirits.

"We pushed the Germans back in France and Belgium and by late summer had advanced further east than we had ever been during the war. If we hadn't been in the middle of a war with people shooting at us from every village and hay bale this might have been a nice place to visit. The rolling hills, well-kept fields and quaint villages were beautiful and wrapped in deep tradition and history. It was sad to see whole villages abandoned as innocent victims of war left their homes to escape the tyranny of the German invasion.

"As we marched from village to village, my canteen was getting a pretty good workout—filled during the day and drained by my men in the evenings. We enjoyed those gatherings and became as close as men can be under these circumstances, like brothers almost." Masumi saddened as he thought of the men who hadn't made it home.

"I took special interest in the lifestyle of these rural French and Dutch families. They lived in small but beautiful, well-kept farmhouses on small plots of land and enjoyed a private, peaceful existence. At least they did before the Germans invaded. These people lived off the land and fended for themselves. They didn't work in regular jobs but they worked hard for themselves. I liked the concept of being a farmer and having that independence to be in charge of my own destiny and not have to answer to someone yelling at me to sweep a floor or take out some garbage. For me this appeared to be an ideal way to live and raise a family. The farmers enjoyed the outdoors, planted and harvested crops and led a relatively independent life. It was the same across the countryside and from nation to nation. It didn't matter if they were French, Austrian, or English, the rural lifestyle had an alluring call for me. It got me thinking about life after the war and the possibility of having one like those generous and kind people.

"In September 1918, I was promoted again, this time to Lance Sergeant. I had gained the confidence of the men. Colonel Ormond was also promoted and transferred, removing the racial barrier that existed between us. His replacement Major Whidden MacDonald and I got along much better and he appreciated the work ethic and loyalty of the Japanese Canadian soldiers. He had been with the Tenth when we joined and knew firsthand what we did for the battalion.

"Near the end of September, our unit was moving to Cambria, France when we encountered German machine gunfire. Oura was badly hit, and he was in a lot of pain. I dressed his wound and the medics took him back to the hospital unit. I thought he was going to be okay. But on October 6th, I learned that he died from the wound." Masumi paused, lost in his thoughts and memories as his audience offered a respectful silence.

"My oldest and best friend, Joe Kumakichi Oura, had been killed. A simple salmon fisherman from Steveston, British Columbia, a loyal Canadian soldier had died serving his country. I was devastated." Masumi choked back tears.

"He had been appointed to Corporal at the same time I was promoted to Lance Sergeant. We had been through so much together, so close from the very start. I have never gotten over his death. Even to this day it makes me sad to think about it. It was so close to the end of the war as it turned out. What a useless waste of life! He was buried in the war cemetery in Etaples, France.

"Life was a blur for me after that. I was sent on two weeks leave in November 1918 while the Tenth Battalion made its final march on Germany. I rejoined my unit on December 10th as we marched into Cologne. The twin spires of the massive cathedral there were visible for miles before reaching the city. Our arrival was bittersweet. Not surprisingly, the German people were not nearly as happy to see us as the French had been. For them this was defeat. We had to behave with dignity and compassion and this was my message to my men. We were proud but not disrespectful. My grandfather taught me about how to be a good winner and a good loser, how to respect others and be merciful. This was the bushido way, and this was how we finished our journey.

"I left for England one week after Germany surrendered. You can imagine the celebration going on in London. It was amazing, but because of Oura's death, I was not at all in the spirit to celebrate."

At 10:45 a.m. Masumi rose from his chair and spoke.

"Please excuse me now. It's time for my Memorial Service."

He turned on his small television near his chair and found the broadcast on CBC. The memorial service was being held at the Eternal Flame by the parliament buildings in Ottawa, commemorating Remembrance Day and the fifty-year anniversary of the Battle at Vimy Ridge. Prime Minister Lester B. Pearson was speaking. A Liberal, Masumi remembered. He was the leader of the same party in power when they were interned during the Second World War under Mackenzie-King. The connection stirred Masumi's anger.

For the past twenty-two years Masumi had his own Remembrance Day ritual. As he did today, he dressed in his World War 1 uniform, put on his three medals and Legion pin and saluted his fallen comrades. But he would not attend the hypocritical ceremonies of the government, ceremonies that took place as if nothing had even happened to World War 1 Japanese Canadian war veterans during World War 2. The government wanted to sweep that atrocity under the rug, but Masumi couldn't let it go.

Findlay signaled his cameraman to make sure he filmed Masumi during his tribute. This image would be important in the telling of this amazing tale.

As the clocked reached the top of the hour, Masumi listened to the broadcaster say, "On the eleventh hour of the eleventh day of the eleventh month in 1918, the guns of Europe fell silent. After four years of bitter fighting, The Great War was finally over. The Armistice was signed at 5:00 a.m. in a railway carriage in the Forest of Compiegne, France on November 11th, 1918. Six hours later, at 11 a.m., the war ended."

This proclamation was followed by two minutes of silence. For those minutes Masumi stood at attention saluting his fallen comrades and remembering the events he had just shared with the CBC reporter, remembering the men of the Fighting Tenth Battalion and especially those fifty-five brave Japanese Canadians who sacrificed their lives on the battlefield and in the skirmishes across Europe during the First World War. Tears appeared on Masumi's cheeks as he maintained his stance at attention. The camera caught the emotion in this moment better than any words could ever describe. His recollections were made ever more vivid by sharing them with others. This was why he preferred not to speak of the war.

As Masumi ended his salute and shifted to an at ease position, he glanced around the room. Amy, Lucy and Nancy were all in tears again as they watched Masumi pay his tribute. "We are all very proud of you," Amy said, generating agreeable nods from other family members.

Findlay gave Masumi a little time to compose himself from the emotional experience. The interview was over and he had enough material to share a fantastic tribute to Masumi and the Japanese Canadian war veterans and to those who lost their lives in World War 1.

"Thank you very much for sharing this very personal part of your life with me today, Mr. Mitsui. I am honored that you have recounted your story for us. You have given our viewers a chance to understand exactly what it was like during World War 1 and the great sacrifices made fifty years ago."

Looking at his cameraman, Findlay whispered, "Get this film edited for the six o'clock news. This is a story of the war that has never been told. You can see the feelings of betrayal in the man's eyes as he stands in honor of his fellow soldiers and in defiance of his government! This is our lead story tonight."

CHAPTER SIX

Between the Wars

Loyalty and Duty
...the ideas of being faithful, devoted, true, and obedient. The warrior practices unconditional loyalty and trust towards others.

Hamilton, Ontario, November 11, 1967

"Father, wake up. Mr. Ken Adachi is here to see you."

"What? Who? What have you gone and done now, Amy?" Masumi asked in a confused and half-awake state looking up at the stranger standing in front of him.

"Oh please, don't wake him," said Adachi.

"Oh goodness," said Amy. "He drops off all the time. He'll probably fall asleep once or twice while he's talking to you. Just poke him a little bit but don't make any sounds like explosions. He doesn't like that at all." She winked and grinned.

"Father," she spoke a little louder. "It's Ken Adachi, the Japanese writer from Toronto."

"Maryland, actually," Adachi corrected her.

"Let's keep it simple," she suggested. "He knows where Toronto is."

Masumi slowly, and a little painfully, rose from his chair, looked around the room to get his bearings and tried to remember what day it was and why the house was full of people. Seeing his blue blazer and medals hanging on the side chair, he began to remember the time and place.

"Yes, yes, Mr. Adachi," Masumi said with an enthusiastic handshake. "I have been looking forward to speaking with you. Amy tells me your family was interned in B.C. in 1942 like us. Come, please. Sit with me here." He pointed to a couch near his chair.

"Coffee, Mr. Adachi?" asked Amy.

"Yes please, two creams, one sugar."

"Please tell me about yourself and why you have come to meet with me and my family today," Masumi asked.

"Well, to start, I am a second-generation Japanese immigrant. Like you and your family, my family was interned during World War 2. We were located in Slocan, B.C. I was thirteen years old at the time. After the war, I started a writing career with the *New Canadian*, a Japanese Canadian newspaper. I taught literature at the University of Toronto and I'm currently a teacher at the University of Maryland. I am very passionate about the stories of Japanese Canadians and, from what I know about you and your family's experiences, these are just the kinds of memories that need to be told."

"That's am impressive thing for you to become a university professor from a start in an internment camp, Mr. Adachi. Well done!"

"Thank you for that and for speaking with me today, Mr. Mitsui," Adachi began. "It is an honor to meet you and I look forward to hearing about many of your experiences as a Japanese Canadian."

"Well, if you watch the six o'clock news you can learn all about me," Masumi said with a smirk. "That CBC news guy, Findlay, just left about an hour ago and I told him all about World War 1."

"I'm sure it's very interesting," said Adachi. "I'll try to watch it. But what I am working on is a bit different. I'm writing a book addressing racism, a history of Japanese Canadians. At eighty years old, you have a lot of history as a Japanese Canadian and some very interesting experiences from what I have been able to discover.

"I have researched the riots of 1907 and many stories about Japanese Canadians in World War 1 as well as some of those in World War 2. I also have firsthand knowledge of the internment camps and the years following the second war. But, a time gap for me—because it is before I was born—is the period immediately following the First World War. If you can, please recall for me what life was like in Canada when you and the other Japanese Canadian war heroes returned to Canada. How did you re-enter society, and were you treated differently when you returned than you had been treated before the war? Were you ever able to reintegrate into the life you once led before Pearl Harbor?"

"Yes, it certainly was an important period in my life," responded Masumi. "We were so very happy, jubilant really, since the war was over and we could finally return home. But, at the same time, we were damaged, and no one comprehended or predicted how we would be affected in the years ahead. After World War 1 they called it 'shell shock' and then after World War 2 it was called 'combat exhaustion.' Call it what you like. We were all messed up for a long time. Some men took their own lives. Others drank heavily, while some found the help they needed in friends and family." He looked around the room in appreciation at his family members gathered again to hear more of his story. Clearly this was his outcome. His family had been his safety net. Sugi and his bushido beliefs helped him adjust to life after the war.

"As we returned to British Columbia after the war, we were once again 'Japs' who were taking jobs away from white Canadians. We were still foreigners. But it was a different story for a grateful Japanese community. They built a cenotaph in honor of the 227 Japanese Canadians who went to war for Canada."

"I've seen the memorial many times," said Ken. "It's a fine tribute situated in a very public area for all to see."

"I'll start my story on the ship returning from England," said Masumi. "That was when we all had time to think about how lucky and thankful we were to be alive, how good it would be to see our friends and family and get back to a more normal way of living which didn't involve killing and trying not to get killed."

Deck of the RMS Carmania, April 12, 1919

Two years had passed since the memorable battle on Vimy Ridge. The physical and mental scars of the bloodshed and carnage of those years were etched deeply into the bodies and psyche of all the Canadian war veterans, now homeward bound. The past two days at sea had put miles of distance between the soldiers and the battlefields they fought on, but the memories traveled with them on the RMS Carmania. And they were likely to travel with them for the rest of their lives.

Sergeant Masumi Mitsui and Corporal Sainosuke Kubota stood together by the railing at the bow of the ship as it crashed through the waves and the mist of the choppy northern Atlantic Ocean. The wind and spray felt good on their faces thanks to the warmth of the sun on a refreshing spring day. Nearly three years ago they started this adventure together and now they were on the last leg of their journey. The coast of Canada beckoned them home. They were finishing it together. Their friend, Joe Oura, had not been so lucky. His absence was in both of their minds as they headed homeward, leaving him behind.

"How do you feel this morning, Masumi?" Kubota inquired.

"Glad to be alive," he responded. "I'm still limping a lot and my finger will never be the same, but I'm grateful to have survived the shelling, bullets and poison gas. When I look back and think about Oura, Matsumura, Sugimoto and all the others who died and are left behind, I am humbled."

"I agree. We are most fortunate to be going home when so many other Canadians gave their lives and are buried in Flanders or a dozen other small cemeteries across Europe. What are your plans when we get home?" Kubota asked.

"I'm going to get busy living. Masumi has been single too long and he needs a wife and family," he grinned, as if saying it in the third person would make it so.

"Will you go back to the hotel in Victoria and try to get your old job back?"

"No, I'm tired of working for other people and being treated badly. I deserve better. I hope the sacrifices we made in this war will change minds about Japanese people and new opportunities will be open to us, but I fear it will be the same."

"What then?" Kubota asked.

"You know all the small farms and farmhouses we passed across Europe?"

"Yes, it did look like a peaceful, idyllic life, at least before the Germans ransacked the countryside and the war destroyed their villages."

"Well that lifestyle really appealed to me. I think I want to be a farmer. I want to get married, have a family and work on my farm. I want to live in peace and enjoy a stable family life. I missed out on it as a child and it's something I want." He looked up as though a version of his perfect life floated in the sky just ahead.

"Do you know anything about farming, Masumi?"

"Nope. But I didn't know anything about fighting either and I'm still here to talk about it. How hard can it be? People have to eat, right?"

"And you are a hard worker, one of the hardest working men I know. I'm sure you will be a great farmer."

"Thank you. What about you Kubota san? What will you do?" Masumi inquired.

"I think I want to go into business in some way. I want to use my brain, not my back for a while. I like the way Japanese people were treated in Calgary and think I will try and build my future there."

"Let's make sure we stay connected when we get home. Let's not get so busy we don't have time for friends," Masumi suggested.

"Agreed," pledged Kubota.

They fell silent for a long period, gripping the railing while enjoying the soothing motion of the ship rising and falling in the ocean waves. Sea birds flew back and forth across the ship waiting for some waste discharge to scavenge and light clouds meandered across the sky as the men looked to the horizon. Their futures seemed bright ahead.

The novelty of the ocean spray started to wear off, so they found their way back inside for breakfast, heading aft along the starboard walkway. As they approached the door, they came across a soldier huddled on the metal life jacket storage box with his left arm in a strangle hold around a metal fire bucket. Getting closer, they recognized Masajiro Shishido plunging his head into the bucket and heaving like death itself was grabbing his intestines. It was a horrific, gut churning wail, making Masumi and Kubota wince as they looked at each other. Kubota giggled. Masa had been in a similar position yesterday. Their friend had been throwing up for two days at sea. Masumi grinned too and then shook it off, trying to be serious.

"Masa, how are you doing?" He was genuinely concerned for his fellow soldier's well-being.

"Not good, Sarge," said Masa. "I think it would have been better if they had shot me back in Europe rather than to die like this."

"You're not going to die," Masumi assured him. "We only have six more days of sailing."

The suggestion of six more days and nights of this agony caused Masajiro to puke even louder and longer than before. Kubota turned away as he burst into laughter. Even the always serious Masumi was having trouble keeping a straight face as he tried to give comfort to Masajiro.

"A little while ago I felt this tickly bit in my throat and I swallowed it back," Masa described. "I was pretty sure it was my asshole coming up."

That did it. Masumi burst out laughing and Kubota was on the deck heaving himself, not from seasickness, just gasping for air as he laughed so hard.

Composing himself, Masumi said, "Maybe the ship's medic has something for you."

"A bullet is all I need, Sarge," pleaded Masa. "Just put me out of my misery!"

Still unable to talk, Kubota crawled to the cabin door waving at Masumi to stop because he couldn't catch his breath from laughing. Masumi grinned and suggested to Masa, "Maybe some soup?" His comment triggered another round of heaves from Masajiro. "Okay, not soup then."

Kubota crashed through the door and Masumi followed, feeling he was close to losing control as well. He wasn't being helpful to his ailing friend and he knew if he stayed any longer, he would be on the floor with Kubota in hysterics.

God, it felt good to laugh again.

"I'll send...the medic...out to...find you...my friend," promised Masumi as he suppressed the laughter. He found Kubota in a lump on the floor inside still convulsing, gasping for air and laughing all at once.

"You're a mean man, Kubota," Masumi kiddingly scolded him.

"I can't help myself." He rolled onto his back. "I feel really bad for him. I'm just really glad it isn't me."

The transatlantic voyage felt like it would never end. Soldiers were anxious to get home, but they had no control over the speed or direction of their journey. And, while they enjoyed some pleasant and humorous moments during the trip, there was also a lot of time to be reflective, alone with their thoughts and memories of the years at war.

For Masumi, this was a time to assess his achievements as a soldier and as a man. He looked back on the days leading to his enlistment, his training and ultimately his years as a soldier. He was mostly thankful to be alive. His survival was due to a combination of luck and the backing and protection he received from his fellow soldiers. His thoughts went to the many men and, in particular, his fellow Japanese Canadians who would not be returning to their friends and family in Canada. He thought often of Oura, and he cried every single time. His death was the lowest point for Masumi in a war filled with tragedy and sorrow.

The sleeping quarters on the Carmania were cramped; four bunks to a small room. Some had the luxury of a window but the inside rooms were small boxes with stacked bunks. Masumi didn't care. The bed was nice, compared to field conditions, and they were warm and dry. But even in such close quarters he periodically felt alone. Alone with his thoughts and memories.

As Masumi laid in his bed at night, unable to sleep, with his own horrifying recollections flashing across his mind, he thought about his actions as a warrior. Had he honored his father and grandfather by staying true to bushido and the way of the samurai? Was there honor in fighting for his country even when it meant killing other men—young men, most of whom probably didn't want to be fighting and die any more than he did?

Masumi had been benevolent and merciful whenever he could be. He showed compassion and let people live when killing was unnecessary. He cared for his fellow soldiers in their times of need, both emotional and physical. He also felt he had been courageous as a soldier by hiding his fear. He'd been a good leader in battle and in the safer confines away from the front lines.

But most of all, Masumi felt he had shown a duty to his country and his fellow Japanese Canadians by enlisting and fighting for the important things he valued as a Canadian and as a man of Japanese descent. That was his greatest achievement. He had fulfilled his duty and, above all, would have made his ancestors proud. They may never know of his actions, but this is what he had hoped to accomplish by leaving his homeland and beginning a new life. He could wear his uniform with pride. It wasn't samurai armor but it was his modern-day version of the clothes of a warrior. And he could march tall knowing he was a good leader and a brave soldier.

Calgary, Alberta, April 23, 1919

The demobilization of the Fighting Tenth Battalion occurred in the early hours of April 23rd, 1919 at the newly built Mewata Barracks in Calgary. Upon disembarking from the Carmania in Halifax, the unit traveled by train to Calgary, making many stops along the way where the locals paid tribute and celebrated the war victory with this now famous infantry troop, the Fighting Tenth. Different battalions departed along the way, in Winnipeg, Regina, and Moose Jaw, but Calgary was the home base to many of these men and they were all anxious to see friends and family. For the Japanese from British Columbia, the ride home was not yet over, but their journey as soldiers would end here.

Thousands of people lined the streets in Calgary as the battalion made its final march to the barracks from the train station. The troop fell into formation in the new parade yard to the east of the barracks. A marching band played non-stop and people cheered, waving their hands or banners above their heads. The British ensign atop a flagpole could be seen by everyone, a symbol of their freedom, of their victory in the worst conflict in the history of the world.

Military and political officials gave speeches to a loud and boisterous crowd. The energy level of the rowdy spectators was contagious as everyone embraced the end of the war and the reconnection of families and friends. Flags and bunting adorned every building on the grounds. In this environment, the Japanese Canadian soldiers were treated as equals. Alberta had always been a friendly place for them and many, like Kubota, were considering the choice of making this province their new home. The thought of returning to those turbulent times and unrest on the west coast made them anxious for change. They'd had a little taste of equality during the war and wanted it to continue.

Now a Sergeant, Masumi played a leadership role as a noncommissioned officer. He wore the stripes proudly and took his role seriously. This was his dream, to be a leader of men. The final days as a soldier in service to his country made him prouder than at any other time in his life.

The formalities ended with the issuance of final salary payments and discharge papers. Not having spent much money during the war, this check along with his savings since joining the army would be the start of a payment on the farm he dreamed of owning, a down payment on his future life. The government would also be providing loans to returning soldiers to help them re-establish themselves after the war.

The following morning, just over thirty Japanese Canadians from the 10th Battalion boarded a westbound train for the last leg of their journey home to Vancouver. In all, over 170 Japanese Canadians survived the war. Many would return to B.C., but others felt the racism and hatred toward them there wasn't worth returning to. They had no ties to that part of Canada and, after traveling the world for the past two years, they were more confident in their ability to adapt.

On the train, sitting beside fellow Military Medal recipient, Toku Iwamoto, Masumi asked, "What plans do you have when you get home, Toku?"

"I want to fish again," he replied without hesitation. "The salmon runs are so good there. I can make an excellent living for my family. I'll get a small boat and nets and spend my days on the water enjoying the peacefulness. I have a new respect and value for life, Sarge. For the rest of my days I will always be grateful to be alive."

"Well said, my friend," agreed Masumi. "I share your feelings. We can hold our heads high with honor, knowing we fought for our country and for freedom. We were both awarded the Military Medal for bravery, you and me, and this recognition means something."

"What will you do when we get home, Sarge?" asked Toku.

"I haven't told anyone this, but I have been writing to a woman in Vancouver while we have been at war. Her name is Sugi Shin," Masumi confided. "She was married to Tetsuzo, but he died before the war, so she and her young son have been on their own for some time now. She sent me a letter from Canada when we were shipped off to Great Britain. I think she had feelings for me. Her early letters just told me about home and offered support for me during the war. But, as time went by, we started sharing our feelings more. We have been talking a lot, and I think we may get married when I return."

"You old dog, Sarge!" Toku jabbed him in the ribs with his elbow.

"No, no," Masumi quickly responded in defense. "She is a very nice woman and a good mother to her young son. I would be lucky if she would have me. She knows about farming too, so she would be a good partner to help me live out my dream to own some land and be my own boss."

Both in their mid-thirties, Masumi and Sugiko felt drawn together. They had known each other for about four years, but Sugi had been married and Masumi had gone to war. During his absence, their feelings for each other kindled; their relationship stirred by letters back and forth across an ocean. Masumi wrote from his heart, thinking there was a real possibility he wouldn't live to ever see Sugi again. Her responses in return were open and honest. These were the characteristics Masumi wanted in a wife.

Vancouver, British Columbia, June 1919

The train traveled much of the journey from Calgary to Vancouver through the Rocky Mountains in the darkness. Masumi slept in short intervals, anxious about his arrival home and about seeing Sugi for the first time in over two years. Much had happened to both of them in that period. She was now a single mother, and he had nearly been killed on numerous occasions. They had been critical support for each other from a distance during very difficult times and had built a basis for a relationship through their correspondence. At first, Sugi admitted to Masumi, she felt guilty writing to him. What would people think? Masumi calmed her and made her feel better about herself. She liked that he could be a source of strength for her when she felt alone. For Masumi, the letters from Sugi kept him going most days. She would probably never know how much he needed to hear from her, and how, through her letters, she made him feel like someone cared about him. The relationship grew from a distance. What would it be like when they finally met face to face after all they had shared in those letters? He still had every one of them. So did she.

The train arrived in Vancouver in the early hours of the morning on April 25th, 1919. At 7:00 a.m. the porter moved from car to car, announcing, "Thirty minutes to Vancouver Terminal Station." His holler woke those still asleep. "Thirty minutes!"

The brakes started an ear-piercing squeal as the train approached the station and slowed to city limit speed. Steam was purged from the brake system and the wheels rattled and clanked as the train finally came to a complete halt.

Like Calgary and the other stops along the westward route, a crowd had assembled to welcome the war heroes home. More flags, bunting and a loud band greeted the soldiers as they disembarked from the train. From the top of the stairs on the passenger car, Masumi scanned the crowd but there were just too many people and he couldn't spot Sugi before he was pushed on by eager soldiers behind him.

But she saw him.

As he reached the ground, he cursed his height, or lack of it to be more exact. He couldn't see anything but necks and shoulders.

Damn, he thought, *I'm going to have to find a ladder or something.*

The station platform was chaos. People were yelling and waving, the band played on, and the train was still making noises trains make—bursting clouds of released steam, squeals and those inexplicable clunking noises of metal on metal as train cars bump back and forth.

Masumi headed toward the main building of the station. Someone grabbed his arm from the side. It startled him. He was jumpy and sensitive to surprises. But this was a good surprise. Sugi pulled herself to him in the crush of the crowd. Closer than she might have planned given her shyness and uncertainty about what this greeting might bring.

Masumi smiled his biggest smile since they won the baseball game in France. He was genuinely glad to see her, and she him. Uncharacteristically he reached for her and pulled her close in a strong hug. She returned the hug on her tip toes with a tight grip on his shoulders. They remained embraced for what seemed like many minutes, feeling warm and safe, a feeling they both needed in their lives at precisely that moment.

Their public embrace was not traditionally Japanese in custom, but it was a Canadian custom. Hundreds of other couples on the platform were expressing their love and thankfulness in exactly the same way, just happy to be in their loved one's arms again after the most agonizing years of their lives.

Masumi wanted to kiss Sugi, but Japanese modesty won out, preventing him from going quite that far. The *honne/tatemae* divide between public expression and private thoughts and feelings was considered to be of paramount importance in Japanese culture. These were difficult cultural habits to ignore. Sugi told Masumi much later she knew right then and there they would marry and raise a family together. She hugged him even tighter and Masumi soaked in the intimacy and love he was feeling. It had been a long time since Masumi had seen Sugi and back then they'd been casual friends. And yet, somehow, they had built a bond across two continents and an ocean through the erratic delivery of military mail during the war.

Finally, Masumi spoke. "I'm so glad to see you, Sugi. I wasn't sure you would be here to greet me."

"Of course I'm here. You're a 'big deal' war hero Masumi Mitsui. I don't want somebody else making off with you!" She grinned. "I'm so thankful you made it back alive. So many men died in Europe. I was afraid for you every day. When I heard about Oura, I cried for days."

"Me too," he confessed as he noticed Sugi's eyes glistening.

Sugi poured her heart out on the train platform. "I've been waiting for this day for months and months, Masumi. For the day you would come home, for the day we could be together. It's been so hard to be on my own and care for my son. Just hold me now."

And that's what he did.

As they walked arm in arm away from the station, Sugi noticed a pronounced limp In Masumi's stride.

"You're injured?" she asked with genuine concern.

"It's nothing," he replied. "A small twist of my knee. It will mend in time."

"I'll have a look at it when we get to my house." Her tone made it clear this would not be optional for Masumi.

Masumi had never dreamed this would be his future when he left to fight in the war, but he was so thankful to come home to Sugi's warm welcome and open arms. His mind was in turmoil from the memories and visions of the horrors of war but her mere presence gave him a sense of grounding and hope. His heart was filled with a fresh elation as he pondered a future together with this woman, raising a family and being a farmer.

Springtime in Vancouver was a great time to fall in love. Trees and flowers bloomed. The days were clear and fresh, and the ocean air crisp. Everything just smelled good. It was a great time for walks on the beach, picnics in the park or hikes in the nearby mountains.

The subject of marriage surfaced quickly between Masumi and Sugi. They both wanted to be married, so when Masumi popped the question Sugi said, "Well of course!" She had no doubts.

Even though she accepted Masumi's proposal, Sugi wanted to get to know Masumi better before they actually married. At first his answers were abbreviated and he didn't ask too many questions. As time passed, and Sugi persisted, he shared a bit more, revealing the kind of person he was, what was important to him and how he wanted to live his life. They enjoyed many long and personal conversations over the next few weeks. She wanted to really know him and understand his character. After all, she already had a seven-year-old son, Dick, and she intended to have more children. Masumi would be a husband and a father. It was important.

On a sunny Sunday in July, all three of them enjoyed a day at Joe's Beach, a lengthy west-facing beach in Vancouver harbor ideal for swimming and enjoying the long sunny summer days of B.C.'s west coast. It was part of one of the best swimming areas along English Bay and a popular recreation area. The gradual slope and the golden sand made this particular beach one of the busiest of a dozen or more spots in Vancouver and the surrounding areas.

Dick built castles in the sand and splashed in the salty waters of the bay. Like every child at the beach, the fascination of digging holes and trenches like moats around imaginary castles could keep him occupied for an hour. He busily transported buckets of water from the ocean to his construction on the beach. Like every other castle builder, he lost the battle as the water soaked into the sand faster than he could carry it from the ocean, but he was determined the next bucketful would be the one to fill the trench and finish his dream castle.

Feelings of family contentment settled in Masumi immediately. The beaches of Vancouver were a world away from the trenches of

Europe. Sun and surf were such a delight in comparison to rain and mud. The day was wonderfully peaceful and beautiful. This was what Masumi needed to reinvigorate himself, restart his life and vanquish the dark memories of death and suffering. He didn't know how long it would take. Would the dark, disturbing memories ever go away?

Sugi had steered clear of asking Masumi questions about the war, but he was having trouble adjusting to a life where people weren't trying to kill him every day. He was troubled by his memories and suffered with great sadness at the loss of close friends and comrades from his battalion. His flashbacks would come upon him at any time day or night and last for minutes or hours as he slipped into periods of depression and sadness.

Later that evening Sugi made some hot tea and snuggled next to Masumi on the couch. As she looked into his eyes Masumi returned her attention. He felt safe and loved. He trusted her, knowing she was very supportive of his needs and condition.

"Do you want to talk about the war, Masumi? Can you tell me what happened there?" she asked.

"I cannot tell you about the horrible things that happened during the war, Sugi. I don't wish to relive those memories and you would be horrified to hear of the pain and suffering."

"But you are remembering them," she insisted. "Maybe if you just talk about it, the memories will stop tormenting you."

"The bad dreams and the sadness will go away I pray. I need to get on with my life, our lives, and try to forget these things."

"Okay, I will try to understand. But tell me this then, why did you decide to join and go to war in the first place? They didn't make it easy for you to enlist. What did you hope to accomplish?"

"I went to war to show my courage and loyalty but mostly to bring honor to the Japanese Canadian people. I believed we could show the white people we want to be accepted as equals. I honestly felt it was my duty to my new country."

"Now that the war is over, do you feel it was worth it? Do you feel you accomplished what you wanted to do?"

"While we were fighting alongside other Canadians against a common enemy, we were accepted, even befriended. Those soldiers will always be my friends, my comrades. But back at home, I can see nothing has really changed I'm sad to say. It's just the way it was. Returning from the war to this city, this province, I find everything in British Columbia is still the same. No one knows we risked our lives, got injured and even died fighting for Canada. No one cares. We are still just Japs.

"Before we returned home, the B.C. government actually reduced the number of fishing licenses to people 'other than white residents.' Can you believe it?" He didn't hide his anger and disgust. "Veterans are exempt from this law, but it is clearly a racially charged choice from the government. I don't understand why they would do that?"

Sugi paused to let Masumi's obvious frustration dissipate a bit before carrying on.

"Well, what *did* you learn from being in those awful battles?" She tried to work around the edges of his memories and get him talking about it again.

"I learned mercy," he recalled. "My samurai grandfather would have been proud of me." Sugi had managed to get him to open up to her a little bit. He wasn't talking about the atrocities of war but he was sharing his feelings. Clever woman.

"I'll tell you this. Many of the German soldiers who fought against us were forced into the fight. Most of them didn't want to be there but had no choice. I never killed anyone who wanted to surrender. I wouldn't let the men in my unit kill enemy soldiers who begged for mercy. And we did show them mercy, benevolence and compassion. In return, the Germans learned we were not wicked. We were fair and we treated them with respect, even as prisoners."

Sugi let the conversation end at that point as Masumi was clearly agitated and not enjoying himself, which was partly why they had gone to the beach earlier.

"So, what will you do now, my hero?" she asked, changing the topic. "What else can be done and how far are you willing to go to gain equality and acceptance for Japanese Canadians?"

"We must convince the B.C. government to give Japanese Canadians the right to vote. It is the right thing to do. Kubota told me Japanese Canadians in Alberta are already allowed to vote in both federal and provincial elections, so why can't we do the same here in B.C.?

"We will go to parliament in Victoria and we will fight." He clenched his fist with dogged determination. He would need help to mount a serious challenge. He would have no trouble gaining help from members of the Canadian Japanese Association. They would advocate for equal rights for Japanese after the war. But he wanted to rally the war veterans because they represented a much stronger voice right now.

Sugi had planted a seed of an idea in Masumi, and on his walk back to his home in the evening, he started to build a plan. Letters from commanding officers; a better understanding of the laws in Alberta franchising Japanese Canadians; meetings with elected officials; these were all necessary. And Masumi needed to take a leadership role, in part to replace his friend Yasushi Yamazaki who had returned to Japan after the war. Masumi needed to join the Canadian Japanese Association and speak on behalf of all Japanese immigrants in British Columbia. As a decorated war hero, they would listen to him. And he needed to join the Royal Canadian Legion and get endorsement for Japanese veterans to gain the right to vote. He had a lot of work to do!

The next morning Masumi returned to Sugi's home to help in her garden. She had planted vegetables, strawberries and a few local flowers like hydrangeas and rhododendrons which grew into large, colorful bushes in the rich soils and moist salty air of British Columbia. Today they weeded the vegetables on their hands and knees, digging in the dirt. Masumi and Sugi both loved gardening and watching things grow and it was a good time together, a good time to plan.

Out of nowhere Sugi blurted, "Chickens!"

"What?" he asked.

"I said chickens!"

"I heard that part. What are you talking about?"

"We could be chicken farmers."

"How do you farm chickens?"

"You get little chickens, you feed them until they are big chickens and then you sell them. You told me you wanted to be a farmer, Masumi. This is a good plan. And we can have some layers too and sell the eggs," she continued. "Every day you feed the chickens, and in the morning, you go collect the eggs and sell them."

"Well, it sounds easy."

"Well it's not! It's hard work every day. They get sick, they fight, and they stink. But we can make a good living as chicken farmers."

"Do we have enough money to get started?"

"I think land is too expensive around Steveston. I've been looking into it. But if we go back into the country and stay close to the river flats, the land is a lot cheaper. There is uncleared land available from the government in Hammond. If we combine our money and we get a veteran's loan, we can do it."

Sugi's idea was music to Masumi's ears. Ever since he saw the small farms across Europe, he had dreamed of such a life. He didn't remember sharing this dream with Sugi, but he must have done it in his letters and she got busy investigating their options. She was prepared with a plan.

"Okay," Masumi agreed with a broad smile on his face. "Let's be chicken farmers. Yessiree, I'm gonna be a chicken farmer!"

In early August 1919, just three short months after returning home from the war, Masumi and Sugi married in a small ceremony in New Westminster, B.C. in front of a small gathering of friends including Masumi's friend Sainosuke Kubota. Masumi looked distinguished in a new gray suit. Sugi wore a soft pink cotton dress and held a small bouquet of flowers. They were clearly in love and anxious to begin a new life fulfilling the dream they had when they both came to Canada more than a decade ago. Young Dick was dapper in his small suit and tie and it was clear to everyone he would be joined by siblings very soon.

One important person missing from the wedding celebrations was Masumi's mentor and friend Yasushi Yamazaki. The man who had organized the Japanese Canadian troops for the war effort had returned to Japan to take on another new challenge in his life. That's just how Yasushi was, always seeking a new challenge. Masumi was even more sad his dear friend Oura was not there, but he gained strength in the fact his life was turning out as he had dreamed it would. His future would be filled with joy and success, with a large family of children and grandchildren. He pledged to honor the Mitsui name and the family traditions of Japan and be a good Canadian at the same time.

Hamilton, Ontario, November 11, 1967

"Is this the kind of story you were looking for Mr. Adachi?" asked Masumi. "It might be a bit more personal than you care to hear."

"Oh yes, Mr. Mitsui," Adachi replied. "This is exactly the theme I wish to explore and the story that needs to be told. I didn't mention this to you, but the working title of my book is *The Enemy That Never Was,* and your experience tells the tale perfectly. You are such an honorable man, a credit to the Japanese people. While many people, mainly politicians, saw the Japanese people as a threat, they were really quite the opposite. They were good people like you and Sugi, like my own parents and hundreds of other immigrants and Canadian-born people of Japanese descent who were never a threat at all. They just wanted to be the best Canadians they could be. This is exactly what I want! And please," he said as an aside, "call me Ken."

"That is fine with me, Ken. You call me Masumi too please." He felt a trust and comradeship with Adachi in their very short time together.

"I feel like I know your wife after listening to you talk about her, but we have never met," Adachi continued. "I am so very sad to learn she is ill and living in a nursing home. It must be very difficult for you after everything you have gone through together. I wish I could have met her years ago. She sounds like another person of strong character, a fighter."

Now it was Masumi's turn to reach for the Kleenex box. "We were a great team, she and I." He wept openly and wiped both of his eyes.

"She worked hard and she was so supportive of my desires to gain equality for Japanese immigrants as Canadian citizens."

"I want to hear all of it, Mr. Mitsui, about rebuilding your lives, about the vote and, especially about your lives during and after the Second World War. But first can we talk about the tribute paid to the Japanese Canadian war veterans in 1920? Tell me about the construction and ceremony around the marvelous cenotaph in Stanley Park. What did it mean to you?"

"Yes, yes," Masumi said as he pictured the magnificent thirty-five-foot tower symbolizing the memory of Japanese Canadians who served in all of Canada's wars. "The Japanese merchants in the Vancouver area collected $15,000 and built a fantastic tribute to the men who served in World War 1. Japanese soldiers serving in the second World War and the Korean war were added later.

"For me it was an important symbol of loyalty and sacrifice. It is in a beautiful location that can be seen by all who come to the park. You can't miss it. And it pays tribute, showing all Canadians that the Japanese soldiers, just like all the other Canadian soldiers, risked their lives, and for fifty-five souls, lost their lives in the process. This sacred place is special to me but it's a long way from Hamilton. I hope I get to see it again in my lifetime.

"The ceremony to light the flame took place on the third anniversary of the Battle of Vimy Ridge. It was a beautiful Vancouver day on April 2nd, 1920. I remember it well," he recalled.

Vancouver, British Columbia, April 2, 1920

Masumi saw the man in a Corporal's uniform standing on a slightly elevated knoll, a woman by his side. The man looked out from Stanley Park over the inner harbor of Burrard Inlet separating Vancouver from North Vancouver. It was a cloudy day, threatening rain. That was April in British Columbia. The Corporal scanned the crowd of dignitaries in suits and special guests in uniform looking for someone. When he spotted Masumi he called out excitedly.

"Masumi, Masumi, over here," yelled Sainosuke Kubota in the direction of the crowd. "It's good to see you here, old friend. I thought you would come."

"Hello, Sainosuke san," replied Masumi. "You look well. Business must be agreeing with you." Sugi, who was accompanying Masumi smiled and bowed to Kubota.

"Sugi, it is very nice to see you here today too." Kubota bowed respectfully in return to Masumi's wife. He had only met Sugi at their wedding, but he liked her from the outset. It was clear she and Masumi were happy together. "I would like you to meet my wife, Hide." He turned and brought her forward in greeting. Kubota had returned to Japan shortly after the war to visit his family and came back to Canada with his new bride. She was very traditionally Japanese as she stood steps behind Kubota, head bowed and hands together in front.

The occasion bringing them together this day was the unveiling of the Memorial Cenotaph in Stanley Park commemorating the men who had fought in the World War. It was a towering sandstone column, a white marble Japanese style pagoda with a terra cotta roof on top housing an eternal flame. The structure sat on a twelve-sided polygon base with each side representing a petal of a flower naming the location and date of a famous battle during the First World War. Bronze plaques around the base of the tower listed the names of survivors as well as those who lost their lives during the war. The central plaque stated:

World War I
Japanese Canadian War Memorial
This monument is in lasting memory of the 190 who
answered the call of duty for Canada and to the 54 who
laid down their lives in defence of freedom in the great
war. Their names are engraved on the monument erected,
April 2, 1920.

"This is a wonderful memorial wouldn't you agree, Kubota?" Masumi asked.

"It fills my heart," he replied. "It makes me proud to be a Japanese Canadian. Excuse me now, I have been asked to say a few words today. I will be back soon. Can you stay with Hide please?"

"Of course. We will get to know her and tell her all about you," Masumi said with a big grin.

"Don't believe what he tells you, Hide," Kubota backed away with a jokingly nervous look on his face. "Masumi tells many tales that contain only small amounts of truth." He flashed a large grin.

During the ceremony, a Japanese Canadian business man wearing an expensive-looking gray suit acknowledged the many soldiers who were attending the tribute ceremony.

"This monument is a tribute to all the brave Japanese Canadians who fought for Canada in the war," he began. "Your bravery and sacrifice did not go unnoticed in the Japanese community." This subtly implied the rest of the people of British Columbia might not care to remember the role the Japanese people played in the war. "May we never forget the Japanese men who fought, especially the ones who died so the Allied forces could win the glorious victory. And thanks to the Japanese business community who generously donated the money so Mr. James Benzie here could design and supervise the construction of this magnificent tribute." He swung his open hand high in the air in the direction of the cenotaph.

Kubota had positioned himself beside the dignitaries who had been responsible for the construction of the cenotaph. After being personally introduced by one of the hosts, Kubota shared a poem he had composed for the occasion:

> *Although you are gone you are not dead*
> *Surely the setting sun will rise again for you*
> *Your heroic spirit will live in our hearts*
> *We take the torch from your hand to fight and carry on.*

As a final gesture, Kubota saluted the memorial as a soldier and then bowed graciously as a friend. Masumi couldn't hold back tears as he too remembered his fallen comrades and considered the ultimate price they had paid.

After the ceremony, Kubota rejoined Masumi, Sugi and Hide.

"Now what lies has he filled your head with?" Sainosuke asked.

"Mr. Mitsui told me you were a cook during the war," Hide replied.

"Ah, well that was true, at first," he replied as he looked at Masumi and raised his hand playfully as if he was going to smack him. "But that was a mistake and I transferred to the infantry as soon as I could. They don't make cooks into corporals you know!" he proclaimed, proudly pointing to the two flashes on the sleeve of his uniform.

Changing to a more serious topic, Kubota turned to Masumi and asked, "How is progress on gaining the voting franchise for Japanese Canadians here in British Columbia going?"

"Not well I'm afraid. We all thought...hoped by volunteering to fight for Canada we would be respected and accepted. We thought the government would change its mind about giving the franchise to Japanese Canadians. But nothing has changed," Masumi said sadly.

"Shinobu san contacted the B.C. government on our behalf, through the Canadian Japanese Association, requesting a change to the law. It never even went to a vote before parliament. They just said no. You are lucky to have the right to vote in Alberta," Masumi continued. "It is unjust and unfair that our people here in British Columbia are not treated as well."

"You must find another way to force the issue," suggested Kubota. "The 10th Battalion is behind you, Masumi. Is there some way you can use the strength of Canada's military branch to speak on your behalf?"

"I don't know, but the veterans and the Japanese businessmen are united in our goal to secure the franchise for our people!" Masumi glanced at his wife. "Sugi and I have some other news to share with you. We are expecting a baby in August!"

"That's wonderful news," said Kubota. "The first Mitsui *nisei* in Canada! You will have to name the baby after me." He flashed his familiar grin.

"You would have to convince Sugi of that," said Masumi. "You'd have a better chance of convincing the government to give us the vote!"

The Mitsuis purchased seventeen acres in a village known as Hammond, B.C. in the summer of 1920. The purchase of land from the Soldier's Settlement Board was possible with money Masumi has saved during the war, his war bond, a special program from the provincial government encouraging land development, and a loan from the bank. The land was flat, and it needed clearing before it would produce crops, but Masumi got busy building chicken coops and in one month they purchased their first batch of chicks.

"Today we are chicken farmers my love," proclaimed Masumi proudly. It was the beginning of their business as a family.

Pregnancy aside, Sugi worked as hard as Masumi to clear the land, build a home and start their farming business. This was Japanese culture they were very familiar with—their family life and their business were one and the same. They lived where they worked, and in time, their children would work there too. The work required to set up the farm was too heavy for Dick but he was keen to be a part of this new adventure.

Learning to be a successful chicken farmer wasn't without its challenges. Having someone tell you chickens stink, and actually smelling live chickens is not at all the same. They had a sharp and penetrating smell that reached inside your brain by way of your nostrils and made your eyes water and your head hurt. But there was no going back now. Somehow, they had to change their mind-set from suffering the smell of chickens to imagining it was the smell of money. Maybe one day they would reach this mind-altering plateau, but not any time soon!

They also learned they couldn't run as fast as chickens. The chickens would often escape the confines of the chicken coop and run for freedom. But the lure of getting fed at some point in the day always brought them back. This insight only came to Masumi after many rounds of running after escaped birds. Sugi got a great kick out of seeing him try to catch a chicken that didn't want to be caught. The sight of Masumi running after a white blur with his hands low in front of his body always brought a chuckle and made her day. Masumi even thought, in some instances, Sugi was an accomplice in the escape, just so she could laugh at him in pursuit of the runaway.

Starting a family was a big decision. Not a family of baby chicks, a family of baby people. Masumi had always wanted to have a family, but before Sugi came into his life he wondered if he would ever experience the pride and joy of being a father. His dream became a reality when the doctor emerged from the delivery room of the Royal Columbian Hospital in New Westminster in August of 1920. Masumi and Sugi's first child together, Amy Emiko Mitsui, was born that day. She brought joy and hope to their lives. Every two years following, the scene was repeated as George Hideo next joined the family, followed in another two years by girl number two, Lucy Sumiyo. Harry Hideharu was the last of the Mitsui children, born in December 1926. The Mitsuis followed a tradition developing within the Japanese Canadian community of giving the children a Canadian name to help them assimilate in the country. But they honored their Japanese heritage by also giving them a second Japanese name.

Sugi's son Dick was now fourteen years old, rounding out the family with these four small children under six years of age and an expanding poultry farm. All this kept the Mitsuis very busy, but in a fulfilling way. The workday started early and chores always needed doing. Masumi managed to stay involved in voting franchise discussions within the community. This continued as a priority for him and many of the returning veterans. He communicated regularly with Kubota in Calgary and Saburo Shinobu, an officer with the Canadian Japanese Association in Vancouver.

He learned of a plan by the veterans to establish the Royal Canadian Legion with branches for service men across the country. Local agencies or "branches" would manage the many issues resulting from over half a million men returning to Canada after the war. Matters like pensions and medical administration required a unified voice. The Japanese Canadians felt their right to vote was exactly the kind of problem a local branch of the Legion would sponsor.

However, when Masumi approached the newly forming branch, he was told Japanese soldiers would not be allowed to join the B.C.

Branch. Technically they had joined the war effort in Alberta but, truthfully, the white veterans administering the affairs of the branch didn't want them there. Racism once again reared its ugly head from a source Masumi found both surprising and disappointing.

Undaunted, he and the other Japanese veterans contacted the national base of the Canadian Legion in 1926 with an application to form their own Japanese Canadian branch. They were granted the ninth charter of the Canadian Legion and became known as Branch #9, a Japanese Canadian veterans' organization, which quickly embraced many issues of racism and inequality affecting their members. First on their list was to gain the franchise to vote in British Columbia. Finally, they felt, they had the voice the provincial government could not ignore.

The Memorial Service at the cenotaph in Stanley Park in November of that year marked the seventh ceremony there since the monument had been erected. However, this was the first-year members of Branch #9 of the Canadian Legion presented arms and colors as a branch of the military. Their banner was a purple flag with gold tassels around the edge and the British ensign proudly displayed in the upper left corner with "Japanese Branch No. 9 B.C., The Canadian Legion B.E.S.L." printed in a gold banner across the center. It was a proud moment for Masumi, Shinobu and the other vets who helped organize the Legion Branch.

Hamilton, Ontario, November 11, 1967

"Well done, Masumi," Adachi broke in with a short round of applause. "These are wonderful accomplishments for you, your family and the veterans in such a short time after the war. The cenotaph, the Legion Branch and your farm, not to mention a young family. You must have felt very satisfied."

"Well no, not really," Masumi said. "Yes, having our four children along with Dick was very fulfilling and joyful for Sugi and I, and things were better within the Japanese Canadian Community. But our requests for the right to vote, starting in 1920, continued to be denied and many of our returning veterans, as well as local residents in the fishing community, were being forced out of the business by white fishermen, with help from the elected officials. It was criminal!" He pounded his fist downward on the arm of his aged chair.

"Japanese fishermen had to deal with the B.C. government reducing the number of fishing licenses year after year. The fishing community got together to decide who needed the work most and who would suffer the least hardship considering their age, family and ability to get work in other places. One year the government decided to prohibit gas engines for the Japanese boats. Can you believe it? They had to use sails to fish while the other trawlers and seiners breezed by under power."

"That's right!" piped in Hiro. "I was there when it happened. We had the deck stacked against us and no one speaking for us. Didn't matter if we were veterans or not. They just wanted to run us out of town. To starve us out really."

"The cutbacks continued," Masumi said. "Ultimately, other industries like farming and lumber started to complain the displaced Japanese fishermen were finding work on farms and in the lumber camps at the expense of white British Columbians. Then they got upset. The cutbacks for fishermen finally stopped in about 1930.

"Sugi and I were lucky we had our farm and could be independent, but general laborers were having a very difficult time. I hired a couple of men here and there, but I wasn't big enough to have regular work for others."

"What about wages?" Adachi asked. "Were they at least the same?"

"No, not at all. In 1925 the minimum wage was $.40/hour but Japanese got paid $.25/hour. Nobody said anything. The employers justified it by claiming the Japanese were used to living with a lower class of accommodation and food. So, even though they were forcing this poverty on the Japanese people, they would turn it around on us saying we were unfair competition for jobs because our cost of living was lower than the average person! You can imagine how this angered me," Masumi concluded with his teeth gritted and brow furrowed.

Pausing from his story he called out, "Amy, could we have some tea for Ken and Hiro please?"

"Coming right up, Dad," she replied.

"So, things went back to the way they were before the war. This is what you are saying, right?" Ken said.

"Absolutely. Maybe worse," Masumi said. "Japanese families like ours started having babies. This didn't sit well with the racist theories. Now we were plotting a takeover, they ranted. And they were educating our children in their schools like it was part of a complex, sophisticated, subversive Japanese plot.

"We all did what we had to do to survive and earn a living. Men and women worked the fields, cleared land and worked at whatever they could to make a dollar. The harder we worked, the more criticism we received. It was very disheartening."

"Given all the things you could have spent time and money on, you decided to press the matter and go after the voting franchise, right? Why did you feel that was important and how did it finally get approved?" Adachi asked.

"Ah, now there's a chapter of this story worth telling," Masumi said with a satisfied grin forming on his face. "With the Legion Branch #9 certified in 1926, the veterans decided to use our platform as a way to work for Japanese rights in Canada. It was part of a national organization and in 1930, the national Legion gave our chapter unanimous backing to attempt to gain the franchise in British Columbia. I remember the annual meeting of Legion Branch #9 right after Christmas in 1930."

Vancouver, British Columbia, January 6, 1931

"The results of the vote are final gentlemen," announced Saburo Shinobu, acting as the scrutineer for the Branch #9 election. "It is fitting our new president has actually voted in a Canadian election during the war in Europe. He knows what it feels like to exercise his franchise and he will lead our efforts to gain this right for all Japanese people in British Columbia. Please join me in congratulating our newly elected president, Sergeant Masumi Mitsui."

A loud ovation followed the declaration. Masumi was a popular choice among the veterans. The result was a foregone conclusion, but one requiring the following of Legion procedures. Masumi had worked tirelessly for the Legion since its inception in 1926. He was a quiet leader who did more of his convincing with his actions rather than his words. He did this all the while raising five children and managing his successful broiler and layer operation in Hammond. He was passionate about the role of the Legion in the community and in the uppermost matter at hand, the right for Japanese Canadians to vote in Canadian provincial and federal elections.

Masumi rose to accept his new role as president.

"Thank you, my friends." His thoughts went to his mentor Yasushi Yamazaki. How would he take on this new challenge? With gusto and courage. "I pledge to serve in this role as a loyal veteran of the war and a citizen of Canada who just happens to be of Japanese descent. I consider it my duty to finish what we began when we all enrolled in service to our country as soldiers. The white veterans in British Columbia wouldn't accept us as members of their legion so we have come together once again to find our place in this country and fight for justice and civil liberty." Masumi's brief acceptance speech was met with a loud roar of support from his peers. The enthusiasm charged him with energy to take on the tasks they confronted.

Their first order of business was already on the docket. They were to travel to Victoria during the Spring Assembly and make presentations to the legislature, one Member of the Legislative Assembly at a time. Their goal—the right to vote in provincial elections for Japanese Canadian veterans—was only a starting point in the minds of the Legion members. It was a step towards full enfranchisement for all Japanese Canadians of voting age.

Straight of Georgia, Vancouver, British Columbia, March 30, 1931

Nearly three months later, Masumi and a contingent representing the Japanese veterans of Legion #9, headed to the Victoria legislature.

"How does it feel being back on a boat heading into Victoria Harbor over twenty years after you first set foot in Canada?" Shinobu asked as they stood outside on the deck of the B.C. ferry. Weather permitting, Masumi preferred to travel on the outside rather than the inside of ships.

"My heart is racing a bit," Masumi admitted, taking a quick check on his feelings. "But I'm not sure if it's from the memories of so long ago, the anticipation of the job at hand, or the fact I'm on a damn boat again! I think the latter. I just hope I can get a good night's sleep. We have a full day ahead of us tomorrow with a lot at stake."

Masumi would have loved to stay at the Empress Hotel where he was once employed, but the nightly room cost was well above the Legion's budget. Nevertheless, it would have been satisfying to enjoy the luxury of his old workplace as a guest. A lot had happened to Masumi since those first days in Victoria. It was a different time and a different place, where he now represented many thousands of immigrants to Canada instead of just one.

"Masumi, I read this morning the Japanese House of Peers in Tokyo decided against giving Japanese women the right to vote," said Shinobu as they looked west from the bow of the ferry.

"It's interesting about voting isn't it," pondered Masumi. "Here, the ones who have it—the whites—protest against Japanese acquiring it. In Japan, men who have the right, exclude women. Being on the have-not side, I have a sympathy for those women in Japan. But we are fighting the same fight here in Canada, men and women. It's like the white and Japanese Canadians in Europe during the war. There, we were on the same side, fighting together, and then we came home and settled back into colored segregation. We all have a built-in prejudice and it can expand or contract depending on the surrounding circumstances. Understanding those circumstances and using them to our advantage will help us succeed for Japanese men and women in Canada."

"I am happy you are leading this delegation, Masumi san," said Shinobu. "You are definitely the right man for this job."

The Branch #9 Legion had doggedly lobbied British Columbia politicians since its inception. The Japanese Canadian community supported the initiative for more than a decade. Their unwavering message—a request to grant voting rights to people of Japanese ancestry living in British Columbia. Other provinces in Canada did not discriminate against the Japanese, allowing them to vote in municipal, provincial and federal elections. But in British Columbia the roots of racism lived on in the legislation of the land. Clause 5 of Bill 135 stated Japanese could not vote in British Columbia in either provincial or federal elections, full stop.

Early in 1931, Masumi hoped the lobbying would pay off. Perhaps it was the passage of time since the war, those ten plus years. Or maybe it was the fact many of the elected members of parliament were also veterans. Or maybe simple common sense would prevail on the argument. Whatever the reason, the Legion executive learned the Provincial Elections Act was being brought forward in the provincial legislature. This included provisions for the granting of voting privileges to Japanese Canadian war veterans. The legislative member sponsoring the Bill was MacGregor MacIntosh, a Conservative and a Scottish-born immigrant to Canada.

There was no certainty the bill would result in a positive decision and Masumi and Shinobu planned to meet with every member of the house to try to convince them to pass the motion. Joined by Sainosuke Kubota, adding another war veteran to their entourage, Masumi, Shinobu and four other Japanese Canadian businessmen from Vancouver would begin their campaign with members of parliament the following day.

Standing at the base of the staircase in front of the main building of British Columbia's legislative buildings the next morning, Masumi and the Japanese entourage paused to take in the full meaning of their mission. This mission was for all Japanese Canadian veterans, but especially in honor of those who did not return, those who would never be able to vote.

The legislative buildings sat prominently on the south slope of Victoria Harbor, adjacent to the Empress Hotel. Much like other Canadian legislatures, it was an intimidating and noble structure representing all the gravitas of the decisions made within its walls. The delegation was scheduled to meet with Member of the Legislative Assembly (MLA) MacIntosh and an assembly of Conservative MLAs at 9:00 a.m. Finding one member's office in the labyrinth of halls and corridors of this massive structure proved to be one more challenge for this committed group. Finally, they located the office and were greeted by MacIntosh, a military man if ever there was one. He stood erect and stiff, sporting a short and bristly mustache common to British military leaders of the day. His dress was formal, a three-piece pinstriped suit, and hair carefully coiffed and greased back from his forehead like he had just come from a swim.

"Gentleman, welcome to the B.C. parliament," greeted MacIntosh. "I took the liberty of inviting some of the friendly votes from the House. You don't have to spend time lobbying these gentlemen as they already support my bill. Please allow me to introduce you."

"Gentlemen," he bellowed to gain the attention of the MLAs engaged in numerous side conversations. "Here are the representatives from the Japanese Royal Canadian Legion Branch #9. Advisor Saburo Shinobu, Secretary Sainosuke Kubota, and branch President Masumi Mitsui. They are joined by several Japanese businessmen from Vancouver." Masumi then introduced the other members of their contingent to the MLAs. The seven Japanese Canadians representing the Legion stood and bowed their heads in respect.

"When these gentlemen heard the assembly was going to discuss the franchise for Japanese Canadian war veterans, they reached out and asked if they could come and present their own case," continued MacIntosh, turning to Masumi and the others. "Gentleman, like these men, I was not born here in Canada. As some of you may know, I was born in Scotland, and came to Canada as a young man. And yet here I am, a member of the Legislative Assembly of British Columbia. Sadly, the Japanese who immigrated here do not even have a say on who fills these legislative chairs. The time must end when we look upon men like these fellow Canadians and see a foreigner, a threat, or even worse, an enemy.

"We've heard the same arguments many times. They will take our jobs.

They will undermine our culture, change our way of life. And I expect we will hear such arguments again. I am sponsoring this bill to right a wrong. It is a bill requiring us to treat all immigrants to Canada in a fair and equitable manner. I asked you here to meet these men and to listen to what they have to say, support the motion I have tabled, and exert any influence you can on other members of parliament to endorse this vote in a nonpartisan manner. These war veterans risked their lives for our country on the battlefields of Europe. They have earned their right to cast a ballot as Canadian citizens and I am sponsoring the bill to make it happen!"

After the introductions and a brief conversation with the MLAs present in MacGregor's office, the contingent excused themselves in order to promote their cause with other elected representatives.

As they traveled the many hallways of the legislature and met with one MLA after another, they learned some elected officials endorsed the contingent's views.

One empathetic MLA said, "I fought in the war myself. As far as I'm concerned, you vets have earned a place in Canada and the right to vote."

Others adamantly opposed the proposal, some for personal reasons and others as a representation of their constituencies' views on the Japanese people. Those members representing the vocal and militant fisheries industry, for example, remained steadfastly opposed to any support of the Japanese Canadians.

One racist MLA said "You will never get my vote to give you any more rights than you already have as long as I have a seat in this assembly." They weren't counting on his vote.

After a morning of one-on-one and small group meetings, the delegation took a break for lunch.

"The vote is going to be close. Would you agree, Masumi?" Shinobu asked, looking at his compatriot.

"Very close. But we are closer than we have ever been before, so this is the time for us to work harder," Masumi said with determination. "We are working for all Japanese Canadians now. It is our duty to represent them and gain this important victory. Where do you think we stand on the vote count?"

"By my count we have fifteen 'Yes' votes, sixteen 'No' votes and six 'undecided,'" summarized Shinobu. "We still have a chance."

～

The vote in parliament that afternoon was a tie: eighteen "For" and eighteen "Against," with one abstention. The Speaker of the House cast his vote "Against" which defeated the bill in first reading.

MacIntosh met with the Japanese contingent after the vote outside parliamentary chambers. "What can I say, gentleman. I am sorry we did not win today," He looked slightly defeated.

"Is it over?" asked Kubota. "Is that it?"

"Only the first round of voting is over," replied MacIntosh. "A second round will be held tomorrow,"

"Why should we expect the second round to be any different?" asked Kubota.

"Well, it's a long shot but there is one MLA, Alexander Manson, who abstained from the first round of voting."

"Why did he abstain?"

"I don't know. But he is planning to participate in the vote tomorrow, and he has agreed to meet with you in the morning to hear you out."

"Then we will bring our most convincing argument."

"He has agreed to meet with one of you. Just one though. Whomever you choose."

The Japanese men looked back and forth at each other, knowing full well who should meet with MLA Manson.

～

The next morning Masumi walked boldly down the middle of the corridors of the legislature in search of Alexander Manson's office. The lingering limp from his knee injury during the war, exacerbated by all the walking on the hard floors the day before, created a distinctive gait. However, his straight posture and squared shoulders revealed his confident military manner and determination. Entering Manson's office, he was met by an aide and immediately led in to meet the member of parliament.

"Hello. Welcome. Please, come sit," greeted Manson.

Masumi bowed his head and took a seat.

"How are your accommodations? Do you like our city?" Manson inquired.

"Yes. I lived here once. When I first came from Japan."

"Yes, of course. And when was that?"

"1908."

"Mr. Mitsui, I told Macintosh I would hear you out. And now here we are. I must admit, I am torn on this decision and now it appears to be mine to make. I realize this affects a great many people, so I am taking this very seriously. I am open to hearing what you have to say on the matter. Please proceed."

Masumi didn't respond right away. In fact, he remained silent for a long moment pondering his approach.

Masumi stared out the window, at the rising sun. During that moment of serenity, he gathered his thoughts, drew on the guidance and wisdom of his grandfather and Yamazaki and began his compassionate argument.

"My grandfather was a samurai warrior. A powerful man, not in size, but in spirit. He taught me the way of the samurai. The way of bushido."

He had Manson's attention.

"And my father, he was an officer in the Japanese Navy. From the time I was a small boy, I believed it was my destiny to follow in our family tradition, to be a warrior. When I came of age, I tried to join the Navy, but I failed their exam. I failed my family. I felt as if I had dishonored all of them, those who were alive and those who were already gone. I had no job, nowhere to go and no opportunity in Japan. It was a difficult decision for me, but I believed leaving Japan and starting a new life somewhere else was the right thing to do. I also knew I had to prove to myself and my family that I was a man of courage and honor.

"I came to Canada. Only a few Japanese came that year. I tried to build a new life for myself here. A new tradition. A new family. It was the Japanese community here in Canada who welcomed me. It was the same group supporting Japanese men to join other Canadians in the war. I was afraid they would not want me. Where could I go if I failed again?" He looked Manson hard in the eye. "You love this country don't you Mr. Manson? There is nowhere else you would go or want to be?"

Manson nodded.

"This is the same for me as well." Masumi gestured to himself. "Nowhere else. This is my home now. When Canada entered the war, I knew I had to join. It was never a choice for me. It was my duty. Fighting was the only thing to do. The right thing to do. And so, I fought. I followed in the footsteps of my father and his father and his father before him, in the samurai tradition. And yet, when I returned home from the war, one of the lucky ones to have survived, I was met with rejection from my fellow Canadians. Still, I am not wanted here. Do you know what that feels like?"

"I can't say I do."

"It is truly unimaginable. But for us, it is our life every day. And this is why I come before you today, Mr. Manson. I ask you, like I once did, to make the only choice you can. Give Japanese Canadians the right to vote. Not because you want to. Not because we are asking. But simply because it is the right thing to do."

Seven representatives of the Japanese Canadian community were the only people sitting in the viewing gallery, nearly thirty feet above the parliament floor on the afternoon of April 1st, 1931. The House Speaker sat immediately below them out of their view. Masumi saw many faces of members they had spoken with over the past few days. MacGregor MacIntosh gave them a quick wave. The House Speaker announced the opportunity for members to address the assembly on proceedings and Macintosh rose to speak.

"Mr. Speaker, assembly members, I would like to introduce to our session, members from the Canadian Japanese Association and the Royal Canadian Legion Branch #9 from Vancouver, who have joined us for the important vote we have before us today. Please welcome Saburo Shinobu, Naburo Murakami, Rikuzo Hoita, Nobuhei Watanabe, and Legion Provincial Secretary Robert MacNicol.

"I will add, Mr. Speaker, that two members of this group are veterans of the World War in Europe. These two men fought bravely all across Europe including Vimy Ridge, Hill 70 and Passchendaele. Please join me in welcoming Corporal Sainosuke Kubota and Sergeant Masumi Mitsui, who was decorated with the Military Medal, the British War Medal and the Victory Medal. Gentlemen, it is an honor to have you attend our proceedings today. Please join me in welcoming these guests."

The introduction was met with a smattering of clapping and some modest table thumping. If the applause coming from the members was any indication of the vote, this wasn't going to go well. The next hour was agony for Masumi, listening to various members speak for and against the motion.

Racism is alive and well, even in parliament, thought Masumi. The issues of Japanese stealing jobs from whites was raised. So too were concerns over assimilation in the population, something Europeans managed due to their similar skin color and customs.

Ian Mackenzie, the Liberal MLA from North Vancouver who had won his seat by the slim margin of only thirty-two votes, was the most vocal in opposition to granting Japanese veterans the vote. His constituents included a vocal fishing industry who were aggressive in opposing any rights for Japanese whether they be voting in elections or fishing the coastal waters. They just wanted them gone. Mackenzie's views reflected this very clear message from the people he represented. His tone bordered on hate and contempt for the Japanese people in general and these representatives in the gallery specifically.

"Mr. Speaker," Mackenzie began, "Many of my constituents are West Coast fishermen. I speak for them when I say there is no place in British Columbia for the Japanese. For over thirty years Asians have been coming to Canada, working for lower wages and failing to become part of the community of Canada. Granting them the right to vote would only endorse the dangerous threat they pose to overtake our province and even our country. Their children are now attending our schools, and they are undermining our culture and our identity. One in every eight babies born in British Columbia is Japanese," dramatically raising both arms. "We are under threat of our province being taken over by immigrants and their next generation born on our soil. Giving them the right to vote in any manner is an unwise decision."

"Do they realize we are sitting here listening to what they are saying?" Kubota whispered to Masumi. "It's nothing less than insulting. They speak about us as if we are less than human."

"Not everyone though," responded Masumi as MacIntosh rose in rebuttal.

"Mr. Speaker," said Macintosh, "my esteemed colleague from North Vancouver fails to acknowledge Japanese Canadians get paid less for doing the same work. It isn't their choice to work for less money. We allow this to happen." He paused to let this sink in then gestured to the gallery. "Those men up there risked their lives in defense of our country. They are honest hard-working people, the very characters we ascribe to all Canadians. I submit, Mr. Speaker, these are the best of Canadians, not the worst. We should be ashamed of the manner in which the B.C. government has treated them. Asians have voting rights in Canada's other provinces. Only British Columbia lags in righting this wrong." Staring directly toward Alexander Manson, he continued, "Mr. Speaker, I ask all members of parliament, regardless of party line, to do the right thing and vote 'Yes' to this motion. It would be a gracious and just act for men who fought under the flag of the British Commonwealth. Thank you."

Alexander Manson remained silent but listened intently. Masumi and the others watched him closely, trying to get an inkling of which side of the argument he was leaning towards. But he was a seasoned politician, stoic and impossible to read.

When the debate ended, the Speaker called for the final vote on the motion. One by one the constituency names were called to respond. "Yea" from some, "Nay" from others. Manson, from the riding of Omineca, was near the end of the list.

"The member from Omineca?" called the Speaker.

The men in the balcony all held their breath.

"Yea," said Manson.

That was it, wasn't it? But they had to wait until all thirty-seven votes had been cast. There was no certainty someone hadn't changed their mind as a result of the debate. Shinobu was keeping track of the vote as they reached the members from Vancouver, then Victoria and finally Yale. Before the voting reached the last MLA Shinobu looked to Masumi and said quietly, "Nineteen! That's it. We won!"

Seconds later the Speaker called on the member from Yale and announced "By a margin of nineteen to eighteen, the Yeas have it. The motion is passed."

In an instant, seven pairs of arms were thrust in the air in a cheer of victory. The Japanese Canadians were jubilant. They broke out in boisterous cheering and celebration, hugging and dancing in the elevated parliament seating, defying death if anyone were to fall in the gleeful skirmish. They were simultaneously happy, hopeful, satisfied and exhausted. Each man congratulated every other man in the balcony—no words, just smiles and nods as they rejoiced in the voting result.

They'd done it. They'd won.

The House gave them some time to enjoy the victory and make a lot more noise than they were supposed to make. This was a deeply emotional and hard-fought victory, and they deserved a moment to enjoy the results of their efforts. The cheers and applause from the balcony continued for several minutes, joined by some of the members of parliament in the House. Eventually, an usher suggested they leave the gallery. Half giddy, they complied and marched out with a final wave of gratitude to MacGregor MacIntosh and Alexander Manson.

Even though the motion only gave the vote to war veterans, through their efforts they had become the first group of Asian Canadians to win the vote in British Columbia, a province notorious for enacting a long list of racial exclusions with respect to the franchise. Their efforts represented a major breakthrough in Canada's constitutional evolution to a full democracy, paving the way for others of Asian origin, a process eventually leading to the recognition of the political rights of all Canadians. What they had accomplished was unprecedented in Canadian history.

Vancouver, British Columbia, April 1, 1931

The news of their success in Victoria had reached Vancouver long before they arrived, and throngs of Japanese Canadians turned out to welcome them home and celebrate.

As the B.C. Ferry approached the Vancouver dock, it looked to Masumi as if half the Japanese population of Canada was waiting for them. Many of the Legion members were there, some in uniform and others in less formal legion attire. People were yelling, smiling and waving their arms wildly. Others had remained in their cars to honk horns loudly as the ship came in. On the dock, excitement and jubilation awaited them, similar to the greeting the military troops received as they returned home from the war just over ten years ago. A good feeling to be sure.

Upon disembarking, the men were swept away in a noisy, horn-honking seventeen-car procession through the streets of Vancouver, finally arriving at Stanley Park. As the procession wound its way toward the cenotaph, the words of the song "It's a Long Way to Tipperary" could be heard echoing from the woods as the gathering proceeded arm in arm through the park.

Sugi and their son Dick finally caught up to Masumi in the procession.

"I'm so proud of you Masumi!" She squeezed him with unabashed delight.

He was glad to see them and emotional after the grueling two days. The implication of their accomplishments had time to sink in during the ferry ride. This wasn't the final goal—the vote for all Japanese Canadians. It was only the vote for returning veterans. But it was another first for these soldiers and an important, solid example of fair and equal treatment as citizens of Canada. This meant something, and Masumi had played a major role in the outcome. Maybe he made this happen by convincing Alexander Manson to vote in favor. Who knew? But it didn't matter. What mattered was they were victorious, and he could share this success with his family! This was more important to Masumi than he had realized, until the emotions of the moment finally sunk in.

As the sun set and the raucous crowd had settled, Sainosuke Kubota stepped to the base of the cenotaph and once again respectfully recited the poem he had written in honor of the fallen Japanese soldiers. This was the cause these men had fought and died for; the reason this memorial had been constructed. It was a good day for Japanese Canadians.

Hamilton, Ontario, November 11, 1967

"All Japanese Canadians owe you and your colleagues a great debt of gratitude Masumi," said Adachi. "You broke down a barrier, and we all benefit from your actions to this day and forevermore. You were right, that was a story worth telling. I hope I can do it justice in my book.

"It's sounds like you were fortunate to have the support of MacGregor MacIntosh, Alexander Manson and the Conservatives to push through the vote."

"Well you would think that on the surface," Masumi replied with a curious look. "But it was not what it appeared to be."

"How's that?"

"There were actually more Conservatives who voted against the motion than for it, seventeen to eleven. And even though they didn't have the majority in parliament, the Liberals were more in favor with seven to one. One Independent Party member swayed the outcome in our favor. The vote ran along personal feelings rather than party lines. We appealed to the veterans.

"Another odd element to the story is while MacIntosh voted in favor of war veterans' voting rights, several years later, when it came time to vote on issues affecting Japanese Canadians, it turns out he was actually very anti-Japanese, preferring our people be expelled from Canada. The Liberals turned on us too when the new Co-operative Commonwealth Federation (CCF) party started supporting the Japanese franchise. The Liberals told people a vote for a CCF candidate was a vote to give Asians voting rights, and the Liberal party was opposed to granting Asians the right to vote. We didn't have many friends in politics in the thirties.

"As far as finally getting the voting franchise, it took many more years to reach that status for all Japanese people. As I'm sure you know, Ken, the final decision to grant the vote to all of us didn't come for another eighteen years—to the exact day in fact, on April 1st, 1949. So many horrible things happened in those intervening years, virtually all of them bad for people of Japanese ancestry."

"I'm sure you are referring to the Second World War and the internment of all Japanese Canadians," Adachi guessed. "But I would like to learn more about your life and those of people like you in the next decade. For me this is an interesting period as the next generation of Japanese Canadians, well, Canadians of Japanese descent to be more accurate, entered the world."

"You are right about that, Ken," Masumi agreed. "The 1930s was a decade filled with distrust and hate and a building animosity towards Asians in general and Japanese in particular."

Slightly puzzled, Adachi asked, "Can you tell me why that was so?"

"Yes, I can," Masumi responded. "Events happening several thousand miles away had a strong and unexpected influence on those of us here in Canada. Across the Pacific Ocean, Japan was engaged in an aggressive territorial dispute against China over Manchuria. Even though Japanese Canadians had nothing to do with any of the horrible actions Japan was responsible for committing against China, we were blamed and resented. This is a period of Japanese history that shames everyone of Japanese descent today," admitted Masumi. "Personally, I was disgusted and ashamed of the actions of our military. Japanese soldiers were accused of murdering hundreds of thousands of Chinese civilians and raping tens of thousands of women. It was disgraceful. These were not the actions of a people whose society is based on the teachings of Confucius and the beliefs of bushido. The war was fought in China, so my family was safe in Japan and my father was retired from the Navy. But the actions of the Japanese soldiers fighting in China stretched across the Pacific Ocean.

"In Canada, our businesses were boycotted, and our community was detested, not just by Chinese Canadians but by everyone. Adding this to the stress of the Depression, the 1930s were very hard on all Japanese businesses. We clung together and supported each other. Unlike the war, when whites and colored held strong together with a shared belief, this time we were the singular enemy."

"Not surprisingly the local Chinese refused to do business with Japanese farmers," Masumi added. "Now we were hated by another cultural group. Can it get any worse, I wondered? Well, actually it could, as it turned out.

"There was growing suspicion illegal Japanese immigrants were being smuggled into Canada by way of Vancouver Island. That's why MacIntosh turned on us. His riding was on Vancouver Island. Rumors surfaced suggesting Japan was secretly trying to take over Canada's West Coast. Of course, it was all nonsense and there was never any evidence, but these stories added fuel to the beliefs of those who wanted us to be kicked out of Canada. Our enemies spread these rumors and incited fear and hate in their constituents. By the time we got to 1940, it felt like we had hit bottom and might never recover. I had no idea what the real bottom was though. I learned that in the next five years." He looked forlornly to the floor as if gazing into a deep abyss, memories flooding back to him.

"Stepping away from politics for a bit and before we get to your memories of World War 2, what else comes to your memory when you think about the 30s?" Asked Adachi. "Start with some of your family memories. Tell me what life was like on the chicken farm and in your community."

This opening from Adachi caught the ears of all four Mitsui children who had settled in around the two men to listen to more of Masumi's recollections. He never talked much about the early days on the farm. For all of them this was a rare opportunity to hear some rich family history. At this stage in their lives it was more important than ever to have some understanding of the past, when they were children some forty years ago.

"Sugi and I worked very hard in the early years starting the farm," Masumi began. "We cleared land and marketed our chickens. We learned a lot in those days—what to do and what not to do. We learned disease can kill a flock in a hurry. You lose everything and have to start over," he recalled. "Dick was only ten years old when we started the farm and we had all four kids in the early 1920s, so it was a bit crazy around the Mitsui home."

"I'll bet it was a very busy home Masumi," said Adachi. "What specific memories do you have about your family and your farm from those years?"

Amy couldn't resist the opening. "Yes father," she piped in, "tell us why you sent George to Japan." She giggled and sent a conspiratorial look towards Lucy. She then looked across to George with an impish grin knowing he was embarrassed by the story of his trip to Japan. He gave her a scowl in return.

"I'll get to that," Masumi promised. "But I can tell you the thirties was a difficult decade for everyone. The country was in a depression you know."

"Yes, The Depression was a difficult time for everyone," acknowledged Adachi. "How did it affect you and your family?"

"While not as bad as many people's during the thirties, our lives were still very challenging. Sugi and I had five children to care for along with managing a small business requiring more than twelve hours of work every day. Prices for food were low. Most people didn't have any money anyway so there was a lot of difficult times for many," Masumi recalled. "They called them 'bread lines' and 'soup lines' where people who had nothing were forced to take whatever they could get. By comparison we were lucky. We had food, a house and our health.

"The federal government started deporting people, sending them back to their homeland. The Japanese felt particularly vulnerable as this is exactly what the B.C. politicians had been trying to achieve for years," Masumi shared. "Fortunately, for us, they prioritized immigrants in jails or hospitals as a burden to the public. Those people were deported. We had jobs and paid taxes.

"As if things weren't bad enough, a fire in 1935 destroyed a large part of our home. We had to rebuild at a time when we barely had enough money to live. This was one of the greatest tragedies we faced as a family, but we persevered and built a grand home for us to live in."

"I remember that day," George said. "I was thirteen at the time. I came riding home from school to find fire trucks. The flames and smoke were everywhere."

"We were lucky not to lose the chicken barn and birds," Masumi recalled. "That would have been an even greater disaster."

"It took over a year for us to get back into our new home. Remember that Amy?" George asked.

"I sure do," she said. "Lucy, Harry, Mom and I lived with the Kawamoto's while Dad rebuilt the home. You, Dick and Dad moved into the shed attached to the chicken coop."

"I can still smell chicken poop!" griped George. "That smell will never leave me! Yuck!"

"We didn't have much money, but we all worked to maintain the farm, all seven of us," added Masumi. "The kids had their chores. In the evenings we would play games, do homework, and once in a while, I would tell them stories of ancient Japan and the samurai."

Port Coquitlam, BC, November 1932

"Sit down, sit down," Masumi directed as he held his hands outstretched, palms down in an effort to calm the children. The family had gathered in the living room after dinner clean up. The room's lighting was subdued due to the shorter days and longer nights. Everyone gradually quieted at Masumi's urgings. They knew he wouldn't start until it was completely quiet. Father had promised to share some stories of samurai warriors tonight, generating an air of excitement in the children. They were always eager to hear more stories about this special legacy of their ancient ancestors—people who were actually related to them as part of the Mitsui clan. Their enthusiasm pleased Masumi. He fondly remembered those evenings he spent with his grandfather, learning all these legends. It fulfilled a dream for him to be able to retell those stories to his children.

"The legend of the samurai in Japan goes back many hundreds of years," Masumi began, the same way he began this story every time he told them a chapter. "The samurai were an army of brave warriors, first formed about 1300 years ago in ancient Japan. There were no police forces or laws. Instead, there were feudal lords called 'shoguns' who had built their own armies to defend their lands. The warriors who defended those lands were known as 'samurai.' They were paid to fight, to kill and, if necessary, to die for their shogun. There were similarities between our ancestors and the lords and knights of Medieval Europe at the same time in history," Masumi observed. "Each warrior wore armor, carried a sword and bow and often fought on horseback. They defended a lord or king who lived in a large home or castle on feudal lands farmed by peasants.

"The word 'samurai' means *one who serves.*" Masumi bowed before the children to indicate humility and servitude. Masumi could tell by the children's responses that they loved the animation he included in his stories as well as his reverence for ancient Japan and their forefathers.

"You have heard me speak of bushido or the way of the warrior. These are the great teachings of the samurai masters who became part of Japanese culture and a way of life for our people. We have much to learn from our ancestors and the samurai who are responsible for the way we conduct ourselves today," Masumi reflected. "It goes back to Confucianism and Zen Buddhist teachings which have very powerful and meaningful beliefs. But we will get to that a bit later," he promised.

"Samurai also had a gentle, cultural side to them identifying with the fragile, fleeting beauty of the cherry blossoms, for instance. These fearsome warriors wrote poems about cherry trees and held extravagant cherry blossom viewing parties and ceremonies. The cherry blossom doesn't cling to the tree until it withers, but falls in its prime, the same way a samurai imagined himself dying in battle.

"In preparation for war each samurai warrior commissioned an elaborate suit of armor made just for him. The suits were combinations of iron, bronze, copper and polished leather for protection, along with colorful lacquered wood and papier mâché for decoration. Many small sections would be laced together in elaborate shapes to create sleeves, breastplates, thigh and shin protection for these magnificent outfits. They would weigh between twenty-five and forty pounds! Imagine trying to fight an opponent with that weight on your body. This showed the strength and skill of the samurai fighters.

"In their body armor designs, warriors paid tribute to dragons, animals like the rhinoceros or large deer, and even flames. They carried razor sharp steel swords—katanas and wakizashis—perfectly matched for strength and suppleness. The scabbards were made of gold and bronze and the handles of wood, leather and even the skin of stingrays.

"When a horde of these warriors in their fierce-looking armor charged down a hillside, it would strike terror into the hearts of the opposing force. The samurai would yell and scream to generate panic in their targets. It was truly a fearsome display.

"In battle, samurai warriors were known to chop off their fallen enemies' heads and present them to their lord." Masumi carried on in a crescendo of volume ending with a loud stamp of his foot as he acted out a beheading and then looking at his hand holding an imaginary head by the hair in the midst of the children. They would shriek with disgust and fear as he ran about the room waving the imaginary head in their direction, forcing them to recoil. The girls shrieked especially loud, while the boys joined in the imaginary battle, waving pretend swords at pretend enemies.

After everyone calmed down and the nervous giggling subsided, Masumi continued with his tale of the Mitsui family's place in this history.

"Now I will tell you about our clan, the Mitsui clan. In the years following the formation of the first great clans in Japan, many wars occurred between rival lords. Power shifted between families based on which shogun reigned supreme. In one great battle called the Onin War, which lasted ten years during the 1400s, the city of Kyoto was burned to the ground. I can tell you though it is once again a beautiful, historic city which I remember seeing during my journey to Canada twenty-five years ago.

"The Mitsui clan can be traced back to the 1100s," he boasted. "We were a proud family of warriors serving many noble shoguns over the centuries. Your great grandfather was one of the last samurai warriors to serve the Emperor of Japan, thirty years before I was born.

"After centuries of fighting, into the late 1600s, Japan entered into a time of peace. No wars were fought and so there were no paying battles for samurai. Our family was in great need of money to finance our army, so one of our ancestors, Takatoshi Mitsui, started a business enterprise making soy and sake, a business that later expanded into dry goods retail and, more importantly, merchant banking. Through these enterprises the family split in two parts. One was a most powerful family of merchants and industrialists in Japan. The other part continued our long tradition as a warrior clan. I know this part is boring." Masumi nodded to George who paid less attention as the story shifted away from warriors. "And not what you want to hear about, but it is how we came to be who we are and how our samurai were able to serve the Japanese Emperor for over 200 years. The businesses flourished in Edo, Kyoto and Osaka for 150 years, but the family bank was by far the most profitable and helped the Mitsui remain powerful.

"The Mitsui men became shrewd businessmen and sided with the Emperor during difficult times. This resulted in favored status for the Mitsui clan as power returned to the Meiji government during the Restoration in Japan. But this was also the beginning of the end for samurai as powerful businesses overtook the government and placed their own Emperor in charge. At their request, he ordered an end to samurai."

"The warriors lost their high position in Japanese society. They were forced to surrender their swords and were forbidden to wear their hair in the formal topknot style of the samurai. In 1877 the samurai tried to form a rebellion in an effort to regain their power, but their efforts were thwarted and many of them committed *seppuku* or ritual suicide as a last expression of failure as a warrior.

"Why would they do that father?" Amy asked, not understanding their reasoning.

"For warriors it is important to have honor above all else," replied Masumi. "They pledged this honor and loyalty to their lord when they became samurai. It was part of who they were. The disgrace of not being able to be a samurai was just too much for many of these men. They were soldiers without a war and decided they would rather die than go on living in disgrace."

Amy's question reminded him of his own seppuku. Of course, he didn't actually committed suicide, but he had felt disgrace and he had left his family to strike out on his own, leaving them behind as if he had died. He wondered about the sadness his grandfather must have felt in the years after he was stripped of his privilege as a samurai.

His mind drifted briefly to his family in Japan. His only close living relative was Tomo as his grandfather had passed away shortly after he came to Canada and his father had died just before Masumi went to war.

"What about bushido?" Lucy asked bringing his attention back to the small room and his family, focused on his every word.

"Yes…yes of course, Lucy," Masumi responded coming back to the here and now of the evening. "Bushido…bushido," he repeated for emphasis and gravity.

"Bushido means 'the way of the warrior' in English. It is a code of conduct samurai warriors followed in their daily lives, a roadmap of proper behavior. There are eight themes of bushido: justice, benevolence, respect, honesty, duty, courage, self-control and honor. My grandfather taught me bushido when I was just about your age. He told me it would take a week to learn the themes and a lifetime to learn the meanings. I follow these teachings myself and get great inner strength from them. They have helped me through difficult times in my early years in Canada and also during the war in Europe.

"There is a right and a wrong way to live your life, my children. Bushido is the right path."

Hamilton, Ontario, November 11, 1967

"Marvelous, Masumi!" Adachi praised. "The foundations of bushido, the history of Japan, and specifically the samurai, these are things not well known by our current generations. It's an important history of our culture we should remember as our heritage and something we should celebrate as a community. Good for you for passing these stories on to your children."

"I sure remember those evenings," said Amy. "It was so much fun to learn about our family history and the stories of Japan. Lucy and I are planning a trip there to see all of those wonderful places ourselves."

"What other memories come to mind as you think back to the thirties?" Ken prompted.

"One good thing I can remember was the arrival of all those trees from Japan." Masumi was enjoying this walk down memory lane, but he also knew the worst memories of his lifetime were yet to come as the story unfolded.

"What was that about?" asked Adachi bringing Masumi back to his original thought.

"You may not know this, but all of the beautiful cherry blossom trees planted around the city of Vancouver were not in British Columbia at all until they were sent from Japan. In 1935, Kobe and Yokohama made a gift of three hundred trees to Vancouver as a gesture of friendship. Japan was trying to build better relations with friendly countries, and Canada was home to a lot of Japanese nationals, so it was a goodwill gesture between the two nations. They sent more trees much later, in 1958 I believe, and some of those were planted around the cenotaph in Stanley Park. These beautiful trees are a wonderful reminder of my early years in Japan with my family. They were special to my grandfather too," he recalled as the memory of cherry trees and samurai flashed back to him again.

As Masumi paused for a small break, the girls went into action. They couldn't wait any longer. Amy made eye contact with Lucy and nodded her head towards Masumi, encouraging her sister to rekindle her earlier request to get her father to talk about George's embarrassing story. "Tell us about George getting in trouble and having to go to Japan, Father," said Lucy, feeding off the earlier jab by Amy. The girls loved to get in their shots at George whenever they could. It was payback for years of teasing by George and his friends when they were all younger. "I remember George was shooting a BB gun and got in trouble with the police!" she added, throwing a little primer fuel on the narrative fire.

"Why don't you mind your own business!" George shot over at Lucy. "Nobody wants to hear that story again."

"Yes, we do!" chorused Lucy and Amy. "Tell us about George and the Graham boys', Father!" Amy added some of the details to remind Masumi and help get the story going.

"Ah geez," George moaned. "Here we go."

"Those Graham boys were a very bad influence on George," Masumi waded into the story like it was his idea and he had started it, even though the girls had lured him into telling it. Amy and Lucy smiled gleefully at each other and Masumi knew he had taken their bait. George was in for an uncomfortable time in front of their guest. The girls lived for moments like this.

"Yes, boys in the country with guns and too much time on their hands, a combination spelling trouble," recalled Masumi.

"They were around eighteen years old, I think," said Masumi. "Full of no good if you ask me—George too! They were shooting out street lamps on the backroads and the rural police caught them. Damned if those buggers didn't get one over on the officer and steal his car one night. After a wild ride they ended it by driving the car into Buntzen Lake in Port Coquitlam."

"I wasn't driving the police car," said George in a weak defense.

"You knew it was wrong though, didn't you?" Masumi flashed a hard look in George's direction as if it had just happened a couple of days ago.

This was just too sweet for Amy and Lucy as they giggled at George's discomfort and admonishing all these years later.

"Yes father," George conceded. "Of course."

"Well you were just lucky I was on good terms with Officer Stafford at the RCMP. I spoke with him and promised I would personally see to it you never did anything like that again. So he agreed to let you come home with me. Those Graham boys could still be in jail for all I know!

"That's when I decided to send you to Japan to stay with my brother Tomo and learn some humility and respect," continued Masumi. "Children are raised differently in Japan, better I would say. They respect adults, they follow rules, they do what they are told. Here in Canada it is not the same. It is not good here. Great benefit came from George going to Japan for three years. He returned with respect and maturity."

"I also came back with the family wakizashi," said George.

"A samurai short sword?" Adachi asked.

"Yes," George replied. "You know a bit about these I gather? It is the Mitsui clan's small samurai sword. Many swords were destroyed in the Meiji Restoration when the samurai class was dismantled. Like father just said, my great grandfather was one of the last samurai. And then again, after the Second World War, even more Japanese swords were destroyed or grabbed as souvenirs by soldiers. We nearly lost ours as well during the internment. Father can tell you that story. But I was given the opportunity to bring the sword to Canada and give it to the family's current samurai, our father, Sergeant Masumi Mitsui.

"In Japan I lived and worked with my uncle and learned a lot about their culture and history, my ancestral identity," explained George. "My father's bravery fighting for Canada in World War 1 is a source of great pride with the Mitsuis in Japan and they were honored to send the sword to him as he upheld the pride and the service of samurai in our family's history.

"As I look back on those two years I spent in Japan, I am glad father sent me. I returned to Canada in the summer of 1941 as war tension was escalating in Japan and international conflict increasing. I didn't want to get mixed up in it. Father is the samurai in this family, not me," he concluded with a nod of respect to Masumi.

Their work done in successfully dragging George through the public humiliation with one of their favorite family stories, the ladies suggested a brief rest was in order. "Let's take a little break and have some food, shall we?" proposed Amy. Everyone must be a little tired and a lot hungry. I know I am." Amy, Lucy and George's wife, Nancy, headed off to the kitchen to prepare salad and break out the casserole dishes they had prepared for the day.

As they left, George leaned over to Ken Adachi and said, "Would you like to see the sword Mr. Adachi?"

"Most definitely," he replied eagerly. It was a rare opportunity to see an authentic samurai sword, especially one with the provenance of the Mitsui family.

"I'll be right back," promised George.

Lucy and Amy put out a wonderful dinner spread. Ken Adachi and the Mitsui family enjoyed the evening on this Remembrance Day and national Centennial. Even the grandchildren had been captivated by Masumi's stories—and the food—as they settled into small crevices of the couch or on the floor with pillows and blankets.

"This is quite a family treasure, Masumi," acknowledged Adachi as he examined the samurai sword. "I'm sure it has great meaning and reverence for you and your family."

Masumi smiled. "It certainly symbolizes to me the 'Way of the Samurai.' It's magical and mystical to think about where it has been and what adventures it must have been a part of. But for me, it is a symbol of bushido and the lessons I learned from my grandfather, respect, courage, honor...characteristics like these. So yes, it means a lot to me but not at all in a violent way. More in calm, serene, gentle way."

"George mentioned you nearly lost it. How did that happen?"

"Well this kind of leads into the next phase of the story," replied Masumi. "It starts several months after George returned from Japan, on one fateful day in December 1941. A day that turned our family's life and the lives of all Japanese Canadians upside down. It is also the cause of my continuing anger with the Canadian government. I have never forgiven the government for what they did to me, my family and all Japanese Canadians. This chapter of our life started when the Japanese bombed Pearl Harbor."

"Wow!" Adachi exclaimed. "That's quite a lead in. I would very much like to hear your recollection of that day and the years following. This is really the essence of my story. A story about a perceived enemy of Canada masquerading as Canadian citizens. A story about Japanese Canadian first and second generations, issei and nissei, who were seen as a threat to the country. A story about the enemy that never was. Please tell me all about it."

CHAPTER SEVEN

Pearl Harbor and Internment

Courage
...to surmount pain, insecurity, and doubt in an effort to defend one's own self or others.

Honolulu, Hawaii, USA, December 7, 1941

On the morning of December 7th, 1941, the Japanese Navy and Air Force launched a coordinated attack on the U.S. bases at Pearl Harbor, Guam and Manila in the Philippines. They also attacked British bases in Hong Kong, Singapore and Malaya.

The attack on Pearl Harbor destroyed or disabled twenty-one ships and over three hundred aircraft, all part of the Pacific Fleet. Two thousand four hundred men and women were killed and nearly twelve hundred others injured. The intent of the attack was to disable a large portion of the American fleet, preventing it from interfering with the Japanese conquest of the Dutch East Indies and Malaya. The attack focused on U.S. battleships, as they were considered the strength of the U.S. Navy. The losses were expected to be demoralizing to any potential U.S. military effort. The Japanese hoped the Americans would stay out of any further conflict in the Pacific. In hindsight, it's safe to say they sorely misjudged the reaction of America.

Conflict between Japan and China had been escalating for most of the 1930s. The United States had sided with China and other smaller nations by cutting off war supplies to Japan. These actions were perceived as hostile towards Japan, damaging an already tense relationship. Talks between Japan and the United States failed in November of 1941 and the main Japanese attack fleet sailed for Pearl Harbor on November 26, 1941, just days later.

Port Coquitlam, British Columbia, December 7, 1941

George burst into the chicken barn just after 2:00 p.m. on Sunday afternoon.

"Father, come quickly to the house. You must hear what is happening!"

"What is it George?" Masumi recognized the urgent tone in George's voice.

"It's the Japanese Navy. They attacked Pearl Harbor!"

"What are you talking about?" Masumi asked incredulously. "That makes no sense to me. Why would they do such a thing?"

Confused and shocked, Masumi caught up to George and entered the back door of the house where he found Sugi and Amy listening to the radio. They both sat with their mouths hanging open, in obvious disbelief, to the loud and rapid words of a newscaster on the radio.

"What is it?" Masumi asked. "What has happened?"

Sugi was first to respond "The news reporter says the Japanese have bombed the U.S. Navy station in Pearl Harbor, Hawaii. The United States is not in the war against Germany and Japan. Why would they do this?" she added, echoing Masumi's thoughts.

"This is military strategy, Sugi," responded Masumi as he reckoned back to his days as a soldier and the extensive planning that went into preemptive strikes such as this. "The Japanese must have anticipated the United States entering the war against them and have taken action to cripple them before they can join the fight."

Masumi had been struggling with the current global conflict that pitted his homeland against those countries he had fought to protect in the First World War. Since the Second World War started, two years earlier, Canada had been sending soldiers to Europe and Asia to aid in the fight. But Masumi hadn't felt the need to join up as some Japanese Canadians had done. He felt he was too old to fight and probably wouldn't pass the physical anyway with his bad knee. He also had responsibilities at home with his family. This attack changed that.

As he listened intently to the radio, his emotions raged. He was angry at the Japanese for ambushing the United States. There was no honor in this attack. He knew this would reflect badly on himself and his family in the local community. He wondered what he should do, now that the war had escalated and moved closer to home.

Immediately after the bombing on December 8th, 1941, the United States declared war on Japan. Canada had already declared war on Italy and Germany in 1938 as part of the British Commonwealth and now added Japan to the list that same day.

Prior to the bombing of Pearl Harbor, there had been no indications of a perceived threat to North America from Japanese immigrants living there. However, they had been under scrutiny as possible spy threats. The Canadian federal government and B.C. provincial government had been actively registering all Japanese citizens living in Canada in preparation for any potential hostilities from Japan towards Canada, and to manage any potential insurgence within the country. Several politicians also used this platform to gain popularity with constituents who could vote, by casting aspersions on Japanese Canadians (who could not vote). In addition to MacGregor MacIntosh in the B.C. government, the Japanese Canadians had an even bigger enemy in Ian Mackenzie, the federal Member of Parliament from Vancouver Centre. An immigrant from Scotland himself, he openly hated the Japanese and worked day and night to prevent them from gaining any level of equality or basic human rights. He was a hateful man with power and access to the Prime Minister. He advocated sending all Japanese Canadians to Japan— immigrants as well as those born in Canada.

The tension level in British Columbia in particular, was very high. Fishermen were under close watch as rumors circulated, incriminating them as spies acting for the Japanese Navy. The high emotions associated with the actions of the Japanese toward China was also a source of suspicion and wariness towards the Japanese locals. Already reeling from the difficult times of the thirties the Japanese merchants were now suffering from boycotts and trade barriers exercised by the white community. Their living conditions had gone from bad to worse.

Port Coquitlam, British Columbia, Canada, December 9, 1941

As usual, Masumi was in the chicken barn and on the job by 6:00 a.m. Feeding birds and pen clean-up was a labor he had learned to love. He'd known nothing about raising chickens and farming when they bought the small farm with the veteran's loan and savings shortly after the war. At first, he had one small building with two hundred birds, but over the years he had added on, modernized the pens and feeders and had become very adept at producing high quality broilers. The population of the lower mainland had grown from 140,000 citizens in the early 1920s to 400,000 by 1940. Demand for chickens had multiplied and Masumi was able to earn a good living for his family. Like the Japanese fishermen who came to Canada and proved to be better at fishing than the Canadians, Masumi dedicated himself to his vocation and quickly excelled among his peers. His morning routine consisted of filling the feeders and water systems and removing the racks that caught the chicken poop as it fell through the cages. In one end and out the other he often thought. Masumi honored his flock and treated them respectfully even though their ultimate fate was a short life once they reached market weight.

Farming chickens was not a job for a lazy man. Masumi worked hard every day and did the work himself. Sugi's responsibility was clearing land, which they then used to grow broccoli for chicken feed. She also had a family vegetable garden and a large area dedicated to strawberries which were as much a hobby as another source of income for the Mitsui family. But Sugi's specialty was dynamite. She blew up stumps and rocks like they were pebbles in her way. Masumi still had to cart the carnage away but only after Sugi blasted them free of their earthly bondage with a half stick here and a whole stick there. She got quite a delight out of her work. As their four children grew, they too worked on the farm alongside them, and together they enjoyed a comfortable life. Even after that devastating fire in April 1935 that destroyed part of their home, they were able to rebuild and succeed in their farming venture. Hard work trumped bad luck every time.

But today his mind wasn't on farming, it was churning over a decision he knew he had to make. At fifty-four years of age he did not look or act like most men that age. Thanks to his work ethic, he was fit and strong and felt confident he was making the right choice. When faced with tough decisions or confused about life's complexities Masumi always gravitated back to the ways of bushido. Not only was this calming, but it also gave him a frame of reference for right and wrong.

The attack by Japan on the U.S. naval base at Pearl Harbor two days earlier had been a horrible shock to Masumi. His homeland had executed a cowardly and heartless attack on a country friendly to his new home. It crossed Masumi's mind that, had he been accepted by the Japanese Navy back in 1908, he might have been involved in the events of this tragic day. The thought of that made his stomach turn with conflict. He was a loyal Canadian citizen and his children were born in this country, but he still felt a kinship and loyalty to Japan. It was his homeland after all, and his brother still lived there. The inner conflict he felt that day was a deep and painful sadness unlike anything he had experienced before.

He tried to make some sense of what was happening. He was a Canadian veteran of a war in which Japan had been an ally. Now his ancestral homeland, his country of birth had sided with Germany and Italy in the Tripartite Pact against his new country along with other nations in the Allied Forces. In spite of feeling conflicted, torn and confused, he knew what he had to do.

The bombing of Pearl Harbor plunged the United States of America into the Second World War and he knew Canada would stand by its allies, both the Americans as well as the European countries embroiled in another global conflict. He had served Canada bravely in the First World War and he believed that he should volunteer to fight for his country again, if he could.

⁓

He could not explain what had happened at Pearl Harbor just forty-eight hours ago, but he knew that it was wrong. No one should behave in this manner. It was a cowardly act that brought him shame as a Japanese man. He could not change what had happened, but he could act in a manner that showed how he felt about this atrocious action. This was not the Japanese way, the bushido way. Canadians should know that he and his fellow Japanese Canadians were not to blame for the atrocity of the bombings. They should honor his courage to stand in opposition to his ancestral land and on the side of North America. After much contemplation he had made up his mind.

He went into the kitchen to find Sugi and tell her of his decision.

"I don't understand," she said. "You are too old to fight. You sacrificed so much already in the Great War. Why do you feel you have to fight again? We have five children. Who will manage the farm? We need you here with us," she said with a crack in her voice that betrayed her emotional upset to Masumi's news.

"Canada is our homeland now," replied Masumi. "When I became a soldier in 1916, I pledged to defend my country. It is my duty to that promise that I must now honor." The strong sense of commitment, loyalty and service to his country was evidence of Masumi's honor. Above all else, this was a driving motivation and core belief which had guided him and his ancestors for centuries. He was, after all, a descendant of Japanese samurai, the most dedicated and fierce combatants of any nation or culture. Now the descendants of these warriors were declaring war against his new homeland and its allies. He went back over thoughts that had been running through his brain. This made it much more personal. If he had to, he decided, he would fight against these Japanese invaders. They did not hold the same beliefs and values as he did, and they were waging war against his country, Canada. That was all that needed to be considered. He would enlist again and give his life, if necessary, to defend his family and his country.

"I must do this, Sugi! I am strong and experienced, and I can lead troops into battle. Even if they say I am too old to fight I will show them they are wrong! Or I will find some way to serve my country in the military." As he went on explaining his choice, Sugi listened intently. Masumi recapped his thoughts. He had weighed the risks and his responsibilities to his family. He had thought about all the friends and fellow soldiers who had fallen at Hill 70 and at Vimy Ridge in France. All their names were there to see on the cenotaph plaque in Stanley Park. He struggled with this decision, but he was driven by his deep-seated belief in his pride as a Canadian. This country had accepted him when he immigrated here over thirty years ago. It had provided him with a decent living and a wonderful family, and fueled a sense of accomplishment.

"What will you do and where will you go?" Sugi asked.

"I don't know" replied Masumi "But I will serve in any way I can. I am a soldier and we owe everything we have to our country." He knew he still had some work to do to convince Sugi that this was the right choice. Leaving his wife and children to manage the farm while he went off to war was definitely not her first choice and he needed her to support his decision.

She will come around, he thought. *She will see that I am right.*

"With George back from Japan—thank goodness he came back when he did, or he would have to stay there during this war—he can help with farm duties. He is a man now."

At dinner that evening a sombre mood prevailed. The events of the previous days were already affecting the children in school. As Japanese Canadians, they experienced racist comments and slurs on a regular basis. It wasn't as bad as when Masumi came to Canada in 1908, but they certainly dealt with their share of hurtful comments and outright hatred. After Pearl Harbor, the unfiltered hate and vitriol directed towards the Japanese students in the schools reached new heights.

"Why did Japan do this horrible thing?" asked sweet, young Lucy. "How could anyone be so awful? My classmates yelled 'Go home Jap!' and they spit on me!" she said, choking as her eyes welled up in tears. "But Canada is my home. I was born here. I have never even been to Japan and I don't speak Japanese."

As Lucy related her experience at school, Masumi became enraged. This only added to his belief that he must show his loyalty to Canada and instill pride in his children for their father's bravery and dedication. To him, this seemed like the best solution. As they finished dinner, he told them his decision.

"Amy, Lucy, George, Harry, I have made a decision. I am going to enlist in the army and fight for Canada. It is my duty as a soldier and a Canadian to join this battle and fight for our freedom. It is also something I have to do as a Japanese man. White Canadians must know that Japanese Canadians fight for Canada in this battle, not for Japan. This will mean hardship for all of you to keep the farm going while I am gone. I am counting on you to work hard and help mother until I am able to return."

As he spoke, he could see the expressions of sadness on all of their faces as they quietly listened to him. Lucy cried openly now. He knew the hurt of racism firsthand and was anguished that his children had to experience this ugliness. Children could be ruthless to each other, and it was impossible for young people to ignore the hatred directed at them by their peers.

How do children learn this behavior? They are most certainly not born with hatred and racism as part of who they are, he thought. It came to them from the world they lived in, their families, their friends and from watching and listening to others who were filled with this contempt.

As much as Masumi displayed courage in his intention to enlist to fight again, he knew his family would have to muster even greater courage in the weeks and months ahead, likely for as long as this war lasted and even beyond. This would truly test their inner strength and commitment to behave in the way he and Sugi had taught them. To respect the very people, fellow Canadians, who acted out in the most despicable of ways towards people of Japanese descent. And even though this conflict involved European countries, the same thing was not happening to immigrants from those countries involved like Germany and Italy. It was only directed at Asians. The hate dug deep, agonizing Masumi as he understood how his children were suffering for something they could not change.

The nature of the courage Masumi would have to display over the coming years was not at all what he envisioned as he contemplated going back to war. The courage he would need to summon would test him in ways he could never imagine. But the brave Masumi Mitsui, the distinguished World War I veteran, never got the chance to volunteer. Japanese Canadians were put in a holding pattern while government officials argued back and forth about what to do with these "aliens."

Canadian Legion Branch #9, Vancouver, B.C., December 9, 1941

As a veteran and President of the Japanese Legion Branch #9, Masumi knew they must make a statement of support to the Canadian government. It must be very clear where the loyalties of all Japanese Canadians were during this difficult and tense period. Masumi called an emergency meeting of the branch executive and together they drafted a telegram to send to the Canadian Prime Minister. He and the other members of the Legion board knew the RCMP had been cataloging all Japanese immigrants in Canada, starting around 1937 when Japan invaded China. The government had the means and the knowledge to target all Japanese Canadians. Positive action would be required by the Japanese community to calm concerns and stem the overt hostility directed towards them from both the Chinese, and now white Canadians.

"This is an excellent statement, Shinobu," Masumi declared as he read the message Shinobu had drafted. "Well done!"

The members of the Japanese Branch of the Canadian Legion, BESL are resolved to pledge their unflinching loyalty to Canada, as they did in the Last Great War, and furthermore resolved to make supreme sacrifice in defence of Canada in this unprecedented crisis which faces her now. Although they are well on in years, they are fully prepared to serve in the defence of the principle for which Canada stands whenever and wherever their services are required.

"I will telegraph it to Ottawa in the morning," Shinobu said. "It is very important we show the support of the Legion and our war veteran members."

"I am going to the registration office on Monday to sign up," added Masumi.

"You are crazy, old man," chuckled Shinobu. "You know they won't take Japanese volunteers and they definitely don't want old worn out relics like you!"

"Laugh if you like, but you know this is the best way to show whites what we stand for, that we are loyal Canadians."

"You are braver than me, Masumi. Good luck to you."

Port Coquitlam, British Columbia, Canada, March 16, 1942

In mid-March, two officers from the local RCMP detachment came to Masumi's house and took him from his family. He was locked behind barbed wire in a holding facility at Hastings Park, the local horse racing track and barns. This was the protocol for senior male family members. Sugi was given instructions to pack a maximum of 150 pounds of personal items per person and leave the rest of their belongings in the basement where they would be safe. They would be notified when a bus would pick them up and be moved to the Hastings Park detention area pending assignment to an internment location.

As it turned out, not only was Masumi not welcome as a soldier in the Canadian army, it was becoming more and more evident that he and his fellow Japanese Canadians were not at all welcome in British Columbia. The persistent racist venom directed towards them day in and day out had been something they lived with over the years, but since Japan had been fighting with China, and even more so after the bombing of Pearl Harbor, the suspicion and overt anger had escalated, often becoming physical. Japanese people were beaten and threatened by other citizens of the province and officials decided something needed to be done "for their own protection." The general consensus of the provincial government was; better to act proactively than be sorry later when something bad happened. The powder keg situation could explode at any moment and the government felt action was necessary to show leadership and also to protect the lives of the Japanese Canadians during the uncertainty of the enactment of war measures. This was the politically expedient solution and the general public was pressing for action based on the fervent vocalizations of several overly impassioned politicians.

The incarceration actions by the B.C. government fueled an already volatile situation and the local politicians were happy to throw verbal gasoline on that emotional fire. This was an unprecedented opportunity to further their efforts toward deportation of all Japanese Canadians from Canada. It empowered them to restate their claims that Japanese were sneaky and treacherous, and this was representative of the character of the Japanese Canadians living in British Columbia. "Clearly, they cannot be trusted" was the common theme from many provincial and municipal politicians. At no time was it considered that most of the Japanese Canadians living in Canada at the start of the Second World War were actually Canadian citizens, born in that country.

Immediately after the bombing, the government ordered the seizure of 1200 Japanese owned and operated fishing boats on the West Coast. Fifty-Nine Japanese language schools were closed, as well as three Japanese newspapers. One English language newspaper, issued by a Japanese publisher, was allowed to remain open. All of those printed in Japanese were ordered closed for fear of communication of inciting commentaries or transmitting espionage in some way to the general population in their native language. This was all done in the interest of "national defense and security," according to the Prime Minister, Mackenzie King. He made the decision in order to avoid domestic violence and in his words "to prevent the possibility of excessive punishment of Canadians now being held as prisoners in Japan." Acting on pressure from various B.C. associations and on advice from the Japanese-hating MP, Ian Mackenzie, who favored full deportation, the Prime Minister took the line of least resistance without any consideration for the impact on Japanese Canadians who would suffer great emotional and financial devastation by these decisions.

Japanese Canadians also lost their jobs. Businesses like CP Rail, local hotels and sawmills fired Japanese workers to avoid worksite hostilities and labor disputes. Once again, the only people paying the price were the Japanese Canadians.

Both the RCMP and Canada's armed forces saw no present danger from the Japanese Canadian community in Canada. But their views were not considered. The opinions that ruled the day were the agenda-based sentiments of politicians who continued to stoke the fires of hate and racism in an effort to expel all Asians, Japanese in particular. Their motivations were more personal and political than the interests of national security that they hid behind.

In the days and weeks to come, the federal government enacted the War Measures Act, giving them power without question or review to restrict, control, evacuate, detain and even deport anyone they chose. The Prime Minister decided the practical political solution was to follow the American lead and intern all Japanese Canadian residents for the duration of the war. This would calm the unsettled masses and silence the rabid politicians who were intent on complete expulsion. How this was going to be done had not been determined, but it would most certainly involve detaining all Japanese Canadians and seizing their personal property.

Apparently, the British Columbia Security Commission recognized that a Japanese community leader like Masumi, fluent in English, could be an asset in the internment process. As a result, he had been recruited by the government to act as an interpreter for incoming internees. This was special consideration given to Masumi as a Canadian Expeditionary Forces veteran.

It didn't feel very special to Masumi at all! He was given an office at the racetrack office building. He and his family were re-united in the converted barn area just before Christmas when the bus delivered Sugi, Amy, Lucy and Harry. George and Dick were allowed to remain on the farm to tend to the chickens.

Finally reunited with her father, Amy burst into a succession of questions without allowing Masumi to respond. "Father, what is going to happen to us? What is going to happen to our home? Where are George and Dick?"

"Slow down Amy, slow down." He tried to calm her. The rest of the family all looked at him hoping for some explanations.

"I don't like it here," cried Lucy. "It stinks!"

"I know, I know," said Masumi. "We are here for our safety according to the RCMP. I don't think we are in danger. It's an excuse to get us to leave Canada. The boys are still on the farm looking after the birds," he replied in answer to Amy's other question. "Sugi, how are you doing?"

"This is very upsetting for me and for the kids," she admitted. "What is going to happen to our new home? How long will we have to stay here?"

"I don't have answers," he replied. "I just have questions, like you. I have been given this Registration Card which identifies me as a war veteran," he flashed the card with his photo and some official government print. "It will help us get better accommodations, but for now we must stay in this disgusting animal barn."

"If we are here for our safety why are they putting barbed wire around the fences? That feels more like we are prisoners than we are being protected," observed Sugi.

"This place they have put us in is barely suitable for animals, Masumi. Why have they crammed us all in here in a place that reeks of animals, urine and poop?" raged Sugi. "Look!" She pointed. "We don't even have privacy, just stalls made for animals!"

The B.C. government had chosen to house the internees in a stable, and that's exactly how everyone felt—like herded animals. For the children this was an adventure. They played with other kids and had the run of the whole complex. For adults this was an entirely different experience—humiliation, anger, sadness, fear—all these emotions overwhelmed the uprooted, innocent victims.

In addition to the horrendous living conditions, the food was not to the liking of Japanese Canadians. The main staple was beef stew and potatoes, not traditional Japanese food and certainly lacking in variety. Not surprisingly, dysentery soon took hold of the general population at Hastings Park. The lack of adequate sanitation and poor hygiene was an optimal breeding ground for the bacteria. At one point, so many people were sick, they stopped using the assigned washrooms and simply relieved themselves in the stable draining troughs. The smell was indescribable, and people started calling the drains *Fluid Drive* like it was a vital artery. At least that added some levity to the repulsive, pungent situation, but it certainly made a bad situation even worse.

Hastings Park, Vancouver, British Columbia, Canada, March 18, 1942

In the early days of Canada's involvement in World War 2, most Canadians didn't know or care about the internment of Japanese Canadians in British Columbia. The world war was a much bigger story and a more personal concern. They believed the Canadian government was acting in the best interests of the country and moving the Japanese people away from the rest of the population must be a good idea given the war against Japan. Even historical supporters of the Japanese Canadians like the Co-operative Commonwealth Federation party acquiesced to the incarceration and seizure decisions. Championing the Japanese community became very unpopular politically and would not help in their attempts to form a government. More politics of racism.

The Japanese Canadians were alone and had no means to oppose the decisions and confinement imposed on them. There was no one fighting for their rights in opposition to the injustice of these actions. These innocent victims of circumstance were powerless to defend themselves and were dispensed with in a quiet, swift manner.

Masumi's Legion associate Saburo Shinobu and his family had also been incarcerated at the Hastings Park barns, so Masumi had one friend in an otherwise hostile environment of tension and distrust towards him.

"Is the situation getting any better for us Masumi?" Shinobu asked. "Will we be able to return to our homes and get our possessions back?"

"No, my friend, it's worse than ever. The government has enacted the War Measures Act which gives them almost unlimited power. They are using that to sell our possessions and imprison us without trial. It looks like we will be given three choices: go to Japan, go to the internment villages or move to other parts of Canada, like Ontario. I am so mad I can hardly even talk about it. And they expect me to tell the Japanese families these are their only options! They have taken my farm and informed me it will be sold, and I will get the money. I don't want the money. I want my farm!"

"What if we refuse any of those three choices?"

"Then you will be sent to a men's prison in Angler, Ontario and your family will be shipped to internment. Many Japanese men have already tried to fight the government and are now in jail."

⁓

The procedure for deciding who was shipped out, when and where, was equally impersonal and harsh. Each night someone from the department would read out a list of numbers that were assigned to the detainees, and those people had to be ready to leave the next morning. It became a common scene to see families loading their personal items on trucks at Hastings Park headed for the train station—next stop, places with names like Lemon Creek, Kaslo, Slocan, Tashme or Greenwood.

During a break one morning, Masumi phoned the farm to speak to his sons. George answered the phone.

"How are you both making out, son?" he asked.

"Good father. Without any new chicks coming in we are reduced to one set of pens. They will be ready to sell in about a week."

"Good work, George. Much responsibility has fallen on yours and Dick's shoulders in the past three months and you have been strong," Masumi said proudly.

"I've had lots of time to think father and I have some ideas. First, I want to tell you I buried the sword by the fence line behind the barn. I don't trust the police who say our belongings will be safe in the basement. Everyone knows we will not be in the house and way out here, unguarded, the farm is a target for burglars. I brought that sword here from Japan and I don't want to lose it," he stated angrily.

"That's probably a good idea. Who knows when we will return and what will happen while the war is being fought?"

"I have been notified I must report to work on a road crew in Strathmore, Alberta as soon as my work is done here on the farm," George informed Masumi. "Dick is being sent to a sugar beet farm near Lethbridge. We have no choice. We will not be able to stay with the family."

"I don't know what is going to happen to the rest of the family," Masumi admitted. "Even though I have a job working for the Commission at Hastings Park I know that will end soon. I don't want to work for them and help send Japanese Canadian citizens to these isolated camps in the mountains. It is horrible for everyone."

"What is going to happen to our farm when we are all sent away father?" asked George. "We can't just leave everything!"

"I don't know," admitted Masumi. No one is telling me anything, but I do know we have lost all our rights as citizens in this country, even people born here, like you. It's a great injustice, a disgrace which I intend to fight with all my energy.

"You boys will be on your own through this George, but you are men now and ready to look out for yourselves. I will look after mother and the rest of the family. You both make me proud today, my son," choked out Masumi. "I have to get back to work. Let's talk later, and you and Dick can speak to mother too."

Returning to his office, he found an envelope laying on his desk. Sitting, he reluctantly opened it wondering what it could be and why someone would wait until he wasn't there to deliver it. As he read through the brief note typed on the single sheet of paper, he understood the nature of this cowardly act. He got up and headed for his family's temporary lodgings in the barn.

"Sugi, I've just received notice that we are to be shipped to an internment camp."

"What does that mean? No one called our number."

"I guess they thought I deserved more than finding out during the number call. It's the same either way." He waved the notice in the air like a sword. "With most of the people placed in camps, they don't need an interpreter anymore, so they are sending us to join the others who were here. The location people are going to now is called Greenwood, an old mining town in the southern part of the province.

"I am so angry," he growled. "How can they treat me this way? I am a war veteran, a man who has shown loyalty to my country by risking my life. And this is how they repay me?" He waved the letter over his head again, still thrashing out at an invisible enemy.

"This is so upsetting, Masumi. What can you do?"

"I don't know," he said in defeat. "But I will speak to the Security Commissioner in the morning. Maybe I will take my gun with me."

"Take Lucy with you when you meet with him. Okay? She will help keep you calm. No gun!"

"Okay. There is no need to worry, but to make you happy, I will."

∽

Lucy and Masumi arrived at the Security Commission office at Hastings Park sharp at 9:00 Monday morning. Masumi was very agitated and hadn't slept much the night before, fretting over what was happening to them.

The commissioner, Captain Harnett, sitting behind his immense, long desk, stood and extended his hand saying, "What can I do for you, Sarge?"

Masumi refused to shake hands and, instead, plunged them into his coat pockets.

"No father!" Lucy reacted, but calmed down when Masumi's hands reappeared holding his three war medals in one and the letter from the government in the other.

"There's nothing you can do *for* me now! What are you doing *to* me? I served my country. You've taken everything away, telling us we must leave with only 150 pounds of luggage. What are the good of my medals?" He threw them across the Commissioner's desk and onto the floor while shaking the letter of assignment he had received the previous day.

The commissioner quickly got down on his hands and knees and reverently retrieved Masumi's medals. Offering them back to him he said, "This isn't my doing, Sarge. I got my orders from Ottawa. There is nothing I can do for you."

"How can your government treat a war veteran this way? Do you question my allegiance to my country?" he asked.

"Of course not, Sarge," the Commissioner sympathized, still holding the medals. "It's just the rules the government has put in place. You are caught in a much bigger situation. This is a War Measures Act. It's the same for everyone. You wouldn't be safe here if you stayed."

This response did nothing to calm Masumi, and he turned and left the office at a fast limp.

Lucy reached over to the Commissioner and took Masumi's medals back knowing he would have a change of heart. They meant everything to him, so this action made it very clear to her how intensely angry he was right now.

"Well what did that accomplish, Father?" Lucy called out as she ran to catch up with him. She knew how mad he was by the fast pace. That was always a clue for the Mitsuis.

"What does anything we do *accomplish*, Lucy?" He emphasized "accomplish" with a sarcastic tone. "No matter what we do and how many times we bow to the abuse of white people, the Japanese are treated like animals!" The years of racism and rejection culminated in this latest and most disrespectful treatment—by the government of all sources.

"I don't have any more cheeks to turn!" he growled. He had never been as angry as he was at this moment. Making things worse, he felt helpless to change anything that was happening to the people he cared about most, his family and friends.

Returning to their family compartment in the stable, Lucy and Masumi sat with the others.

"What happened? Sugi asked.

"No one knows what is going on here," he reported. "There's no plan and certainly no consideration for the good and loyal Japanese Canadians who would be willing to fight for this country. We aren't a safety risk to other Canadians. Do you know they are saying we can go back to Japan? What does that mean? I left Japan thirty-four years ago! And you kids have never even been there or learned the language. Go back to Japan! Nonsense!"

"Father went crazy on the Commissioner," Lucy interjected before Masumi could start again. "He was yelling, and he even threw his medals on the floor. I was afraid he had a gun or was going to do something really crazy. But he made his point." Lucy reached into her coat pocket, retrieved the medals and secretly handed them to Sugi for safe keeping.

"Does that change things, Masumi?" Sugi inquired. "Can we go back to our home?"

"It changes nothing. We can't go back to the farm, at least not until the war is over, I fear. We will not move to Japan. Our only options are to go where they send us or move to the east. At least here in British Columbia we will have some privileges because I am a war veteran, so I think that's our best and only option right now."

"What about Dick and George?"

"George told me they are sending them both to Alberta. He is thinking about moving east and finding work there. I think that's a good idea. He's ready to spread his wings. He's grown a lot since he came home from Japan. Dick wants to stay closer to B.C."

"No! They need to be with us."

"They need to become men now, Sugi. This is their time to show courage. It is a time for all of us to be courageous and strong. Even if we are apart, we are still strong as a family."

On March 19th, 1942, Masumi, as president of the Canadian Legion Branch #9, officially surrendered the charter of the branch back to a sister branch of the Legion in Vancouver. This would mark the end of an important milestone in the Japanese community; a Legion branch dedicated to the Japanese Canadian veterans and fallen heroes of the First World War was no more. It felt like salt on an open wound. This branch represented much hard work on his part and that of his fellow war veterans to gain position and status in Canada's culture.

It took over one month for Masumi to conclude his work, secure possessions at the farm and prepare for the move to Greenwood. Finally, in late April 1942, the Mitsui family, like many other Japanese Canadians, climbed aboard the train at the CP Railway station destined for the interior of British Columbia and a very uncertain future.

The CP Rail station in Vancouver was a center of chaos, as families dragged their possessions to the loading platform and hugged their friends and family, who were being torn apart and sent off in different directions. Many people were crying while some were drawn to outright wailing in grief, as confused and frightened internees loaded on the passenger cars in preparation for departure.

As the train pulled away, those left on the loading dock waved and cried. Their loved ones leaned out windows straining for a last glimpse of their family which was quickly being obscured by distance and steam from the locomotive.

Masumi claimed a window seat so he could watch the passage, a journey that was taking his family away and simultaneously taking everything from him, forever altering their lives and hundreds of others. He had traveled on many trains in his life in Japan, in Canada before and after the war, and throughout Europe during the war. This wasn't new to him, but it was, by far, the most emotionally charged ride he had ever taken.

The rail line took them along the flat lower mainland of British Columbia to the Fraser River, which they would follow all the way to their first stop. At this time of year, the river was at its widest point due to the spring runoff. The familiar muddy brown water churned up the delta soils. They crossed over a trestle bridge to the south side, heading east. The Mitsui farm was just across the river on the north side. He looked in that direction and a lump formed in his throat. Would ever see his home again?

As the train headed east along the southern bank of the Fraser, the Coastal Mountain range loomed closer and closer. Living in Port Coquitlam, they could easily see the mountains in the distance, but he never really appreciated their sheer size. As they moved out of the flat lands of the Fraser River Valley, the train clattered along with the river's edge to the north and solid rock faces to the south. The cliffs, climbing hundreds of feet straight up with not so much as a single tree growing on them, introduced an environment that foretold an inhospitable future. Occasionally, the train would pass a rock crevasse where small creeks poured forth the melting snow and, every so often, they would pass a spectacular waterfall that appeared to be cascading those hundreds of feet off the top of the mountain and landing in a pool right beside the tracks. This was rugged country. It looked like no one lived out here and yet this was going to be their new home. How were they supposed to survive?

In the small junction town of Hope, B.C., the internees transferred to the southern route of the local Kettle Valley Railroad for transport to the derelict mining town of Greenwood and a future full of uncertainty.

"*Hope?*" Masumi muttered to himself as he read the town name on the railroad station wall.

Now that is ironic. That's about all we have left, he thought as he and his family stood on the transfer platform waiting for the next leg of their journey to begin. Hope was all he clung to when he thought about the farm, about George and about how he would be able to take care of his family now.

Although Masumi did not know it at the time, the uncomfortable and lengthy trip from the Vancouver station to Hope turned out to be the short, luxury leg of their journey. The segment from Hope to Greenwood was more than double the distance, traversing an old mining rail route that took them deep into the mountains, along winding, climbing stretches of track which at times seemed utterly impassable. The train rattled along on bumpy tracks through narrow crevasses in the mountain and across wooden trestles that groaned under its weight. Fortunately, the scenic views were to the side, as passengers looked out the windows. If they had been able to see the condition of the rail tracks ahead of them they might have jumped off and taken their chances on foot. It took seven hours for the Kettle Valley engine to haul its load of passengers and freight from Hope to Greenwood. A full twelve hours had passed since they pulled away from the platform in Vancouver. It had been a long day full of emotion and trepidation.

Greenwood, British Columbia, Canada, April 21, 1942

The small village of Greenwood was nestled in the Columbia Valley mountains midway between the Coast and Rocky Mountain Ranges of British Columbia just north of the Canadian-U.S.A. border. It had once been a vibrant, successful mining community but the copper mine had been abandoned and Greenwood approached ghost town status due to plummeting copper prices after the end of the First World War. A few people remained in town or the surrounding area, eking out a living in the general store, the church or the small hospital which served the area. Rural residents operated small livestock and grain and hay cropping farms. The village was a peaceful, secluded homestead of little note prior to the bombing of Pearl Harbor. It was able to sustain a small population, but now selected as the temporary home to incarcerated Japanese Canadians, no one knew how the influx of these internees was going to affect the community. What would they do? How would they all be able to live and survive?

At the outset of the Second World War, Greenwood was home to less than 150 people. Most buildings were in disrepair or boarded up and abandoned. The mine and smelter had been decommissioned for over twenty years. They sat idle and unused, with the towering smokestack from the smelter standing as the only reminder of the past vibrant heydays. The mountain setting and high altitude assured residents that winters would be long and cold and the snowfall deep. The town was accessed by a single highway for car or truck traffic and the Kettle Valley Railroad for rail service. The railway ran parallel to the main street in town in a north-south direction, and the housing was all located on the east side of the tracks. Black and gray mountains rose on either side of the small town and, with several hundred miles to the nearest populated village, Greenwood was at best an isolated municipality for those who preferred that lifestyle. At worst, it was a prison without bars for those who did not.

Arriving on the train, the first thing the Japanese Canadians sighted was that huge brick smokestack rising 120 feet from the dormant copper smelter. In April, the snow was almost all gone but the thin air was crisp and biting as the train pulled to a stop at the station. Waiting for them on the platform was a gathering of what appeared to be local citizens. For most of their lives Japanese Canadians had been the recipients of hatred and mob fury. Large groups of white Canadians gathering together generally turned out to be a bad thing for the Japanese people. This crowd did not appear promising to Masumi as it had all the makings of yet another confrontation between local whites and an invasion of unwanted Japanese immigrants. Masumi and Sugi's children spotted them first—men standing on the platform carrying axes and baseball bats. They looked angry as the train pulled to a stop. This trainload of people was not the first to arrive in Greenwood, but they were certainly adding stress to this mountain community. He worried that their arrival might go badly for the internees on the train. With trepidation and great anxiety about what might befall them, the families disembarked from the train.

As the travelers emerged onto the platform, one man stepped forward from the locals. Wearing a suit and tie, he carried an air of distinction and authority about him as he brandished a warm smile.

"Welcome to Greenwood!" called out local Mayor W. E. McArthur. "We know this is a lot colder here than the places you have been living in, but we warmly welcome you to your new home. These are difficult times, but we hope we can all make the best of this terrible situation. Our home is now your home too."

Masumi leaned close to Sugi. "What a bunch of garbage from another B.C. politician! This is not, and never will be, our home. He doesn't understand that we are here against our will." Masumi and Sugi glanced at the menacing men who obviously did not share the same welcoming spirit as the man who had greeted them. Masumi had seen this hatred in the eyes of white Canadians already, and he knew this was not the end of the racial discontent.

Some of the internment camps, such as Tashme, were new villages created just to house the Japanese. They were completely on their own with no means of support whatsoever. Greenwood was unique compared to most of the other internment locations because of the surprising willingness of the community to accept and house the internees. The local townspeople understood the value in populating their village and had no reservations about Japanese Canadians. This alone set the community apart from so many other parts of Canada that rejected the influx of people of Asian descent. Most of the residents of Greenwood had never even seen a Japanese person before.

"Everyone, please make your way to the Hallet Block on Main Street for your housing assignments. That brown brick building right over there." McArthur pointed. "It's going to be tight living quarters to start, but as we get houses repaired and livable, things will gradually get better."

The occasion at the train station took Masumi back to his arrival in Victoria over thirty years ago. He remembered the crusty, smelly old man yelling at them on the pier and calling them "japs." While their arrival today wasn't the best of circumstances, he appreciated the gesture of Mayor McArthur to treat them like human beings.

Masumi learned later that not all Japanese were as welcome in other small B.C. towns selected as temporary homes for the exiled. In most locations in the interior, Japanese were seen as enemies to be treated with suspicion and fear. Local merchants raised prices, charging more to people who were already being cheated out of their money and property. Some businesses hired Japanese workers but at greatly reduced wages. Detainees had poor heat and no light in many of their lodgings. In some cases, they were forced to live in tents or thin-walled uninsulated shacks as temperatures plummeted to -40 Fahrenheit during the winter. There was an allocation of one blanket per person. Curfews forced Japanese to be indoors by 10:00 p.m. Their new homes had indeed become prisons without bars.

By comparison, Greenwood was the best of a bad situation. Masumi and his family actually had a house to live in, but it still felt like a prison to him.

~

Masumi's status as a World War I veteran continued to provide special privileges to him and his family. Just like his role at Hastings Park, he was given the job as an interpreter. Additionally, he was assigned by the local Royal Canadian Mounted Police to act as a local enforcement officer for the B.C. Security Commission. This role pitted him between the enforcement of the internment on one side and his own community of Japanese people on the other. This privilege was a nightmare for Masumi and a role he was not at all interested in playing. It was his job to keep the peace. That meant dealing with complaints—of which there were many—and explaining to his friends why they didn't have enough food or water or heat and why they couldn't return to their homes.

After completing his nightly rounds one evening, Masumi returned to their home in Greenwood. He was greeted at the front door by Sugi.

"Why do you even bother going out at night Masumi?" she asked. "No one is breaking any rules or planning secret attacks for goodness sake!"

"I know," he replied. "I just don't want to give the government any excuse to take anything else from us."

"Like what? Our clothes? We don't have anything left to take! The Japanese are angry with you because it feels like you are one of the police instead of one of the prisoners."

"But we are prisoners!" he exclaimed. "All of us!"

"Well I know that and so do you, but we've become isolated because you work for them. The Japanese think you are a spy for the government. The call you Banana, Masumi, yellow on the outside and white on the inside."

"That is wrong!" Masumi was insulted by the implication of this moniker. "I am proud to be a Japanese Canadian and I have spoken up for our rights many times. These people must know that."

"They do, but they are looking for someone to be mad at, and you are the first person they see."

"Ahhh!" Masumi threw a hand in the air. "What can I do?"

"Father," Amy interrupted, "they told us we would be able to go back to our home, but mother told us they sold it. What has happened to our things? What has happened to the farm?"

"The government lied to us," he replied with restrained anger. "I cannot tell you how much this upsets me and your mother. You know how hard we all worked to build the farm and our new home. We deserve to be treated better. It's one thing to be hated and persecuted by ignorant people but when we become the target of the political action of government officials, we have no way to fight back or defend ourselves."

"I just want to go home," cried Lucy. "All of my treasures and my clothes are in that room you built downstairs. If they sold our house what has happened to our things?"

"I don't know what will happen," said Masumi. "The government seized cars and boats and personal property along with over seventy farms in the Fraser Valley. There are over 20,000 people of Japanese descent in British Columbia. I just don't see how they can lock us all up for the length of the war."

Or even longer, he thought to himself but dared not say that to his family.

"This just keeps getting worse and worse." Masumi collapsed into a chair. The anguish and misery of losing everything they owned, uprooting and separating his family and now becoming ostracized from the Japanese community was too much to bear. It was harder and harder to dig deep to find that heroic courage his grandfather taught him some forty-five years ago.

"Let's leave here and go to Ontario," Sugi suggested. "In his letters George says that Japanese are treated much better than in the west."

"No! Our home is here, and we cannot leave the farm. We will stay and we will get it back after the war."

"The farm has been sold Masumi. They sent us $2,735, a tenth of what it was worth. We will never get it back."

"Then we will get a fair price! We will force the government to pay us what it is worth."

Sugi would not press him on this decision, but she knew that what she said was the right choice. He just wasn't ready to give up, at least not yet.

All the enterprising, hard-working new arrivals to Greenwood wasted no time settling into their new accommodations which were a huge improvement to the rank smelling, crowded stalls of Hastings Park. The Mitsui's house provided privacy and a decent roof over their heads but they were unsettled. This was not their home or a place of their choosing. It was unbearably cold in the winter and agonizingly boring most of the time. A paradise to some who called Greenwood home, it felt like a prison camp to the Japanese.

The Mitsuis were overwhelmed by their experiences of winter in the mountains of British Columbia. It was a beautiful place in the spring and summer, but no one had prepared them for the harsh winters. Even wearing every article of clothing they owned, they were still freezing. The old home they lived in couldn't keep out the sub-zero temperatures and bitter winds. The snow was deep, making it difficult to get around, especially for Masumi with his persistently painful knee injury which had advanced to an arthritic condition. For people used to the climate of the Fraser Valley, the mountain winter was just too much to bear.

As springtime came to the Rockies, the new residents were treated to an abundance of color and renewal of life, typical in a mountain rain forest. The sights and smells of fresh growth along with the decay of pine needles and old forest offered a unique and invigorating outlook to their new lives. Gardens were planted, clothes lines were constructed, and signs of life surfaced all over Greenwood. The people of the community—white people and people of color—spent time getting to know each other by hosting picnics, parades and dances where they shared food and stories. The community came to life with a transfusion of new blood and the Japanese culture and work ethic. In the final count, 1,203 Japanese Canadians were sequestered in Greenwood for the war.

Amy and Lucy, along with several other Japanese Canadians, volunteered at the local hospital. They made the best of the situation. Sugi's penchant for saving everything kicked into high gear. She was well-known as a pack rat for all things. Her life had been a constant battle of being without. So much so, that she never threw anything out that might have some small value in the future, in her eyes at least. It was amazing what she could do with a small amount of wool or a scrap of fabric. Tough times required this type of frugal behavior and Sugi was a master, just as she had been with sticks of dynamite two decades earlier.

Masumi and Sugi tried desperately to show a good front for the children, but it was hard to hide a multitude of emotions including anger, frustration and sadness. Masumi contacted the B.C. Security Commission regularly in efforts to get a fairer price for his farm. He wouldn't have sold it for ten times what he was paid because it meant more to him than the monetary value. The farm was core to who he was, proof of his success in life. It was more than a home or a business; it defined the Mitsui family, their lifestyle and their commitment; it was the end result of his family working together to build something that was theirs. And it had been torn away from him. This disrespectful, unjust action was something he could not, and would not, forgive.

During the slow and empty days during their internment, Masumi gradually became more sullen. The pressures of his unwanted supervisory role, or watchdog as it made him feel, the separation and unsettled family situation and the crushing loss of his farm, all weighed heavily on his heart and his mood. How much was one man meant to endure?

The harder I work, the more I lose, he thought. He felt life was dealing to him from the bottom of the deck and he was doomed to failure and heartache. He started to drink more than usual to deal with the boredom, depression and psychological pressures that were building inside and tormenting him. These were hard days for Masumi and he spent many hours building an even greater internal rage towards the governments of British Columbia and Canada. They had lied to him, lied to his fellow soldiers of the first war and lied to the Japanese Canadian community.

Conditions were difficult for all Japanese Canadians, not just the Mitsuis. Another devastating outcome of the internment was the separation of family members. Very often the oldest males were conscripted to work in road camps and farms, leaving the wives and children to fend for themselves. Older children were initially sent to schools in different locations than other family members until public outcry opposing the payment of education for Japanese ended that practice. Not the fact that families were torn apart, but the opposition to paying for the education of Japanese children! The fact that 18,000 of the internees were born in this country, and were lawful Canadian citizens, didn't matter.

During the early period while the family was posted in Greenwood, George lived and worked in Alberta moving around in a variety of jobs. His first job was working on a road crew out of Strathmore for the balance of 1942 and part of 1943. Dick worked on a sugar beet farm until 1944. Both of the older male Mitsuis moved to Ontario in 1944 in search of a better life. The family always managed to stay in touch by mail or telegraph, but it was years before they were finally reunited.

The Mitsuis had been spared this emotional upheaval of separation, other than Dick and George, but with them finally moving to Ontario, the ties that bound them to British Columbia were fading. Late in the summer of 1944, Masumi picked up a telegram from George and was reading it after dinner. Sugi waited until he was finished so she could hear from her son who she missed terribly.

As Masumi read George's message he began clenching his fists and frowning.

"He will not join the military!"

"What?" asked Sugi. "What are you talking about?"

"He is telling me he is thinking about signing up to join the war."

"That's nonsense. Why would he do that?"

"He says the government is now signing up Japanese to act as interpreters. He wants to know what I think about that."

"What are you going to tell him?"

"I am going to tell him if he joins the military, I will disown him! How could he even think about doing this after what the government has done to our family?"

"Maybe that's the best way for him to earn money, Masumi."

"Well he can find another way, one that doesn't make it seem like we agree with the way we have been treated and that now we are willing to help the government."

The next morning Masumi hurried to the telegraph office and sent a message to George.

> *Got your message STOP If you join the military, I will disown you STOP.*

George got the message.

Worried about Dick and George and fed up with the work he was asked to do, Masumi continued to struggle from day to day. He had failed in every attempt to get a fair and just settlement for his farm. He would keep fighting for the justice he felt he was due, but not from Greenwood anymore, he decided.

"I think we should move to Ontario and get back together with Dick and George," Masumi announced after dinner.

Four faces simultaneously beamed with grins from ear to ear. "Yeah!" they chorused and the sisters danced.

Everyone had reached their limit with the weather and the substandard living conditions. The people of Greenwood had been nice enough, but this was never going to feel like home. There was no going back to the farm; it was lost. George told them life was better in Ontario. The racism wasn't as bad and there was an opportunity to find work and rebuild their lives.

"Send him a letter, Mother," instructed Masumi to Sugi. "And tell him we are on our way. He will need to find us all a place to live and hopefully some work, so we can start our lives over again."

The Train Ride, October 2, 1944

The government of British Columbia was more than happy to provide five one-way train tickets for the Mitsui family to leave the province. This was an open offer to all interned Japanese Canadians during the war. The government's goal wasn't just to move Japanese Canadians away from the coastal area but, rather, to eradicate them from the province entirely. If they went to Japan, fine. If they went somewhere else in Canada, fine.

It took a couple of months to make all the necessary arrangements for paperwork and logistics but finally, in October of 1944, the Mitsui family was packed and ready to leave Greenwood behind. It also meant walking away from their farm and any lingering hope of ever getting their property returned to them. This stung Masumi the deepest of all. He had worked hard, endured great opposition and hatred from the white community and earned success in spite of those obstacles. Having his efforts and the legacy for his children torn away from him, and suffering even greater humiliation and intolerance, cut deeply into the heart and soul of this proud man.

Moving to Ontario meant another long, uncomfortable ride on a train. But this ride was an escape from imprisonment and a pathway to freedom. For that reason, they all knew they would do what that had to do without complaint. For the next five days and four nights the Mitsuis lived on an eastbound train. Their journey started by heading west, back to Hope, B.C. and then connecting with the Canadian Pacific Railroad for the long cross-country trek to Toronto.

"Maybe this time passing through *Hope* will bring our family something positive," he whispered to Sugi.

"Let's *hope* so." She smiled at Masumi.

⁓

In his fifty-plus years on earth, Masumi had seen many parts of the world—Japan, much of Europe during the war and the west coast of Canada—but nothing prepared him and his family for the glory and rugged beauty of Canada and their visual experience through the windows of the transcontinental train.

From the railroad transfer station in Hope, BC, the train started to climb through the mountains to the Rogers Pass, the route through the Rocky Mountain range. Along the way they traveled on trestles across rivers and streams, through straight and curved tunnels and even an incomprehensible spiral tunnel cut right into the side of a mountain. The Canadian transcontinental railway was completed before Masumi was born, back in 1885. Even then, immigrants from Europe and China were the primary work force put to the task of this massive, dangerous construction project. Many men lost their lives in avalanches during the construction of the railway, mostly Chinese.

The family spent hours just staring out at the unimaginable splendor and the vast, unpopulated areas along their journey. On this occasion the symbolism and foretelling of what might lay ahead lifted their spirits.

Like Greenwood, the climate through the mountains was clear and cold, but it was autumn and very beautiful. They spotted hundreds of animals in the mountain fields and streams—elk, deer, moose and bears—typical North American wildlife. These were creatures the children had never seen before and they were excited. They made a game of spotting wildlife, but it had to be a "confirmed sighting," that is, more than one person had to see the animal for it to count. This kept Harry in check from claiming every rock or tree stump was a bear or a wolf. Late in the afternoon, the train pulled in to the town of Banff, Alberta where travelers could get off and stretch their legs. Some passengers embarked while others disembarked at this location. The train was refueled with coal and water, and mail was exchanged.

During the station stop, the Mitsuis looked south from the station platform to the flat side of a slope of rock named Mount Rundle. Masumi could visualize how this magnificent mountain had been created during a seismic shift of epic proportion. Lower down the mountain, nestled in the valley, was what appeared to be an enormous magical castle. Made of huge brown and gray stones and a copper roof turned green by oxidization, the "castle" was the Banff Springs Hotel. Masumi recognized the building as it bore a strong resemblance to the Empress Hotel in Victoria, both built by the CP Railroad. The sighting of the hotel brought back a flood of memories from Victoria for Masumi—his arrival in Canada, his work as a servant in the city and his return to the B.C. parliament to secure the vote for Japanese Canadian veterans.

The next stop on the journey would be Calgary, another location filled with positive memories of his years serving as a Canadian soldier. The thought of a return to the welcoming spirit of a city that took him in when he was rejected in B.C. added a little more fire to that positive emotion brewing in his heart.

Surprisingly to Masumi, he was enjoying this journey much more than he thought he would. While still painful, the act of leaving the weight of his past behind was liberating. His family's future was uncertain to say the least, but he had taken these risks before, so the feeling was not strange. His whole family showed great courage in taking this next step in their life journey. He was proud of them all.

From a peak of 4,360 feet, the CP train began its descent to the prairies. Winding a path downward from the pass and through the foothills of the Rocky Mountains, it stopped in Calgary for some passengers and then headed east through the plains of western Canada. Known as the breadbasket of the world, the Canadian prairie landscape was all cropland with little in the way of trees, buildings or any real sign of life. Traveling through much of Alberta and Saskatchewan at night, there was still enough light from random farmhouses and moonlight to appreciate the grandeur of these fields and the sheer size of the landmass dedicated to agricultural production by hard-working Canadian farm families.

So much land, so few people, thought Masumi. Not like Japan at all. Harvest was in full swing and the activity in the fields, working by moonlight all through the night, was surprising and amazing to them.

The train made stops all along the route in cities and towns across the prairies and Ontario, in places with pure Canadian names like Medicine Hat, Swift Current, Moose Jaw and Portage la Prairie.

Continuing east past Winnipeg, the train passed through the longest and least populated areas the Mitsuis had ever seen. From school, the children knew this area as the Canadian Shield. The route passed along a hundred kilometer stretch of the second largest lake in the world, Lake Superior.

This truly is a magnificent country, thought Masumi, *so big with so much natural wealth and beauty.*

By the third day Amy, Lucy and Harry were bored with the novelty of the train, and the confines of their seats wore everyone's patience. Harry took to investigating other cars and parts of the train he could visit without getting in trouble—mostly. On one afternoon he meandered back to their seats and plopped on the bench.

"Where on earth have you been, Harry? What have you gotten into?" Sugi asked sternly.

"Just wandering around, Mother," he replied innocently.

"Well you are filthy. You need to go wash and get that black off your face and hands!" she ordered. "Where were you?"

"I was just looking out the window between the cars."

"Well you've managed to get the top half of you covered in soot from the steam engine."

Amy and Lucy peered across at Harry and Sugi as she was giving him a harsh lecture. They saw Harry's black face and hands and the grime on his shirt and they burst out laughing. The whites of his eyes provided extra contrast to his soot covered faced, an irresistible sight that had them in full convulsive laughter.

"What?" Harry asked, looking at his sisters with confusion and innocence. But that just sent them into greater hysterics.

"Here, take this towel and cloth to the washroom and clean yourself up. And don't leave a mess in there behind you!" she yelled after him as he slumped off with his chin on his chest.

As the journey neared its end, everyone was feeling cabin bound and anxious for the trip to be over.

"How much longer?" Amy pleaded on the fourth morning.

"We will be arriving in Toronto tomorrow morning," Masumi responded.

"What are we going to do when we get there?" asked Lucy.

Trying to take some of the pressure off Masumi, Sugi responded, "George is going to meet us at the train station. He has arranged a place for us to stay and hopefully some work for Father."

"I am excited to see George," admitted Amy. "We fight sometimes but he is my brother. I love him, and I miss him."

"Me too," piped in Lucy.

"Girls," Masumi interjected, taking the opportunity to explain their situation and manage their expectations. "We have the clothes on our backs and in our bags and a little bit of money to pay for things for a while, but we will all have to find work as quickly as we can except for Harry who has to finish school. Hopefully George has found jobs for us."

"I am going to work too!" said Harry. "I don't want to go to school anymore!"

"We'll see," said Masumi. But Harry would be eighteen this year. He was probably right. The urgency to earn some money and find a place to live would be the priority for the coming weeks and months.

Toronto, Ontario, October 6, 1944

"Father, mother, over here," George waved excitedly as he spotted his family disembarking from the train. He was genuinely glad to see all of them, even his teasing sisters. He had been on his own for two and a half years, ever since the RCMP had taken his family to Hastings Park.

Masumi spotted George and headed towards him, but it was Sugi who got to him first as she charged the crowd like only a mother trying to get to her child can do. It was reminiscent of her charge to greet Masumi on the train platform upon his return from Europe after the war in 1919. Masumi watched as she hugged George, probably tighter than he had ever been squeezed in his life. She was very emotional over the reunion. George was glad to see her too. In turn, everyone greeted George with a hug, including Masumi who was not known for outward shows of emotion. But the family had been through so much hardship and separation, and the mere fact that they were all together again was a huge emotional lift.

"It is so good to see all of you," said George with uncharacteristic emotion. "I arranged temporary lodging. It is a hostel with nine other families living there. Everyone is trying to get settled and find homes and jobs. I think we will have to go outside of the city to find something that will be best for us. I have a lead on some work at an orchard near a town called St. Catharines."

"I have two jobs right now," he continued. "I work part time as a chauffeur and I also work as a gardener. I saved a small amount of money, so I can help with food and rent for you for a little while. I am just so glad to see you all and to know that you are out of that terrible place in B.C. It's much better here for Japanese Canadians. Let's go this way and get you all settled." The climate in Ontario in October was noticeably more to the Mitsuis liking than the B.C. interior where winter had already made a couple of early calls. Here it was still warm. *That would please everyone in the family,* Masumi thought.

There was no "Jap Town" or "China Town" in Toronto in 1944. The Asian population was too small for a cultural community to form. In one way that was good because it meant they weren't targets of racism as a group but, in another way, it was disappointing. The Mitsuis got their strength and sense of community from the fellowship of other Japanese Canadians. From the day Masumi arrived in Canada, he had relied on the kinship and support of other Japanese people. The collective work of Japanese businessmen and laborers helped organize the Japanese military unit under the leadership of Yasushi Yamazaki. War veterans and the Japanese community in British Columbia collaborated on the construction of the Japanese Memorial Cenotaph in Stanley Park and together they fought for the right to vote for World War 1 veterans. In this new city and new province, 2500 miles from their farm, Masumi felt like a stranger in a strange land. This was not the Canada he knew, but the Canada he knew had turned him out as untrustworthy and a danger to society. Even though they had left the dark cloud of hate and intolerance behind in British Columbia, he had little reason to feel joyful.

The living quarters arranged by George did nothing to brighten their spirits.

"What is this place George?" Masumi asked, gazing at the downtrodden boarding house before him as he got out of the taxi.

"It's a temporary boarding house where you can all stay for a week or a month, as long as it takes to find work and pay for something better. They call it a hostel," responded George. "The war in Europe has created shortages and hardship for all Canadians. Everyone is sacrificing for the war effort. This home is not the greatest and it's a far cry from our farmhouse but, under the circumstances, it's the best we will find."

He was right of course. They had little money and needed a roof over their heads, and a cheap one too. This would be a fit on both counts. It was vastly superior to the barns of Hastings Park, but it was a harsh reminder of the accommodations he had encountered when he first arrived in Canada nearly thirty-five years ago. He had come full circle, but now he had a wife and four children to look after. Three really, as George had done well to become independent.

George looked after arrangements for their arrival and paid for two rooms, a week in advance. The Mitsuis discovered they were indeed sharing the large home with nine other families, consisting of Japanese from the west and European families who managed to escape Europe and traveled to Canada for refuge from the war. This really was like the place he stayed when he arrived in Canada—a melting pot of nationalities looking for a safe refuge and a place to make a new start. At fifty-five years of age, he wondered if he had it in him to rebuild his life. But five sets of eyes looking to him for hope and reassurance told him he must find that courage to do what he needed to do.

Once the bags had been unloaded, and all the Mitsuis worldly possessions were in the rooms, they gathered together and had some tea.

"The orchards on the Niagara Peninsula are hiring laborers for the fruit harvest," advised George. "I think we should head out that way tomorrow and see if we can find work and nearby lodging. It isn't chicken farming, but it's honest work and it is farming, kind of," said George.

"That sounds like a good plan. Just so long as we don't hear any more nonsense about you joining the Canadian military and going to war!" growled Masumi.

"No, Father. I got your message loud and clear. I know you are very angry with the Canadian government and I don't want to disrespect your feelings."

"Very well," Masumi concluded. "We are all together again and that's the most important thing. Let's get some sleep and start to rebuild our lives in our new home in the morning."

Hamilton, Ontario, November 11, 1967

"And that's how we ended up in Ontario," Masumi concluded to Ken Adachi. "We moved to a small rental home in St. Catharines closer to available work and Sugi and I got jobs in a peach orchard. George carried on as a chauffeur and gardener for a few months and then found work delivering coal. That's not all you found was it George?" Masumi grinned as he looked over at George and Nancy sitting and listening intently.

Amy and Lucy giggled, and Nancy looked away sheepishly.

"He was delivering coal to Nancy's parents' house and took a shine to their daughter," Masumi explained.

"I met her at a picnic," George said defensively.

"Sure you did son. And who made sure she was at that picnic, eh?" A big grin spread across George's face.

"I don't know what you are talking about!" Nancy looked away in embarrassment but had a tickled smile on her face as she remembered the courting from George prior to their marriage.

"So, this was where you lived for the remainder of the war?" Adachi asked getting back to the main story line he wanted to pursue.

"Pretty much. We took whatever work we could find. Sugi and I worked many different jobs, all low paying, hard work. With their experience from Greenwood, the girls got work in the hospital and Lucy took a hairdressing course during the evenings."

Jumping ahead to the next milestone in Masumi's recollections of the war, he continued. "The war ended horribly for the Japanese. The atomic bombing of Hiroshima and Nagasaki shocked the world and left us saddened for our homeland and the innocent people who suffered from the actual bombing of those two cities. The legacy of radioactivity that went along with those weapons is just now starting to show in babies born to survivors of the bombs. The closest thing to that in the First World War was the chemical nerve gas released by the Germans. That was horrible too, but it didn't kill as many people as those nuclear weapons. Many innocent Japanese civilians died when those two bombs were dropped."

"You are right," acknowledged Adachi. "And I don't condone the action for a second but, President Harry Truman spoke true when he said, *It ended the war.*"

"That it did," agreed Masumi. "And it ended the internment of the Japanese Canadians still confined in those ghost towns, sugar beet farms and labor camps. But these people had nowhere to go. Their homes, their property and livelihoods were taken from them, their dignity was stripped, and their health was compromised. Much like the country of Japan, the outlook for recovery was bleak. We were every bit as much victims of the war, innocent as we were. We still paid a price and do so to this day.

"As you probably know, Ken, the federal government decided the best way to avoid future problems with Japanese Canadians was to arrange for all of them to be repatriated to Japan or declare their loyalty to Canada and be distributed east of the Rockies rather than go back to our communities on the West Coast. Everyone had to report their intentions to the RCMP. Sugi and I and the children were already in Ontario, so it didn't matter to us, but for many this was another disruption to their lives. Deprived of their worldly possessions, these families who opted to stay in Canada were sent to strange new places to fend for themselves. The inhumanity of the process continued. Nearly four-thousand Japanese Canadians decided to return to Japan, disenchanted with the way they had been treated by Canada. I admit, we considered that ourselves, but our children are Canadians and they wanted to stay here so we considered their future and decided to stay.

"Sadly, we were no more welcome in Ontario than in British Columbia. Local residents voiced their displeasure at the arrival of Japanese Canadians to the Niagara Peninsula and there was even one horrible and memorable incident of a cross burning at one of the orchards hiring Japanese labor. Can you imagine how much hate it must take to go to the effort of building a cross and then burning it in effigy towards the Japanese? If we were dangerous in British Columbia, we were no less dangerous in Ontario, they claimed."

"The scope of this hatred and persecution is overwhelming to me," Adachi said during a pause by Masumi. "It's so similar to the racism in the United States toward blacks, thankfully most of it without the violence that has been so prevalent there in the past decade."

"That's true, Ken. Most of the provincial governments were either unwilling to accept Japanese during the war or agreed to only on the condition we would be moved out as soon as the war was over. The only jobs we could find were hard labor and low paying work like cooking, cleaning and gardening. The same unfounded bias and hatred from B.C. followed us to the east—unfair competition for jobs, lower standard of living and an inability to assimilate into the community. It seemed that nowhere in the country could we gain advocacy for our civil rights as Canadians, unlike the European immigrants."

The afternoon had slipped by in a wink as everyone, especially Ken Adachi, had been caught up in the drama of the story Masumi shared with them. Realizing the hour and the strain this session had taken on Masumi, Ken felt it was enough. "It's getting late Masumi. I stayed longer than I planned, and I took a lot of your time today. I want to thank you for sharing your memories with me."

"I am actually glad you came today, Ken. I have bottled these memories inside me for a long time and it feels good to speak of them, especially to someone I feel I can trust to tell the story right."

"I will do my best," promised Adachi.

"You know there is still a lot of story to tell; things that happened to us and to other Japanese Canadians after the war was over. If you are free, why don't you come back tomorrow and we can finish? I'm tired now, but I would like to share the whole story if you are interested."

"Definitely! The whole story should be told. I can come by around 10:00 if that works for you."

"I look forward to continuing the story in the morning." Masumi reached out to shake Ken's hand.

As difficult as this experience had been for Masumi, he felt unburdened in telling this history and wanted to finish. He liked Ken and looked forward to continuing the sharing of his memories and the injustice of it all with him tomorrow. Perhaps this story he was writing would draw attention to the horrible crimes of the government and, in some way, lead to an admission and accountability for their acts. A simple apology would be a great place to start.

Hamilton, Ontario, November 12, 1967

Sharp at 10:00 a.m. Ken Adachi arrived with freshly baked pastries.

"Good morning Amy, I brought some treats."

"Aren't you kind. We like treats here." She smiled. "Father is in his chair in the front room watching TV. You're lucky it's Sunday and no soap operas are on. Otherwise I'd say good luck pulling him away from the TV."

Entering the room Ken greeted Masumi warmly. "How are you feeling today Masumi? I hope I didn't wear you out yesterday."

"It was a full day," Masumi replied. "But I did enjoy many parts of that walk down memory lane, as difficult and painful as some of those memories are for me to recall."

"I'm looking forward to your experiences and stories about Japanese re-entering society and how you and your family managed to rebuild your lives."

"Well let's get started, shall we? The war ended in Europe in May of 1945 but not until September of that year for Japan after the atomic bombs were dropped. So, let's pick it up there.

"The bombing of my homeland with a weapon so deadly and unforgiving as those atomic bombs is a horror that stays with me even to this day," Masumi began. "We now know the real devastation of nuclear bombs, both at the time of the bombing and a generation later as the impact of radioactivity released on the population reveals itself. My heart cries out for all the innocent people whose lives were lost or forever changed as a result."

CHAPTER EIGHT

Life After World War 2

Self-Control
...men should behave according to an absolute moral standard, one that transcends logic. What's right is right, and what's wrong is wrong.

After the Second World War ended on all fronts, the task of what to do with incarcerated Japanese Canadians became a primary topic of concern for many provincial and federal government officials. Both they and the Japanese Canadians settled into the status quo of the War Measures Act. That is to say, internees were safely ensconced in remote locations and the "problem" was suspended. But, with the Act expiring at the end of 1945, and provincial governments keen on ridding themselves of Asians, the debate began. Various provinces agreed to take Japanese internees for the duration of the war, but they were to be moved out once it was over. Well, now the war was over, and cooperating provincial governments expected action.

Many politicians just wanted to send Japanese people back to Japan, but most of the internees were actually Canadian citizens who had never stepped foot on Japanese soil. It wasn't going to be that simple.

St. Catharines, Ontario, March 10, 1946

On an overcast Sunday morning in March, Harry Mitsui, now in his twentieth year, asked his father a question that had been bothering him most of his life. "Why do you think there is so much hate towards Japanese people father? Why do they threaten us? The war is over, but people still treat us differently. They hate us and I don't understand why."

Masumi looked despondently at the floor and, shaking his head, replied, "I wish I knew Harry. I wish I knew." The same question had plagued Masumi most of his life as well.

"I can tell you what I do know. People aren't born hating other people because of their race or religion or politics. If you watch little children, they don't see a difference in people. They just see people. But we are easily influenced by those around us, by our peers, our teachers, our family and our community. Some people say the core of racism is fear. That is, for some reason you can trust anyone who has the same color skin as you, or who believes the same things you do. But anyone who is visually different should be feared and hated. If their cultures or religions are different, they are not trustworthy. It doesn't make any sense but that's what happens.

"The people of British Columbia feared us, I think. They said they didn't like that we came to Canada and worked harder and accepted less pay for the same jobs. And that meant white Canadians might lose their jobs. They said we were happy living in poverty and undermining the white living standards, so we didn't need to make as much money as white people. Now tell me Harry, who likes living in poverty? This explanation also doesn't make any sense.

"In British Columbia, Asians were considered unfair competition because they were superior workers. The truth is, to offset the effects of lower wages, Asians worked longer hours and got more work done than white people just to survive. Those who feared us felt that compensating for a low wage by working harder was unfair to the white workers. We were criticized for having a lower standard of living and then criticized for working harder in order to raise it. Asians were in an unwinnable position.

"But whatever it is triggering this hatred, it's more than racism, Harry. It's bigger than just race. It arouses harsher outward feelings and actions brought about by this deep, inward feeling. There are many names for this hatred, words like prejudice, discrimination, bigotry and intolerance. It has lots of names and lots of faces. I am baffled as to why other immigrants to Canada are not subjected to the same inhuman treatment. In many cases the harshest racism towards people of Asian descent comes from the Europeans who came to Canada at the same time or even after I did.

"But it's not just here in Canada. Black people in America have been treated even worse than Asians in Canada. It wasn't long ago white people in America could own a black person as a slave. The hatred and oppression many white people have for blacks in the United States continues today, even though blacks were freed after the Civil War in 1865, way before I was even born.

"It has been my experience that politicians made matters a lot worse by using racism as leverage for their own benefit spreading doubt and mistrust in the process. I saw it firsthand before and after the First World War. Their actions widened a divide between people in Canada rather than unifying the citizens. Many politicians fueled the emotions of fear and used it as a weapon to advance themselves personally. To me this is inexcusable, but it happened then and it still does now.

"In the end, racism starts with the color of your skin. I think it's just because we look different, nothing else. As I have said many times, other immigrants from Europe are not treated like we are. In fact, many of them are openly racist towards the Japanese! Take that politician, Alister MacKenzie for example. Honorable Minister, my ass! I'm more Canadian than he is, and yet he had the nerve to use his political power to block every effort made by Japanese Canadians to gain the voting franchise. This is the politics of racism, Harry. As long as all Japanese people don't have a vote in this country we will be treated as less than fully Canadian. Politicians don't have to worry about offending Japanese Canadians because their positions cannot be taken from them by a Japanese vote. They can make us the victims in order to gain favor with those who do have the vote.

"It takes many virtues of bushido to endure the things we have faced. I would say we must lean on our courage, our integrity, our self-control and our morality every day of our lives. I can only hope one day, your generation of Japanese descendants, and the ones to follow, will no longer face the ugliness of racism. But I know right now we live with it and through it every day. If a person is lucky enough to be white, they have absolutely no idea what we Japanese and other Asians experience, how crushing it is to our spirits, and how hurtful it is to all Japanese: old/young, man/woman, laborer/businessman, all of us."

Hamilton, Ontario, November 12, 1967

"Finally, in 1949, the restrictions lifted," Masumi said. "All Japanese people were given full rights as citizens, the right to vote and live anywhere in Canada. I was working as a dishwasher at the time. The announcement felt to me as nothing more than a hollow attempt to try and make retribution for the horrible way we had been treated during the war. But it didn't cost the government anything and it didn't help repay us for what we had lost. We were still a long way from being compensated, in the view of Japanese Canadians."

"A dishwasher?" Adachi repeated to Masumi as a question. "You, a decorated war hero and successful farm businessman, working as a dishwasher?" he repeated incredulously.

"It was one of the only jobs available to Japanese. I worked at a diner along the Queen Elizabeth Way after we moved to Hamilton. I mostly kept to myself, put in my hours and minded my own business. I remember on one evening two bus boys were in the kitchen discussing the announcement by the government of the granting of full citizenship and voting rights to Japanese immigrants. Knowing I could hear them, they disrespectfully launched into a spiteful and racially charged opposition to the decision. I don't remember their names, probably never knew them as no one ever introduced themselves to me or attempted to get to know me. I'll call them

Busboy 1 and 2 for my story. Those are much kinder names than what I would like to call them," he added with a grin.

Hamilton, Ontario, April, 1949

"'Can you believe the government is planning to allow Japs to vote?' asked Busboy 1.

"It's a slap in the face to all war veterans and real Canadians," said Busboy 2.

Offering a comment, I stated, "You know, there are many war veterans of Japanese descent from the First World War and even some from the Second World War who fought and died for Canada."

"What do you know about it, stupid old man? No Japs fought for Canada. That's ridiculous!" responded Busboy 1.

"What I say is true," I continued. "Many were decorated war heroes." I did not mention my own role.

"You're an old fool!" stated Busboy 2. "Our country would never allow Japs to join the army and they should never give your kind the right to vote for our leaders."

"These two boys were brash and ignorant and any further discussion would offer no benefit to me or them. Self-control was my best recourse and I chose to leave the conversation on that point. The boys, for their part, laughed at my apparent surrender and enjoyed their obvious superiority.

"The Fifties were another difficult decade for Japanese Canadians as they tried to claw their way out of abject poverty, nourish and educate their children and endure the continued isolation and rebuke from an angry and racist society. Grudges and hatred from the Second World War landed squarely on the shoulders of every Japanese Canadian. Stories of Japanese torture of war captives in countries like the Philippines added fuel to the fires of hatred towards Japanese people as a race. All people of Japanese descent were deemed guilty by ancestry.

"Fortunately, the Canadian economy rebounded after the war and everyone enjoyed an increased level of prosperity. The hard-work ethic of the Japanese people served us well. We all went to work. We lived together, ate together and maintained a frugal existence while saving money for important expenses like a house and basic living needs.

"The second half of the twentieth century started out well for our family with the recovery of the family Samurai sword, thanks to George's clever plan to bury it and return after the war to retrieve it. The sword holds a place of reverence for our family, acting as a symbol of perseverance and strength for us all. It is a symbol of sorts of a proud family history and a reminder of the integrity and honor of the Mitsui clan.

Amy, Lucy and George all married in the fifties, providing just the necessary excuse the Mitsuis needed for traditional Japanese celebrations. Not long after the weddings, grandchildren started appearing on the scene, a total of four between the three oldest children. This was the *sansei,* or third generation of this Mitsui family line living in Canada. It was a satisfying moment for Masumi to look at his four children, their spouses and their children. This was his legacy and even if he didn't always show it outwardly, as was his personality, in his heart he was happy and proud.

The decade also brought some dark times for the Mitsui family. Masumi could only find menial work and depended on the earning power of his children to pay for many of their expenses. He slipped into an uninspired routine of working at unsatisfying jobs, drinking at the Legion and watching game shows and soap operas on TV. His anger toward the Canadian government never faded. He retained his enmity for the way he and other Asians had been treated and fury that he was never able to recover the value of his farm, seized from him during the internment.

For Christmas in 1953, their four children surprised Sugi and Masumi with a wonderful gift. They bought them round trip tickets to Japan. This would be the first time either of them returned to their homeland since coming to Canada. Reluctant at first, Masumi warmed to the idea of traveling back to the land of his birth and his ancestors and to see his brother Tomo and many new family members he had never met.

On March 3rd, 1954 Masumi and Sugi boarded an airplane for the first flight of their lives. With its four propeller engines, the Trans Canada Airlines DC6 was one of the most modern airplanes in the sky, taking them all the way from Toronto to Vancouver in less than six hours. Masumi remembered traveling on the train from British Columbia to Hamilton just ten years earlier. That journey took six days! To him, it was truly amazing.

Once in Vancouver, they returned to the familiar streets of Japantown, streets like Powell, Alexander and Hastings. Much had changed in the ensuing years, due largely to the evacuation of Japanese in 1942. Some Japanese people had returned to British Columbia in 1949 after the government removed the restriction preventing Japanese Canadians from living within a hundred miles of the West Coast. But the area was predominantly populated by Chinese now. They could not bring themselves to travel to Port Coquitlam and visit the farm. The memories and emotions were still too raw.

Two days later, they boarded the Hikawa Maru, a luxurious ocean liner recommissioned and refurbished after the war. It had a grand central staircase, opulent dining rooms and comfortable cabins. This was luxury beyond the comprehension of Masumi and Sugi and they felt a little out of place initially. But the twelve-day journey turned into a daily routine of relaxation and interaction with fellow travelers. It would turn out to be one of the highlights of their lives.

"Look at this beautiful ship Masumi," Sugi said in awe as they ascended the boarding ramp towards the main reception area, even giggling a bit at the experience. She was snuggled close to him with her hand holding his arm as they took in the full luxury of the passenger liner. The opulence of chandeliers, huge murals, polished brass, wood grain panels and elaborate leather and fabric-covered furniture was overwhelming. "It is too much for us," she said.

"Nonsense! We deserve something special like this after all we have been through," replied Masumi.

"Welcome to the Hikawa Maru, Mr. and Mrs. Mitsui," said the ship's concierge, one of the dozen or so uniformed staff waiting in the ship's reception. "Is this your first voyage with us?"

"Well, yes it is," replied Masumi, quickly assuming the role of a world traveler.

"The ship you have just boarded was built in 1930 and carried nationals back home between Japan and the United States in 1941. It was converted to a hospital ship during the war and after the war it was a cargo ship until it was refurbished last year into the magnificent passenger liner you see before you," he recited as he gestured to the inner sanctum of the ship's lobby.

"It looks magnificent!" acknowledged Masumi.

"We hope your trip with us will be an enjoyable one. Please follow this man to your cabin and call on anyone if you need assistance." He pointed to another uniformed employee. This treatment was far different than the welcome Masumi had received as he first set foot on Canadian soil almost fifty years ago.

Maybe there is hope one day we will be treated as equals everywhere, he dreamed.

Sugi and Masumi enjoyed a rare experience of service from white people and a welcoming environment from the crew of the vessel as well as their fellow travelers. During a conversation at dinner Sugi shared Masumi's World War I experience and the honors he had received with another couple. Rumor quickly spread around the vessel of the "legend" among them. Respect for his efforts became quite evident as many of the more than three hundred passengers would greet the couple courteously. The special treatment culminated with an invitation for Masumi and Sugi to dine at the Captain's Table one evening.

"I think I just want to stay on this ship forever," said Sugi one evening in the dining room. "It's just so wonderful!"

Smiling in response, Masumi agreed. "Yes, it's a long way from Hastings Park, isn't it?"

The journey back to Japan retraced the route Masumi had taken to Canada back in 1907—from Vancouver to Seattle to Yokohama by sea and then to Fukuoka, this time by plane rather than train.

Masumi and his brother Tomo had stayed in contact with each other over the years by mail and telephone, sharing pictures of themselves and their families, but it had been forty-six years since Masumi left Japan and they had not seen each other face to face in all that time. Their greeting to each other instantly brought tears to Sugi's eyes as these two men grasped each other as only brothers can.

"Look at you Tomo! You have become an old man," teased Masumi.

"Not as old as you my dear brother," he quickly countered. "I can't wait to hear about all of your family. How is Hideo doing?" he asked, using George's Japanese name.

"He has become a fine man, Tomo. We have you to thank for taking him in and teaching him humility and honor."

"I would like to take the credit my brother. But he already had those things when you sent him to me. He just needed to see how to live with those good characteristics in front of the bad ones. He also has a streak of stubbornness in him along with a willingness to work very hard. Does that sound like anyone you know, Masumi?" At that Masumi grinned, appreciative of the compliment. It had been his brother Tomo he missed most of all when he left Japan. It was good for his soul to be together again.

"And this beautiful woman must be Sugi." Tomo charmingly held both arms open in a welcoming embrace.

Sugi bowed in respectful Japanese fashion which allowed her to hide her embarrassed grin and blush at Tomo's flattery. "I am pleased to meet you Tomo," she replied, moving closer and returning his welcoming hug. "Thank you for inviting us to your home."

"It is our pleasure. Come, meet my family. We have so much to catch up on." He guided Masumi and Sugi through the airport and into his waiting car to travel to his home.

After two weeks of visiting, eating and more visiting, Sugi became impatient to see her relatives just as Masumi enjoyed his time with the many Mitsui family members in the Fukuoka region. It was time to say good-bye, at least for now as they planned to return to Fukuoka before their return to Canada.

From Fukuoka they traveled to Oita Prefecture where Sugi's family now lived. They received the same warm welcome from family that had been apart too long. While staying near Oita, they enjoyed the warmth and healing powers of the many steam baths created from natural geothermal springs. They relaxed in the tranquility of Japan and the rich culture of its simplicity and serenity.

In all, the Mitsuis stayed in Japan for fourteen months, visiting their respective families back and forth, behaving like tourists and rejuvenating their bodies and souls. In Japan they looked like other people and were free of racism and hate. The inclination to stay for the remainder of their lives was strong, but the pull of family was even stronger. So, in May 1955, they boarded the Hikawa Maru for the return voyage to their home in Hamilton and their lives as Canadians.

CHAPTER NINE

The Sixties and Seventies

Justice
...is a deep sense of doing what is right given the situation at hand, based upon reason and judgment. It's about doing the right thing or making the right decision, not because it's easy but because it's ethically and morally correct. And doing so with fervor.

The sixties was a time of great change around the world, most notably in North America. Sex, drugs and rock 'n roll was the mantra, hardly the topics of interest to an aging Japanese Canadian war veteran. But it was an exciting decade nevertheless, with a little something for everyone from music to politics, from the war in Vietnam to the turbulent Civil Rights movement in the United States. It was the decade of the Kennedy's, Martin Luther King, black power, Woodstock and men landing on the moon. For a TV aficionado like Masumi, it was a grand time to be a spectator and bystander-commentator as many of these historic events unfolded before him in the comfort of his living room.

Hamilton, Ontario, August 28, 1963

This most turbulent of decades, which is fondly remembered by those who were there (or those who remember it at least) was, and still is, known as "The 60s" in North America. The Mitsui family, along with many other Japanese Canadians, paid close attention to the escalating tension in the United States triggered by the American Civil Rights conflict between black and white Americans. The claims of prejudice and inequality by black Americans struck a common chord with the feelings of the Japanese people in Canada. Like the Japanese immigrants and their descendants, black Americans were fighting for fairness and equality not privileged to them, based solely on the color of their skin. They looked different and they were ostracized for it.

On the evening news, the U.S. TV stations were covering one of the most significant, non-violent protests in American history. Over 250,000 black and white people, but mostly black, came together for an event called the March on Washington. Masumi was riveted to the screen as he listened to parts of a speech by one of their leaders, Reverend Martin Luther King. He spoke of having a dream where all men are created equal, where men are judged not by the color of their skin but by the content of their character.

"Listen to the words this man is saying, Sugi," Masumi said during a break in King's speech. "The lives of the Negro people in the United States are exactly like ours. What is even worse, they are victims of violence, murder and segregation. It is horrible. It is interesting to me that the Reverend King speaks of the bushido code without even knowing it. He offers compassion but demands respect. He offers loyalty but expects justice in return. We want the same things."

"Their lives are exposed to much more violence than ours," observed Sugi. "We are not being beaten and killed by those who oppress us, but we are still victims of a very similar hatred."

"Yes, you are right, there are differences between our countries. Look at their leader, President Kennedy. He seems to be a good leader, a man of strong conviction and understanding. Our government does nothing for the Japanese, other Asians or even the aboriginal people of this country! We have a long way to go in Canada and the United States to reach the kind of world Reverend King dreams about."

Three months later, on November 22nd, 1963, President Kennedy was assassinated in Dallas, Texas. Masumi wept that day for this man and his family, for the loss of what might have been, for people of color who lost a champion.

Hamilton, Ontario, November 11, 1967

"There is no doubt the world lost a great leader when President Kennedy was assassinated," said Adachi, interrupting Masumi's recollection. "He was a strong supporter of civil rights. We could all feel the momentum of change. I'm sorry to interrupt your story, Masumi. Please continue."

"That's not a problem at all, Ken. We all felt a great loss from his senseless death," Masumi gestured to the nods of agreement of his family members in the room.

"Sadness followed our family just last year as Sugi had a stroke and we had to move her to long-term care," Masumi said softly to Ken. "Time just seemed to run out for her after a life of struggle and hard physical labor. She is nearly eighty now and the heartless march of time caught up with a weak straggler along the way. This has weighed heavily on my heart, watching my dear wife and partner's health fade. Her declining condition made it more and more difficult each day to attend to her health needs and we are forever grateful to the people at the care facility for their kindness. Amy visits her mother every day. Sometimes I go but it is difficult and Sugi doesn't know who we are.

"And here we are now Ken. I'm eighty years old and most of the fight has left me. Sugi has been in the hospital for just over a year now. And I am having trouble with day-to-day things. Harry is a good roommate but Amy and her husband Tak have invited me to move in with them." He leaned closer to Ken and whispered "She will take better care of me as I get older. I'm planning to live to be a hundred you know."

"Based on everything I've learned about you, Masumi, I wouldn't bet against it," Ken replied with a grin. "You are one of the most determined and persistent individuals I've ever had the pleasure to meet. Your stories epitomize the journey of Japanese Canadians. You make me proud to be Japanese *and* Canadian, Masumi. You have been a pioneer and an adventurer, seeking your place in this world. I am in awe of your internal strength and fortitude. The things you have accomplished in your life for yourself, your family and your people are truly magnificent," concluded Adachi with a modest bow in honor of this great man.

"I have my grandfather to thank," said Masumi. "He taught me the eight virtues of the Samurai, the Bushido Code. I have lived my life relying on these teachings for strength and direction. I will always be proud of my Japanese heritage but in my heart, I am a Canadian, just like everyone else who calls this country their home."

"Our ancestors do have wisdom to share, I agree. I have learned much from you in the past two days and my writings will be better for having met you, Masumi."

"This has been helpful to me too, Ken. I think the term they use to describe this process is cathartic. Although it isn't an English word I am familiar with, it sounds right for me now. I'm not an expert on the English language like you are, but I know a word or two here and there," Masumi grinned.

"Cathartic indeed, my friend."

Rising from his chair, Ken Adachi extended his hand to Masumi. "I will leave you now, but I would like to keep in touch with you if that's alright."

"Definitely," said Masumi. "And send me a copy of your book when you are done!"

"I will. I promise," pledged Ken as he walked to the front door, closing it behind him.

Hamilton, Ontario, January 1970

Masumi settled into a life of retirement in the seventies, living at Amy and Tak's home, watching TV in his favorite old tattered recliner and transforming napping into an art form. Amy and Tak offered to buy Masumi a new chair, mostly to get the eyesore out of their house, but Masumi would hear none of it. "It's perfectly fine," he would say. "Why would we get rid of it?" And, of course, he was right. It was his comfort place and throwing it out would be akin to throwing out Masumi—a thought that only entered their minds on rare occasions. His brain was tired, his memory failing and his body weary. His left knee succumbed to the arthritis which attacked ailing cartilage, making walking painful and difficult. Masumi more than willingly accepted transport by way of a wheelchair.

Several days a week Masumi would go with Amy on her daily visits to see Sugi in the hospital.

"Sometimes I think she recognizes me Amy, but mostly she seems completely disconnected from the world," he said.

"She doesn't always make eye contact, or even show that she knows who we are Papa, but I know she hears us. I know her spirit is still with us. Our visits are important to her."

Still in his wheelchair, Masumi sat close to Sugi's bed and held her hand with both of his.

"I miss her so much every day," he shared without taking his eyes off Sugi's peaceful face.

"Me too."

After a seven-year period of convalescence, Sugi passed away in 1973. She hadn't recognized family for many years while she was in long-term care, so visiting was difficult.

Masumi's friend Hiro passed away shortly after Sugi died, so he had few contemporaries to spend time with. Getting back and forth to the Legion was more work than it was worth, even though Amy was always prepared to be his chauffeur. Regular trips for doctors' appointments became the norm although he preferred not to go to them.

One thing hadn't changed for Masumi through all three decades of the fifties, sixties and seventies: his resolve to boycott Remembrance Day ceremonies and conduct his own tradition of honoring fallen soldiers. Every year he would attach his medals to his Legion blazer and stand at attention in his home in tribute. Amy and Tak supported him in fulfilling this most important of traditions.

Hamilton, Ontario, March 1971

In the spring of 1971, a notification was left in the mailbox at the Mitsui home at 490 York Street in Hamilton informing the occupants their house was part of an exciting new neighborhood rezoning plan which, unfortunately, included the expropriation of their home. It was to become a park as part of a larger plan to widen York Street into York Boulevard and modernize the community. At the time, Harry Mitsui was the only original family member living in the home, operating a furniture upholstery business from there.

Harry was sixteen when the family was evicted from their farm in Port Coquitlam at the start of the Second World War. He remembered well the feelings of loss and anguish from that time in his life and he sat there, stunned, as he read this simple letter telling him he was being evicted again! The eviction notice triggered memories of turmoil and heartbreak. It was devastating news.

It was unlikely anyone else affected by this city council decision would have been a victim of the British Columbia internment process. Most certainly no one gave any consideration to the emotional and psychological impact this would have on one Harry Hideharu Mitsui, World War 2 Internee and casualty of one of the harshest and personally violating events enacted by the federal government in Canadian history.

Harry took the notice to Amy and Tak Kuwabara's house the following day to discuss it with his father. Those three, plus Masumi, gathered around the kitchen table with coffee poured and biscuits served.

"We have to fight this father," exclaimed Harry.

"What can you do, Harry?" Masumi asked.

"I don't know, we will say *No, we refuse to go.*"

"Good luck with your battle. The government takes what the

government wants," Masumi responded with a defeated tone and the look of a victim.

"Well not this time," Harry pledged with a clenched fist. "We will fight them in City Hall."

"Not *we*, Harry, *you*. I'm too old for any more fights like this."

"No, you're not. Look at this ridiculous offer of $35,000. That's crazy! Our house is worth much more. I'm going to fight this notice and I'll sue them if I must. They don't have the right."

"Well actually they do, Harry," counseled Tak. "The law of the land gives the municipality legal recourse to expropriate any property they choose, for public use like roads and parks, playgrounds or garbage dumps. You might be able to fight it and sue for things like business loss, mortgage interest penalties and that sort of thing, but that's it. What they say, goes."

"Well it's still not fair! We will fight it!" asserted Harry.

"You, not we, Harry," repeated Masumi. "I don't have any fight left in me."

"Father, tell me you don't remember how it felt to be dragged from our farm in British Columbia," Harry challenged. "Tell me how this is any different. We must stand our ground. I will not leave our home without a fight!"

"Oh, I remember it well, Harry." Masumi closed his eyes, the images of those days seared in his memory. "Those are times I will never forget. But that was a different fight, a fight against racism and hate. It was a fight against powerful people with discrimination driving their actions. This eviction is not because we are Japanese, but more about being in the wrong place at the wrong time. I wish you luck in this battle Harry, but I will not be able to help you."

⁓

Harry fought the expropriation for five years. Masumi kept up to date on what was happening by reading the news in the paper, even though his children tried to protect him from the stress of the whole situation. They feared it would be upsetting for him, a constant reminder of the loss of their farm. When the city was actually ready to start the road expansion in 1976, Harry was given his final notice.

At 8:00 a.m. on July 18, 1976, a Sunday nonetheless, the Hamilton City Police removed Harry from his home in handcuffs, dressed only in a pair of red shorts and wrapped in a blanket, they dragged him from his home, arms flailing and yelling at the injustice. This was just as they had threatened to do if he did not comply with the eviction and forced sell order, but he would not submit. It was quite a neighborhood spectacle. He served twenty-one days in jail for obstructing the police. For Harry, this had become more than an eviction from his home. It was, in his mind, another example of the government's tyranny over Japanese Canadians, at least he tried to make it about that. He stood his ground until the end. Most people who saw the story on the news just assumed this skinny Japanese man in his underwear was a modern-day Don Quixote, swinging at windmills and fighting imaginary foes. A crackpot, eccentric citizen who couldn't figure out what was going on. They had no way of knowing the root of his motivation, or the damage caused to him by the treatment of the government, from events that happened over thirty years ago, four provinces away.

Masumi on the other hand was indifferent to the event. At eighty-nine years old, he had been knocked around and mistreated by governments, by racists, by unscrupulous businessmen and even by bigoted military leaders. He really didn't have it in him to muster retaliation anymore. He could add angry emotion to his reserve of bitterness and stir his pot of antagonism towards government in general, but his days of roiling against injustice were over.

Harry sued the city of Hamilton for $300,000 in an attempt to gain fair compensation for his cost and suffering as a result of the expropriation. However, he was unsuccessful in his efforts.

CHAPTER TEN

Some Final Bows

Honor
A vivid consciousness of personal dignity and worth...having or earning the respect of others. And, importantly, to live and die with honor.

Chedoke Hospital, Hamilton, Ontario, November 10, 1983

In his ninety-sixth year, Masumi found himself in and out of hospitals as a patient dealing with numerous ailments. As it happened, he was a patient at the Chedoke Hospital in Hamilton on Remembrance Day in 1983. He was in the geriatric unit receiving therapy to strengthen his legs. Amy and Lucy hovered over him daily, filling in the gaps in care they felt their father needed. He soaked up the attention.

"Father," Amy said. "Tomorrow you will still be in the hospital. It is Remembrance Day."

"Tomorrow? Are you sure?" he asked in surprise. He never knew what day or even what month is was. At this stage in his life it really didn't matter. Amy knew what mattered to him most were naps and candies, like the ones he always had near his chair.

"Yes, I'm sure. There is a small memorial ceremony in the auditorium here for patients and staff who are unable to make it to a public one. What do you think about maybe just checking it out?"

"No!"

"Hang on now, hear me out," she quickly replied. "This doesn't have anything to do with the government. It's just the hospital paying tribute to war veterans, just like you do every year. This hospital and the staff here have been wonderful to you over the years. We think it would mean a lot to them if you would attend. I'll bring your blazer and medals and you can do what you normally do on November 11th."

"Who is *we*?" Masumi asked. "You and your sister I'll bet."

"Well, yes, Lucy and I discussed it."

"You remind me of your mother you know. Always working on me to do things."

"I'll take that as a compliment," Amy said smiling, feeling she might be getting somewhere. But that was it. The subject was dropped, and Masumi closed his eyes for a snooze.

What happened during that nap will never be known. Did Sugi come to him in a dream and suggest it was time? Did Oura reach out to him from beyond and give him encouragement to attend the ceremony? Or maybe Yamazaki or his old friend Hiro? Or was it his grandfather, the old samurai, counseling him to pay respect in public, to honor his duty and loyalty to his comrades? Perhaps it was a higher power than all of these people from Masumi's past. Perhaps it was even more spiritual. No one knows. But when he awoke, he made eye contact with Amy and spoke.

"Alright. I'll go if it will make you and your sister happy."

"What?" Amy blurted out in shock.

"I said I'll go to the ceremony tomorrow, but only if you bring my jacket and medals."

"I will. I'm...well, I'm surprised. And happy. Yes...happy," said Amy at a loss for words. "We will bring everything you need."

"Okay then. Good," he said. "Where are those candies?" he asked, not wanting to discuss it anymore.

～

The following day, at 10:45 a.m., every single member of the Mitsui family followed behind Masumi as George slowly and ceremoniously wheeled the ninety-six-year-old World War I veteran into the Nash Auditorium. A small crowd, gathered for the ceremony, sat in uncomfortable gray metal chairs set in rows facing a makeshift podium at the front of the converted basketball court. The nets had been ratcheted up on cables towards the ceiling, presumably to prevent an impromptu game from starting in the midst of the ceremony.

Masumi sat straight and proud in the wheelchair, wearing his Legion blazer adorned with three shiny medals, two silver and one gold. But he insisted on walking the last stretch of carpet between the sections of seating to the front seat reserved for him. He wanted to show everyone how well his therapy was coming along and even at ninety-six he was capable of managing himself. His pride had not diminished in his advanced years.

One of the hospital administrators stepped forward to a small podium at 11:00 and spoke to the small gathering. Amy had confirmed Masumi would be in attendance for the small ceremony and they had given the administrative staff some background on his history as a soldier.

"Ladies and gentlemen, we are honored to have one of the last surviving veterans of the First World War in attendance with us today. Sergeant Masumi Mitsui is a decorated veteran of the First World War. As part of Canada's 50th Battalion, he took part in many famous battles including Passchendaele, Hill 70 and Vimy Ridge. Sergeant Mitsui was born in Japan but came to Canada in 1908. Refused entry into the Canadian Forces in British Columbia he, along with more than two hundred Japanese Canadians, traveled to Calgary to join in the war effort.

"In 1942 he and his family were placed in internment in Greenwood, B.C. as part of the War Measures Act. I'm sure, like me, you all find this to be shocking treatment of a man who fought for our country. Please join me in welcoming our honored guest and Canadian war hero, Sergeant Masumi Mitsui to our service today."

With that, the crowd erupted in cheers. The volume of the noise belied the small gathering of people. Masumi smiled and waved briefly but his heart and his mind were already on the reason for being here—to honor to his fellow soldiers. And he did honor them as the ceremony proceeded. After the tributes, playing of taps and salutes to the flag, Masumi was asked to place a wreath of bright red poppies on a memorial table. Once placed, he stepped back, stood remarkably erect and saluted his comrades and all those who died in service of their country, in his war, and the others that had followed.

Virtually every person in room lined up to shake Masumi's hand as they exited. He had never felt so touched by a collection of strangers. On the way out, he quietly thanked Amy and Lucy for encouraging him to come.

"I felt honor and respect from the people who shook my hand," Masumi told them. "You know these are important bushido values. It means a great deal to me to be shown this kind of personal appreciation and courtesy. I'm glad I came today."

Relighting Cenotaph, Stanley Park, Vancouver, B.C., August 2, 1985

A crowd of several hundred people—many of them in uniform—gathered in a full circle around the circular base of the Japanese Canadian War Memorial Cenotaph in Stanley Park, Vancouver. Originally built in 1920 to honor the Japanese Canadians who fought for Canada, it had just undergone a comprehensive refurbishment. One of the reasons for this rejuvenation was the desire to relight the eternal light atop the monument which had been extinguished almost immediately after the bombing of Pearl Harbor. There is no official record of how that decision was made or who actually turned the light off. Government officials, through the media, justified it by claiming Japanese vessels could use the light for navigating purposes to attack the port of Vancouver. A War Memorial Restoration Committee had been established and placed in charge of the repairs which culminated in a ceremony to rededicate the cenotaph.

Sixty-five years after its installation, the monument looked very different. Well, not the monument itself but, rather, its surroundings.

Once visible from the harbor, it was now surrounded by towering evergreens and an assortment of mature cherry blossom trees. Stanley Park had grown around the cenotaph which was in the heart of the park and its complex pathways. The Vancouver Aquarium had been constructed near the monument and thousands of people passed by this central location in the park every day.

This ceremony had attracted people of many nationalities, not just Japanese. The multi-cultural reality of Vancouver and the intermarriage of nationalities made for a diverse audience.

―⁓―

Earlier, in the spring of 1985, the phone rang at the home of Amy and Tak Kuwabara. Amy took the call while Masumi slept peacefully in his chair.

"Hello, my name is Frank Kamiya. I'm calling from Vancouver and I'm trying to reach Sergeant Masumi Mitsui."

"This is his daughter Amy. I'm afraid my father doesn't do very well with the telephone anymore. Can I help you?" she inquired curiously.

"Hello Amy. Of course, I know who you are, but you don't know me. I am on the Board of the Japanese Canadian Citizens Association and I am the Chairman of the War Memorial Restoration Committee. I am calling to ask your father if he would be willing to come to Vancouver in August as our honored guest and participate in the rededication ceremony to relight the flame on top of the War Memorial cenotaph."

"Wow! That would be a great honor for my father, Mr. Kamiya, but he is ninety-eight years old and mostly confined to a wheelchair. I don't know if he is up to a trip like that."

"We understand, but he is one of only two survivors of the Japanese men who fought for Canada in that war and it would be very special if he could be here. He was here in 1920 when they first dedicated it to the soldiers, and we can't think of anyone more deserving than him to be part of relighting the flame. It's a very symbolic gesture and something I think would be meaningful to him."

"I can't even begin to tell you how honored he would be," confirmed Amy. "And you are absolutely right, the importance of the monument to my father is almost indescribable. There are few things more important to Father than the memory of his fellow soldiers and in gaining the respect they deserve. Leave me your number, I'll speak with him and get back to you."

"Excellent," said Frank, giving her his phone number. "I look forward to hearing from you."

─∽─

"Father, you remember the cenotaph in Stanley Park?"

"Of course I do," he quickly replied.

"Do you also remember they extinguished the light at the top, right after Pearl Harbor?"

"Yes, one of the many insults to the Japanese Canadian community!" he replied in disgust.

"Well a man just called to ask if you would be willing to go back to Vancouver and be their guest of honor during their relighting ceremony in August."

"Do you think I'll still be alive in August?" Masumi responded with his usual dry sense of humor.

"Well if you aren't, we can always just roll you out there in a chair and tell them you are sleeping," she parried back with the same dry wit. They both grinned at the thought. "I was thinking Lucy and I would go with you. We can visit some of the places in your past and maybe even go out and see the farm."

"I think I would like to go, Amy. It would be a good way to pay tribute to the Japanese Canadian soldiers. It also shows them we are a determined people. You can try and turn our light out, but we will come back stronger and relight it. Yes, let's do it!"

Amy made the flight arrangements to Vancouver in August and collaborated with Kamiya and the other members of the Restoration Committee to make all the necessary arrangements for the ceremony. For a ninety-eight-year-old man, the challenges of a trip of this magnitude were daunting. The three of them decided to drive to Toronto and fly directly to Vancouver from there. They stayed at the Vancouver Hotel, another in the glorious chain of regal, castle-like establishments, akin to the Victoria Empress and Banff Springs hotels. It was within reasonable distance to Stanley Park and the cenotaph. Frank had arranged for limousine service to meet the Mitsuis and transport them to a parking lot close to the cenotaph. Everything was set for the event.

"Isn't this a glorious day to be outdoors and celebrating such an important ceremony," asked Amy. She was glad they had agreed to accept the invitation to attend.

August 2nd, 1985 was indeed a glorious Vancouver day, sunny and warm, just right for an outdoor event. The ceremony included speeches, introductions and the traditional playing of *Taps*. But even here and now, the lingering feelings of racism persisted. Was it just a coincidence Fred Wynn, president of the Pacific Command of the Royal Canadian Legion was wearing civilian clothes to a military ceremony rather than his formal military uniform or his Legion blazer at least? Many felt his actions displayed a contempt for the fallen Japanese soldiers and that he harbored an enduring animosity towards the Japanese people.

The actual lighting of the tower was anticlimactic to say the least. The lighting was announced, but Amy couldn't see it. The sodium vapor light installed in the top of the tower was designed to last a lifetime. However, it was slow to reach full luminance. The brightness improved gradually as Frank moved alongside Masumi to place a wreath on the base of the tower.

As he waited in his wheelchair Amy took the podium on his behalf.

> *"Our father's proud to be asked to represent all his comrades who are gone before him but who are not forgotten. This is a memorable event for him and he says Thank you, everyone. Thanks, and God bless you all."*

The ancient warrior was in his finest military dress for the event: Legion beret and badge, blue blazer with his Legion pin on his right lapel and his three war medals on the left lapel (still around thanks to Lucy's quick action to retrieve them from his outburst in 1942). Masumi rose from his wheelchair with assistance from Frank Kamiya and saluted his comrades one last time with a crisp movement of his right hand to the right side of his forehead, his hand vibrating in place as he stared straight ahead.

"I've done my last duty to my comrades. They are gone but not forgotten," he said.

After the ceremony Amy moved Masumi's wheelchair into the shade of the cherry blossom trees planted there fifty years ago. She noticed some tears welling up in her father's eyes.

"Are you doing okay, Papa?" she asked. "This has been an emotional day for you, I know."

"I feel very fulfilled today, girls," Masumi said to Amy and Lucy. "Coming back to British Columbia and participating in this ceremony brings back memories of my life as a soldier. From my arrival in Vancouver, enlisting in the military, honoring my fallen comrades, building the monument and being here sixty-five years ago with Kubota and Sugi. This day has also brought back memories of our internment during the second war and then, finally, justice for the Japanese people. Today I can truly say I feel fulfilled and honored as a Canadian."

This was Masumi's samurai moment. He had achieved all he ever dreamed.

The following day the Mitsuis arranged for transportation to take them to what was now known as 1945 Laurier Avenue in Port Coquitlam, the location of their family farm. The road to the home was paved now, but drainage was still achieved by ditches on either side of the road. The fields and property were filled with over seventy homes, but their house, the one they built after the fire in 1935 still stood on the original site.

As they got out of the car to tour the old family farm, Amy pushed Masumi's wheelchair over the rough terrain of the driveway. She was seized with intense emotion, remembering their last night in their home. She was told they would return after the war to their home and belongings. Instead, their farm was sold and they got next to nothing for it. Their personal belongings had disappeared, lost or stolen, no one knew or cared. That was not a nostalgic, fond memory, but a painful emotional one—a stab in the heart.

"Can you picture George sneaking around here nearly thirty years ago and digging up the sword he buried by the back fence?" Lucy asked.

"It seems so long ago doesn't it?" Amy replied. "So much has changed."

Without speaking, Masumi looked up from his wheelchair at the familiar house, now surrounded by an unfamiliar neighborhood and much larger trees, while Lucy narrated what she saw.

"See that, the chicken house that was down there, it's all gone. The brooder house is gone, and so is the well. It doesn't look like the same place, you'd never know it would you now," said Lucy as she pointed to the back yard of the house. Masumi nodded with a sad, exasperated look of *shikata-ga-nai* (*it can't be helped*).

CHAPTER ELEVEN

Redress

In the decades following the 1942 confinement of Japanese Canadian citizens during the Second World War, no acknowledgment was given to the injustice of this action. No attempts were made to compensate Japanese Canadians for their losses—personal, emotional or financial. Masumi tried, without success, to receive a fairer value for his farm and the personal items seized from him in the weeks and months following December of 1941. It didn't take long for him to realize that battling with the governments in Ontario and B.C. was futile. His energies were better spent rebuilding their lives in Hamilton.

There were, however, some survivors and descendants of internment who were younger and not deterred by government obfuscation. They organized under the banner of the National Association of Japanese Canadians with the primary purpose of securing compensation and an apology from the government. Their target was the federal government, not provincial ones and they would not be denied.

Masumi was ninety years old in 1977 when this association started its initiative. He had little interest in reliving this part of his past and no energy to contribute to their efforts. He did believe in what they were trying to do though. His sense of justice was as strong as ever, and he still felt he and his family had been wronged. His anger at the government for their actions at the start of the second war still burned hotly in his memory.

Simultaneously, the same fight was brewing in the United States on the part of Japanese American citizens and descendants of the internment in that country during the war. Their fight was one and the same as Japanese Canadians—their belongings had been confiscated and they had been wrongfully imprisoned.

As restitution, every Japanese American citizen interned during the war, received $20,000 (US) as a redress payment. Their real estate properties had been held in trust as promised and were returned to the families after the war. Ironically, the state of Hawaii which had a large population of Japanese immigrants, never interned any people of Japanese heritage during the war, even though the greatest damage caused by the events of December 7th, 1941 happened on the island of Oahu in Hawaii. History shows Japanese Canadians received the harshest treatment of any Japanese immigrants in other countries.

Amy and Tak kept Masumi informed on the back and forth efforts between the federal governments and the Japanese people in both countries but his interest and comprehension were not what they once were. In Ottawa, it was a contentious discussion that was not progressing well at all, as the Trudeau Liberals resisted making special compensation for a cultural interest group, fearing it would open the flood gates for a multitude of claims by any number of nationalities both indigenous and immigrant. Brian Mulroney and the Conservatives, as the Official Opposition Party, made the statement that if they were in power, they would address these claims. In the federal election of 1984, the Conservatives formed a majority government under Brian Mulroney leading to great optimism on the part of the members of the National Association that their claims would finally be addressed.

In 1985, emboldened by the election of the Conservatives and their promise to the Japanese community prior to the election, the Japanese Canadian Citizens Association commissioned a Price Waterhouse study to estimate the real financial loss suffered by

Japanese Canadians as a result of internment. The investigation found the total loss, expressed in 1986 dollars, exceeded $450 million for the 22,000 internees. An average loss of slightly more than $20,000 for every man, woman and child.

After a series of proposals, refusals and counter proposals, and considering the settlement in the United States, Mulroney's government, true to their word, agreed to compensation of $21,000 for each living Japanese Canadian interned during the Second World War. One noticeable difference in the two country's settlements was the Americans got their land back while Canadians did not.

On September 22nd, 1987, Prime Minister Brian Mulroney rose in the House of Commons and said:

> *"Mr. Speaker, I think all members of the House know that no amount of money can right the wrong, undo the harm, and heal the wounds...Not only was the treatment inflicted on Japanese Canadians during the war both morally and legally unjustified, it went against the very nature of our country, of Canada...Most of us in our own lives have had occasion to regret certain things we have done. Error is an ingredient of humanity, so too is apology and forgiveness. We all have learned from personal experience that as inadequate as apologies are, they are the only way we can cleanse the past so that we may, as best we can, in good conscience, face the future."*

Masumi Mitsui did not live to receive this settlement. He passed away five months earlier on April 19, 1987, just six months shy of his one-hundredth birthday. More importantly, he never received an apology from the government for their actions. His four children received some measure of justice from government officials, but Masumi Mitsui died without ever receiving the one thing he wanted most from those who had wronged him over forty years ago—a simple "We're sorry."

EPILOGUE

Immigrating to Canada

Between 1877 and 1908 approximately 5,000 Japanese nationals immigrated to Canada from their homeland. In 1908, the Canadian government, in response to extreme pressure from Canadian citizens and some provincial governments, negotiated the Gentlemen's Agreement which limited the annual immigration total to 400 males per year. This annual number was subsequently reduced to 150 per year in 1928. In 1940, the Japanese position leading up to World War 2 put an end to Japanese immigration until the mid-1960s. Other Asian immigrants were also discriminated against during this period while people from Europe freely entered Canada to begin their new lives.

The irony of the immigration condition was the complaint that Japanese people did not assimilate with other Canadians while at the same time they were ostracized and forced to remain inside their own communities. Similarly, their wages were discounted while they were criticized for undercutting other workers. Or, by working longer hours to earn enough money to live, they were charged with stealing jobs from whites.

The "immigration dream" of moving to a new country full of opportunity and a welcoming spirit did not exist for Asian immigrants to Canada. Their efforts to develop their own social, religious and economic institutions were also met with negativity and vitriol.

The vast majority of people of Japanese descent in Canada today were born here. They are not immigrants. Yet, somehow, the perception of aliens in this country persists and racism continues.

On Living One-Hundred Years

Masumi Mitsui was born on October 7th, 1889 and died on April 19, 1987. He was six months shy of reaching his one-hundredth birthday. This achievement is a rarity in his generation. Sadly, he died five months before gaining the one thing he wanted in the latter forty-five years of his life: an apology from the government for the mistreatment of himself, his family and thousands of other Japanese Canadians imprisoned during the Second World War.

Living to be a hundred years or more can be a two-edged sword. On the good side, you get to be alive for a long time. But on the bad side, you get to be alive for a long time, and it may not be the way you want to live. The quality of life in our latter years leaves much to be desired in comparison with the enjoyment we experience in our early years.

The rate of change, innovation and the creative spirit have resulted in some amazing advancements over the past hundred years, many of which occurred during Masumi's lifetime. While exciting to experience, it is difficult to keep pace with changes, especially as one ages and one's openness to change and willingness to alter old habits diminishes. As the rate of change accelerates, the willingness and even expectation of "newer and better" is more the norm. Even living to one-hundred years is becoming more common as food quality improves and medical advances introduce life-saving and life extending features.

But is it really worth living to be a hundred years old if one's quality of life is poor, either through bad health, dementia or loneliness? Masumi was lucky. He had a family who cared and he had a genetic stubbornness about him.

It isn't really that we get to choose to live to be one-hundred or not. That's in the hands of fate. By all rights Masumi should have died in Word War 1, likely more than once. He could have given up the fight long before his hundredth year and he most certainly could have been victim to any number of unpredictable events claiming lives each year, whether it be sickness or accident. Masumi literally and figuratively "dodged the bullet" much longer than most and lived to see a strong legacy of family and a prosperous and integrated community of Japanese descendants living as Canadians. That was his reward for a hundred years well lived.

Lessons Learned...or Not?

Is our society less racist today than those who rioted in the streets of Vancouver in 1907? Or when those in political power stripped people of their possessions and forced them into labor camps and internment simply due to their ancestry?

Does a document signed by Prime Minister Brian Mulroney in 1987 change the reality of the way we accept people of different cultures and religions today?

Are we any more tolerant and accepting of those who come to our country just as our ancestors did within the past hundred years?

On February 19th, 2015 the Canadian government passed Bill C-51, the Anti-Terrorism Act. Its purpose was to enact the Security of Canada Information Sharing Act and the Secure Air Travel Act. Bill C-51 gives the Canadian government and the national police force, the Royal Canadian Mounted Police, the power to arrest those who, in their view, *may* carry out an act of terrorism. In the United States the government passed the Patriot Act in 2001 in response to the terrorist attacks of September 11th of that same year.

How are these powers different than the imposition of the War Measures Act in 1942 and the ultimate imprisonment of over 22,000 Japanese Canadians? Both give inordinate power to governments to ignore individual civil rights based on ethnicity.

Where is the balance between caution and ethnic profiling of visible minorities?

From politicians (people with power) to everyday citizens in our communities, has there been any real change in the acceptance and compassion towards people of visible minorities, immigrants or refugees?

Mass killings of innocent people at worship, shopping at malls or traveling to exotic destinations, continue to proliferate in the news year after year. Murder based on the color of a person's skin, their religious beliefs or their political affiliation occur all around the world. We build walls literally and figuratively to keep people out, to prevent them from invading our space. Why can't the human race figure this out?

When we have a common enemy, such as was the case of Allied Forces fighting in Europe, we find a way to come together. But, upon returning to the lives we led before that experience, these same people find themselves drawn back to old feelings and behaviors. Those specific people with names and faces who were comrades during difficult times may be accepted, but that openness and acceptance does not extend in general terms to those cultures we do not know.

Masumi Mitsui represents the best and worst of immigration. His decision to choose Canada as his new home and his determination to survive and thrive in a land that showed him no respect or gratitude demonstrates the extreme lengths people will go to be accepted. It took great courage for him to leave the safety of his homeland and stay here to face the barriers to acceptance and terror in a new land. Canada offered a new home to immigrants of all nationalities but, in the end, we really didn't mean it for all nationalities, just the ones that looked like us. Is that still the case? For many of the Japanese Canadians who fought in World War 1, even giving their lives for their country wasn't enough to gain acceptance.

World War 1

More than 650,000 Canadians served their country during World War 1. Of that total, 66,000 lost their lives in battle. Two-hundred-thirty-seven Japanese Canadians fought for Canada during that war and fifty-five died on those battlefields.

World War 1 was described as the "war to end all wars" or the "Great War" because it was the ultimate confrontation of nations, resulting in personal sacrifice under the most deplorable conditions imaginable. When the war first started, there was an outpouring of support and excitement. Fighting in a war seemed glamorous. But the glamour diminished when the reality set in—years of stalemate, horrible trench warfare, death and injury to thousands of soldiers. It was one of the most horrific wars in the history of Earth and even for those who survived and managed to return home, life was forever altered due to the physical mutilation and psychological wounds they sustained. The soldiers in the trenches were exposed to the most gruesome experiences. Even commanders sending troops off to certain death suffered from the weight of their responsibilities. No one knew what Post Traumatic Stress Disorder was in 1945. At the time they called the ailing soldiers "shell shocked" and assumed it too would pass.

Tens of thousands of soldiers experienced shell shock or combat stress. Many were treated as cowards and some even executed as a result of their fear of combat. The legacy of this appalling experience lived on in the lives of Axis and Allied forces alike long after the Great War.

Cherry Blossom Trees

Japanese cherry blossom trees have become symbolic of the integration of Japanese immigrants and their descendants. Like the Japanese people, cherry blossom trees did not exist by nature in North America. A small number of trees found their way to Canada across the Pacific Ocean and began to develop roots and acclimatize to this new environment. The first seedlings struggled to find their place, but today they have adapted to their new environment, established roots and flourished. From the initial location at the Japanese cenotaph in Stanley Park to the eight-block stretch of Georgia Street boulevard from Boundary to Willingdon, and from numerous parks and boulevards to hundreds of individual yards across the lower mainland, cherry blossom trees are an integral part of the community and a widely anticipated explosion of color and signal of spring in Vancouver.

Similarly, Japanese Canadians have become an integral component of Canadian culture, from arts to politics, and sports to medicine. Third and fourth generation Japanese Canadians, sansei and yonsei, have established themselves as Canadian citizens, excelling in many areas of Canadian society. These are the results of hard work, persistence, dedication and desire of immigrant families like the Mitsuis.

Baseball

Japanese Canadians really were (and still are) excellent baseball players. The Vancouver-based Asahi Baseball Club was formed in 1914 and played out of the Oppenheimer Park in Japantown. They were a formidable team and won the Pacific Northwest Championship five straight years. For the Japanese people in Canada, the baseball diamond turned out to be one of the only places where they could literally be on a level playing field with whites.

From the mid-1920s to 1941, the Vancouver Asahi Baseball Team, with Harry Miyasaki as its manager, won several back-to-back championships. Miyasaki himself, was a former member of the championship team. He trained his team with principles of bushido that Masumi Mitsui so treasured, such as perseverance, loyalty and self-restraint. His new strategic style of play would come to be referred to as "smartball" or "brain ball."

The Asahi club was disbanded in 1942 as players were disbursed due to internment. But the spirit of baseball lived on in the players and they organized games in the camps and even included locals from business, police, etc., creating some community bonding.

A quote from "The Vancouver Asahi Story" says it best:

> *There is no doubt the Asahi Baseball Team influenced the course of Vancouver's baseball culture between the mid-*

1920s and 1941. This story about the Asahi is a story of perseverance in realizing their 'field of dreams.' It is about leveling the playing field, against all odds.

The Asahi baseball team became a symbol of the Japanese Canadian struggle for equality and respect, and despite being disbanded and interned, left a legacy of inspiration for future generations of all Canadians.[1]

What is Masumi's Legacy?

What Sergeant Masumi Mitsui has left for our family is a legacy of which we will forever be proud. This exhibit being unveiled today (in Calgary, Alberta) shows the contribution which the Issei and Nisei made to Canada and the patriotic role which these individuals took upon themselves to become integral and contributing citizens to their new country and culture.

—David Mitsui, grandson of Masumi Mitsui

For more information on bushido, Japanese Canadian internment and the role of Japanese Canadians in World War 1, visit: www.CanadianSamurai.ca

---

1   "The Vancouver Asahi Story," Canadian Nikkei Youth Baseball Club and Shin Asahi Baseball, 2019, https://www.asahibaseball.com/history.html

ACKNOWLEDGMENTS

The writing of this biography would not have been possible without the rich contributions by three of Masumi Mitsui's grandsons, Mark Ishii, Ted Shin and David Mitsui. Their memories formed a framework to build on, from dates and times to family emotion along with their recollections of the deeply held beliefs of their grandfather.

I would also like to extend my thanks to the Canadian War Museum in Ottawa, the Greenwood Museum and the Nikkei National Museum in Burnaby, B.C., and especially the Nikkei's Research Archivist, Linda Kawamoto Reid for their amazing hospitality and support in providing access and insight.

The support and encouragement of my friends and family through the long and detailed process of research and writing kept me motivated. The seed of this story came from my son Shaun who became my collaborator in the telling of this important saga. His partnership was a special and unexpected gift.

—Russ Crawford

1st Canadian Infantry Brigade: The squared red symbol on the spine of the book pays homage to the Canadian Expeditionary Forces. The shape and color of this "shoulder flash" symbolizes the Calgary based 10th Battalion.

BIBLIOGRAPHY

Ken Adachi, *The Enemy that Never Was*: A History of the Japanese Canadians (McClelland & Stewart, 1976)

Barry Broadfoot , *Years of Sorrow, Years of Shame:* The Story of the Japanese Canadians in World War II (Doubleday Canada Ltd., 1977)

Pierre Burton, *Vimy* (McClelland & Stewart, 1986)

Daniel Dancocks, *Gallant Canadians* (The Calgary Highlanders Regimental Funds Foundation, 1990)

Lyle Dick, *Sergeant Masumi Mitsui and the Japanese Canadian War Memorial:* Intersections of National, Cultural, and Personal Memory (Canadian Historical Review, Vol. 91, Issue 3 (September 2010), 435-63.)

Ann Gomer Sunahara, *Politics of Racism:* The Uprooting of Japanese Canadians During the Second World War (James Lorimer and Company, 1981)

Roy Ito, *We Went to War* (S-20 and Nisei Veterans Association 1984)

Tsukiye Muriel Kitagawa, *This Is My Own:* Letters to Wes and Other Writings on Japanese Canadians, 1941-1948 (Talon Books 1985)

Kaye Kishibe, *Battlefield At Last* (Self Published, 2007)

Roy Miki and Cassandra Kobayashi, *Justice In Our Time* (National Association of Japanese Canadians, 1991)

Inazo Nitobe, *BUSHIDO: The Soul of Japan* (Self Published 1899)

Howard Palmer, *Patterns of Racism:* Attitudes Towards Chinese and Japanese in Alberta 1920-1950 (Academic Paper 1980) https://hssh.journals.yorku.ca/index.php/hssh/article/view/39071

Asahi Baseball: Canadian Nikkei Youth Baseball Club and Shin Asahi Baseball, www.asahibaseball.com

Tim Clark, *The Bushido Code: The Eight Virtues of the Samurai* https://www.artofmanliness.com/articles/the-bushido-code-the-eight-virtues-of-the-samurai

www.ingramcontent.com/pod-product-compliance
Lightning Source LLC
Chambersburg PA
CBHW060352080526
44583CB00012B/279